NESTS ABOVE THE ABYSS

ISOBEL KUHN

NESTS
ABOVE
THE ABYSS

Foreword by

ARNOLD J. LEA

OMF BOOKS

©OVERSEAS MISSIONARY FELLOWSHIP
(formerly China Inland Mission)

First published *1947*
Eight reprints *1964-1980*
Reprinted *1983*

ISBN 9971-83-817-6

OMF Books are distributed by
OMF, 404 South Church Street,
Robesonia, Pa. 19551, USA.
and OMF, Belmont, The Vine,
Sevenoaks, Kent, TN13 3TZ, UK
and other OMF offices.

Cover photo by Macquitty International Collection

Published by Overseas Missionary Fellowship (IHQ) Ltd.,
2 Cluny Road, Singapore 1025, Republic of Singapore
Printed by Hiap Seng Press Pte. Ltd., Singapore

Foreword

ONE evening in the spring of 1942 the peace of our quiet Szechwan town was rudely shattered by the appearance of a large convoy of trucks and jeeps as a unit of the R.A.F. Though newly arrived in China, they were already obliged to move house in face of the Japanese advance from Burma. With them, dusty and worn, came a dozen or so Yunnan missionaries, and amongst them the author of this book. That was our first introduction to Isobel Kuhn, I shall never forget her as she valiantly endeavoured in those days to adjust herself to low-lying Szechwan! The proverbial "duck out of water" wasn't in it! She tried to find a quiet spot, but alas! our badly weeded and cramped garden was such a contrast to the beauties and spaciousness of the Yunnan mountains, and the Szechwanese to whom she spoke were so different from the simple, approachable Lisu people. From the second or third day she was eating her heart out to get back! And the reason? Why, she had given her heart, her love, her life to those laughter-loving people of the hills of west Yunnan. Privation, loneliness and fatigue, though hard to bear for one of her physique, could not keep her away longer than necessary. As soon as conditions were easier in Yunnan, off she went on a truck, accompanied only by a young Chinese girl, to make the long, arduous journey back to the West.

It is impossible not to be impressed with the price that had to be paid to bring the Gospel to the Lisu of the Upper Salween Valley in west Yunnan, both by the Lisu from other districts and the incoming missionaries. Experience has shown that the best way of opening up new work is, where possible, first to send well-grounded Christian nationals to introduce the new message and life. In this way many prejudices are broken down and many preconceived ideas of Christianity are avoided. In 1919 J. O. Fraser wrote concerning the need of this area: "This district *must* be evangelized, but I want to find suitable natives to go first." It was a tremendous thing to ask the untravelled evangelists from the Lisu Church of the South to venture forth some sixteen days' journey into a land where food, dress and even speech were dissimilar, and dangers seen and unseen lurked round every corner. They responded for Christ's sake and the account of what they suffered is humbling indeed and brings forth afresh praise to the Lord who gave such enabling grace.

To follow up this opening amongst the Lisu of north-west Yunnan, in 1934 Mr. and Mrs. Kuhn left the last vestige of civilization on the Paoshan plain, and went to live amongst the mountain people of that region (until the Mission withdrew from China due to Communist pressure). Here amidst sin, squalor, poverty and darkness they have radiated the glory of the Master, and shown the redeeming and reclaiming power of the Cross, as these pen portraits reveal. That Isobel Kuhn was able to write so vividly about the doings of the Lisu people is because she lived amongst them and, more still, lived with them; sharing with them their spiritual battles, big and small, and by her understanding sympathy entering into the very thoughts of their hearts. Mrs. Kuhn did not gloss over sin, nor did she omit the failures of one or another, and yet she wrote with a note of triumph as she traced the growth downward and outward of some of the Christians.

The chapter on "Unseen Missionaries" places prayer in its right perspective to the missionary programme. For the experienced prayer warriors there is much here to encourage, while for the uninitiated in this realm of Christian warfare there is the challenge to undertake for the Master a prayer ministry which is perhaps even more precious and difficult, if properly executed, than going to a foreign land.

ARNOLD J. LEA
Assistant General Director.

Singapore 1969.

Contents

Contents

I

The Munition of Rocks

SATAN has a stronghold—isolated and unchallenged for centuries—a great mountain canyon in West China. Its river takes its source in Tibet and its banks rise to the height of eleven to fifteen thousand feet. The tiers of mountain peaks, flung around chaotically on either side as far as the eye can see, are separated from each other by deep ravines and abysmal chasms. Impossible as it may seem, this canyon is inhabited by human beings, for everywhere you look the canyon sides are checked like patchwork quilt with little hamlets and villages, and these almost perpendicular mountain sides are cut up into little squares or oblongs of farmed lands. Human homes, human nests, have been built on little knolls or jutting ridges that offer a scarce foothold—even over a dizzy drop down the bank. You may see them in such precarious positions that you almost hold your breath lest, even as you watch, they slide over the edge and disappear.

Anyone coming to the canyon must prepare to live perpendicularly as long as he stays; he must prepare to sweat and toil up and down steep mountain trails; he must prepare to live isolated from the rest of the world, from civilization with its medical, intellectual, and social comforts; he must prepare to have nature laugh at the feeble speck he is, and to have Satan hurl at him the fury of the hitherto unchallenged, unconquered lion faced in his own private lair. Surely this canyon is Satan's place of defence; here we will find his munition of rocks.

Are the Lisu tribespeople, who have built their nest-homes all over these mighty rocks where Satan reigns, enjoying the peace and happiness of living "the natural life"? (For some have said, "The heathen are happy: why disturb them?") Yes, they are just as happy and peaceful as fledglings in a nest built on a ledge of jutting rock over one of these mountain abysses, when the monsoon winds sweep like a hurricane through the canyon, and pine trees over a hundred feet tall are uprooted and hurled down into space as easily as a child knocks down a twig in his sand pile. What chance has a little nest against such a strength? That wind is one of the munitions of rocks, and, as it hurls itself against the little dove's nest, with the dark gulf yawning beneath, what are the feelings of the poor little nestlings as they cling to the straw and sticks? They are a picture of the so-called "happy heathen" when one of the Sharp Winds of life strikes him. These Winds hit from many directions.

There is *the Wind of Physical Nature*. In the Rainy Season, when the soil is softened by constant drenching, an animal higher up may dislodge a boulder with his foot; that boulder is hurled down into the ravine and woe betide all living things in its path! I had pointed out to me one such that had killed a woman standing in her doorway and had smashed her shanty home. In 1935 a Lisu Christian was sleeping alone in a hut in his cornfield when, some time before dawn, a rock as large as a dining table (they said) got loosened from the heights above and crashed down. It hit his hut, struck the end of his bed, and bed and occupant were shot out of the door and a hundred feet down the mountainside. He was knocked unconscious, but came to out in the open, in the dark, with the rain beating on his face. His hut of a moment before was nothing but a wreck of splinters.

Another young man, going out early to plough after a heavy rainfall, was struck by another such rock and cut in two at the waist. His oxen ran home frightened at the sight of his mangled corpse. Abyss of physical destruction! When will the Sharp Wind hit?

Not only do landslides terrify the little nest, but earthquakes come just as unannounced. In May 1941 we were eating the midday meal in a Lisu shanty, when suddenly the shanty shook violently and we heard a great roar. One called out, "Thunder!" but the sun was shining brightly. Another shouted, "Aeroplane!" and we all rushed out to the edge of the high plateau to see.

No aeroplane was visible, but before us lay a sight such as I had never seen in all my life. The whole opposite mountain range seemed to be belching smoke and clouds of dust everywhere. My first thought was that it had turned into a hundred-headed volcano. Then, however, I noticed that the fires were probably caused by the friction of the earthquake. Soon the whole opposite mountain range was hidden by a barrage of smoke and dust. It was a literal picture of Ps. civ. 32: "He looketh on the earth, and it trembleth: he toucheth the hills, and they smoke."

It did not clear until the next morning, for through the afternoon and long into the night again and again we heard the ominous roar of land sliding. Later we learned the sad details of much of that terror. Just one will illustrate. Forty Lisu were planting corn on a perpendicular field. The survivors said that all the intimation of danger they heard was when the earth shook; they heard a roar, looked up and saw the top of the mountain descending on them! When the dust and shock were over, of the forty persons only seventeen were to be found.

Sharp Winds from a Bitter Height! There is *the Wind of Merciless Heathendom*. In 1938, just thirty or forty miles to the south of us, a young heathen girl killed her husband and eloped with her lover. According to Chinese custom, she had been married (I suppose) against her own will, and when her true love came she eloped with him. They were caught and she was punished by being skinned alive. She was only eighteen years old. Poor little wind-torn nest! What a horrible abyss that is! Contrast with that this other little nest, hit by the very same Wind.

Going out along Sunset Trail one evening, I met a fellow-villager climbing up laboriously. She was carrying a babe tied in a sling in front of her bosom so that it could nurse easily. On the mother's back was a tall basket full of corn on the cob. The basket was so tall that it towered above her head. As she saw me descending, she rested her load against the hillside and her face lit up with a smile. "Ma-Ma," she said softly, calling me by my Lisu name. "S——!" I replied, greeting her by name. I was deeply moved and said, "How do you come to be carrying such a load? Don't you know that your body is not back to normal yet? This could give you life-long weakness. Where is your husband?"

"Oh, he's at home. But, Ma-Ma, you know him. He never does any work—just lives for the opium pipe. There was no food in the house and the little ones were hungry, so my mother gave me this load, but I have to carry it myself from Pine Mountain." (Pine Mountain is five miles away.)

I was very indignant, for her husband is a big, husky young fellow. "How did you ever come to marry such a man?" I asked.

"Why, Ma-Ma, it was arranged for me. You know our old heathen custom." She went on to tell me of the disappointment to find that the husband chosen for her was almost a devil. He was an opium-smoker, a thief, and would even sell their house furniture when she was absent in order to get money to buy opium. Yet in the telling of this her face was not bitter. There was a sweet peace upon it. As we parted she again thanked the Lord for meeting me and said, "Ma-Ma, take some corn out of my basket; they taste good roasted by the fire. I'd like to give some to you!" But I could no more accept that corn on the cob than David could drink of the water from the Well of Bethlehem. As I left her I thanked my Lord that He can bring an inward peace that passeth understanding, that though the body is suffering, the spirit may dwell with Him in heaven. This little Nest had found the Cleft of the Rock hewn out for her, and when the Sharp Winds blowing upon her were too awful to bear, she could find peace in that Cleft.

Very pitiful times are they when *the raw Wind of Sickness* blows upon them. Knowing nothing of germs, they attribute it to the bite of demons and are terrified and helpless. They think it necessary to make animal sacrifices, and they must pay the wizard or witch also. For such a simple thing as malaria (for which the Salween canyon is notorious) all the livestock, one by one, may be killed off, and the family reduced to dire want. How can they plough such mountainsides without an ox?

Their poverty adds to their misery. I saw a man dying of cancer. His big emaciated frame was just skin-covered bone, yet he had to lie on a bare board day and night with no pillow to ease his pain. When he coughed up spittle they wiped it off with coarse straw paper which scratched his fevered lips mercilessly.

When a really dreaded disease like smallpox comes, they often desert their sick and flee into the fields. The needless sufferings of the sick are indeed a raw Wind. This very thing is one reason why they vie with one another to have the white man establish his home in their villages, for he brings his medicine and "unthinkable" ways of easing pain. Who can dare say, "The heathen are happy: leave them alone"?

There is a little Wind, not comparable with the monsoon, but it blows bitterly on some. It is *the Wind of Helpless Ignorance*. In the canyon a few Chinese schools have been established by the government. They are so isolated that they are not often inspected and the teachers soon become such opium-sots that even the heathen Lisu thinks it useless to send his children to sit under them. For this reason they are illiterate people. Until the missionary came and reduced their language to writing they had no books and could not of course write letters. When one's friend moved to another village, even though only a few miles away, it was like death. Possibilities of meeting again, or of any kind of communication were slim, especially for the women, who seldom travel. Yet when the Lisu are taught, they prove to be as intelligent as the white man. The Christians are keen to learn. An American, looking at a young Lisu Bible student once said, "That is a bright-looking boy. Just under-privileged, that's all." That same under-privileged one once sighed and said to me, "Ma-Ma, you white people are very fortunate. No matter what you want to study—farming, medicine, music, stones or stars, it seems there is someone who can teach you about it. We Lisu have no one to teach us anything, no matter how much we yearn to know."

A Lisu evangelist, being introduced to some American soldiers said, "All that we Lisu have, we owe to the white man." It is sweet to be needed and to be able to share.

But we are not through with these Winds. Daily there blows *the evil Wind of Sin*, blowing softly, wooingly at first, but most destructive of any in its end. Wide yawns the waiting abyss when this Wind blows.

With no shops, no radio, no books, no pleasures to break the humdrum monotony of their farm life, Satan knows the children of men must have some excitement, so he offers wine-drinking, quarrels, gambling, and immorality. When they have gambled away their money, they will often stake their children, their wives, even their own bodies as slaves. So in one night a whole family can be gambled away into life-long slavery.

I said the Wind of Sin blows softly at first. The Lisu are naturally singers and love music; and Satan and sin have given them a set of licentious yodel songs which they call, "Try-to-say-it." On the surface, I understand, it is Nature-talk, as of birds, or the meetings of streams, but each is a metaphor so vile that no Christian Lisu will translate it for you or even repeat it. This suggestive metaphor is often composed spontaneously. At dusk the young men will melt on to the high trails and, as they slip along through the shadows, they will sing a line of challenge, yodelling it at the end. Their voices are carried down the mountainside by the clear air to a group of girls in a village, perhaps, or sleeping in a cornfield to guard the grain from wild animals, and these will answer back. This is where the Try-to-say-it comes in. There are time-used phrases, but if you are clever enough to make up a new one, he must find an answer to it. "Make up a harmless one, for an example," I once asked a Lisu evangelist. So he gave the following:

"I'd give the wide world to have you!" might come yodelling down the mountainside in a strong, young masculine voice.

A girl will take it up and yodel back, "My father's a good shot. You wouldn't dare come near our house!"

And so the musical word-combat, the Try-to-say-it gets under way. In the darkness the singer's position is hidden, indicated only by the direction of the voice. But urged on with home-made whisky, and a humdrum or unhappy day, one can understand the attraction of the unknown, unseen, offered love-call.

One night in a Lisu shanty, all the village around silent and dark, I was awakened. From far up on the high mountain peak towering above us, through the stillness, a chorus of yodels was coming. The clear, strong voices, full of youthful vim, were attractive, and they kept getting nearer and nearer. I understood nothing, discerned no words, but as I lay there unable but to listen, that musical young call lilting through the night made my flesh tingle. And then I knew the power of this "munition" from the Rock Height, and I prayed, "Oh Lord, keep Thine own to-night if there be any who must also hear this. Oh, if I were a heathen girl with no Christ in my heart to quieten me, that call would entice. Thank Thee, Lord, that I am in Thee." And cuddling well into the Cleft of my Rock, I prayed on for younger ones upon whom that Sharp Wind was blowing. Not a voice from the village responded, so after about a half-hour of yodelling, the adventurers passed on and left us. But from then on, I knew why there are practically no pure young Lisu among the heathen. I heard a pretty heathen girl once boast, "There isn't a man in the valley can beat me at Try-to-say-it!" and her husband endorsed her proudly. That it was vile, licentious language in which she was so adept meant nothing to him.

But it is an abyss of destruction that awaits the little falling Nest. The unseen singer by daylight loses his glitter and often proves to be worse than the husband deserted for him. Homes are broken up; deformed children are born; and social diseases take their toll, and other unmentionable miseries perhaps, prove into what an awful pit the little Nest has fallen.

But the Cleft Rock[1] is making a difference. I once asked a handsome young Christian, "Do the girls ever yodel after you?"

"Sure they do—often from a cornfield as I go by," he replied.

"What do you do then?" I inquired curiously.

"Run down the road just as fast as I can!" he answered firmly. I could hardly keep my face straight at the picture thus conjured up, for this particular laddie was noted for his courage and valiance—yet in my heart how happy I was for his answer. He had been studying the scriptures and knew that God says unhesitatingly, more than once, "*Flee* youthful lusts" (2 Tim. ii. 22; 1 Cor. vi. 18). And God has rewarded. Three years ago He gave this young runaway a sweet little Christian wife, one

---

[1] "And that Rock was Christ" (1 Cor. x. 4).

whom an American soldier claimed was "the prettiest girl in the district."

One more Sharp Wind from the Bitter Height. The worst of all Satan's munitions of rocks is *the Wind of Death*; the spiritual hopelessness of the heathen Lisu, which, though pushed to the edge of his daily consciousness, every now and again sweeps in upon him with terror and horror.

A little bamboo hut on the mountainside. It is evening and the family is gathered around the central fire which blazes up and throws a golden light into every cranny of the simple primitive dwelling. Grandparents, father, mother and several children all are concentrating their attention on the little five-year-old son, who is lying on the wooden bed screaming.

"You shouldn't have told him!" expostulates one of the adults. "He is quite small yet. Too bad." (The speaker had no need to mention the death of their neighbour, whom the little boy had dearly loved. It was in all their thoughts.)

"Well, you can't keep it from him," retorts the oldest son. "He's heard the villagers talking about her. And besides he ought not to continue to run to her house the way he does. Her ghost" (in a lowered, fearful whisper) "might get him. She loved him so!"

"Yes, yes," says another, turning pale. "We all have to face this sooner or later. But it was early to tell him that some day he'd be put in the grave. He's only five years——"

"I won't! I won't!" shouts the child hysterically, sitting up and looking around. "You can die if you like; I'm not going to!"

"Who're you that can help it!" sneers his big brother. "Everybody has to——"

"Shut up, will you?" snaps their mother savagely; then, turning to the child, she tried to put her arms around him. "No, of course you won't, A-bi-rao; you——"

"You're a liar!" screams the child. "They say all of us have to die," and again he goes off into hysterical wails.

This is a typical scene, and that little child is the hero of one of the following pages. He told me the essence of that childhood terror, and how the Lisu have no hope beyond the grave, saying that for years after that awful introduction to the fact of death he could not come upon a grave on the mountainside without getting cold all over.

Another young evangelist, in quite a different part of Lisuland, told me he was six years old when he first learned of death, and cried so hard and so long that he was ill for days. Sharp Wind from a devilish height! The Wind may scare the nestlings, but it is nothing to the terror of looking over the side and seeing the gulf yawning beneath! And as for loved ones who must bury their dead—they sometimes weep themselves blind, and some go out of their mind. The Lisu have told me of such.

The wizard of the village may be asked to perform *Ma-mu*. This is an incantation for calling up the dead. Animal sacrifices are offered; the wizard goes through his rites and becomes possessed. He says his soul is wandering up the canyon to the north, searching for the dead one. He will tell what he sees in his search; local places known to all, places farther north known but dimly. Then he will "find" the dead one. When that occurs, the dead man or woman's voice will come through the wizard's mouth and talk to the family. The voice is identical with that of the dead one and makes the relatives sob with excitement. Sad reminiscences of past days or loving greetings to this one or that are accompanied with no word of peace as to the present state of the departed. When the incantation is over, no comfort has been obtained, grief and loss have been newly stirred up, and that is all that a Lisu wizard can achieve. After some years (if I remember rightly) the dead man's spirit cannot be traced . . . he is "gone". No wonder a loving heart grieves itself blind or mad. And other hearts harden themselves. I heard a heathen mother tell of the death of a darling girl of twelve or thirteen. "I was grieving myself ill, so——" She laughed lightly. "Forget her! Make an end of it!" She had hardened her heart and become so shallow that no call for pity or thoughtfulness could evoke a response in her.

"In time past . . . [ye] were not a people, but are now the people of God: which had not obtained mercy, but now have obtained mercy" (1 Pet. ii. 10).

The great heart of God yearned over these lost ones, over these little nests hopelessly perched above the mouth of the awful abyss, and now Lisuland has a Cleft in the Rock wherein to hide when the cruel Wind of Death blows by.

I remember a wooden chapel on a high mountainside. It was packed to the doors for an evening meeting. The speaker was the five-year-old boy mentioned above, now grown up and a well-known evangelist among them. He was relating that story, and went on to tell of a later year when he heard Leila Cooke speak on "I am the resurrection, and the life: he that believeth in me, though he were dead, yet shall he live."

"As she explained that verse," he said, "suddenly the truth of it broke in on my understanding, and the fact of *eternal life*, a life after death, a hope beyond the grave, shone before me. I was thrilled through and through; faith and acceptance of the Saviour were born right then in my soul. It was that verse on the resurrection that brought me to Christ; and I have a feeling that I am not the only Lisu to become a believer because of this truth. All of you who were led to become Christians by the resurrection doctrine, hold up your hands!" And all over the building hands shot into the air and the glowing joy on their faces told its own story.

I have heard the wail of the heathen for their dead and my heart could hardly stand the hopelessness of their agony. But praise God for the refuge of the Cleft Rock, when the Wind of Death sweeps down from the Bitter Height.

One evening as I was viewing the lovely sunset from our front garden, a servant came around the corner of the house, and with a grave face said, "Ma-Ma! Cha-fu-yi is dead. He was drowned in the ravine stream this morning. His parents are just carrying his body home on their backs now."

"Oh, no!" I cried out, for Cha-fu-yi was the darlingest Lisu youngster that I knew, and the pride of his parents. As I hurried up the hill to their house, memories of the wee fellow crowded in on me.

He was always so plucky. When he was very small he had taken sick and my husband was called upon to give him some bitter medicine; so of course, baby-like, he thereafter viewed the big White Man as an enemy who put nasty stuff in your mouth! One day in playing he unconsciously wandered into our front yard and, looking up, suddenly saw John standing on the house platform. Scared, he started to cry and retreat as fast as small legs could take him. John called out to him not to be afraid, but, thinking that was a subtle snare, the little lad was all the more upset. His daddy had taught him to protect himself from dogs by throwing rocks at them, so, as John again called out to him, he stooped down and picked up a big stone to guard himself from the White Monster. He looked so sweet, so baby-brave, the tears rolling down his small nose, the big stone tightly clutched in tiny fist, and the chubby legs trying to run fast in retreat. Valiant-hearted to the last gasp—that was little Cha-fu-yi. What could one say to comfort his parents at such a loss? As I ran toward their house, I prayed in my heart for words, but I had no need for them.

As I came up to the sad scene—the little six-year-old figure was laid out on a plank of wood, Daddy, Mummy, and neighbours all weeping—his father turned to me and said, "It's all right, Ma-Ma. If he had grown up he might have gone into sin." And then we talked of heaven and the joy of the reunion there.

> Thou blest Rock of Ages,
> I'm hiding in Thee.

The stories that succeed this are all of little nests, perched always over the mouth of the abyss, but with a Cleft Rock that follows them through all their storms.

2

Beautiful Feet Reach the Canyon

How beautiful upon the mountains are the feet of him that bringeth good tidings, that publisheth peace; that bringeth good tidings of good, that publisheth salvation; that saith unto Zion, Thy God reigneth!

ISA. lii. 7.

"MAMMA! Mamma!" Cries of delightful terror brought small children running to their mothers to bury their heads on the familiar shelter of the blue apron, while one ear was kept free to hear the exciting talk of the older ones.

"Yes, truly, he is *white*-skinned! My husband told me—he is down there in Li-yi-gwey-pa's house, looking at the creature. I'd love to go too, only I dare not! It *must* be a demon. Who else would have human shape, yet a white skin? And they say his eyes are not black, but the colour of the river and——"

"Then *of course* he's a demon! We all know the demons can take human form. No, I wouldn't dare go either, and I'm so glad the children are afraid to go. Demons steal children," and the speaker embraces tightly the small, excited form buried in her apron.

"But they say he's awfully nice! Such a kind smile, and he talks Lisu and also speaks Chinese. He has other people with him too, that talk the same sort of funny Lisu and they are black-haired, black-eyed and olive-skinned like us. They say they are Flowery Lisu from down the tail of the canyon. That could be true; you know we are called Black Lisu and——"

"Are we?" pipes up a young girl. "Why? We aren't any blacker than the Chinese."

"It isn't our skins, daughter," speaks up an old granny condescendingly, "it's our clothes. We wear this navy blue, but those Flowery Lisu! You should see what they wear"—in a tone of contemptuous disgust—"all red and green and white checks, with cowrie shells to trim the borders of their aprons, and red, blue, and white leggings, and——"

"How do you know, Grannie?" demands Miss Inquisitive. "Where did you see them?"

"When I eloped with A-fu-me-pa—that time we ran off to Burma until the old folks' wrath was appeased. The Lisu across the mountains from here still dress like that. But to go back to this white man—haven' ᴊu girls heard the old tradition that a White Lisu is going .se some day and be our king? If he has Lisu with him, maybe this is——"

At this point a twelve-year-old boy who has stalked up to the group broke into the gossip and exclaimed proudly, "I've *seen* him!"

"Oh, have you? What's he like?" eagerly from the now swelling crowds of timid yet enthralled females.

"He has a nose *this* high," says young Show-off, exaggerating, boy fashion, and carving a nose for himself out of the air, that made the girls scream.

"Oh, how awful. That's a demon, sure! They have noses like beaks; they're part bird, some of them," and thus the conversation swayed back and forth, palpitating with excitement and fear.

The women and children were terrified and would not go near him. The men and some boys of about twelve were bolder and even gathered to converse. They were afraid of his white skin, blue eyes and the high nose we foreigners all have. He stayed only one night and never came again, but the old people still talk of it.

The "Munition of Rocks" was first entered for Christ by James Outram Fraser, whose life is told in the book *Behind the Ranges*.[1] But the strangeness of his white-man appearance so monopolized interest that no one remembers his message. J. O. Fraser was not slow to learn a lesson. This is one of the reasons

[1] *Behind the Ranges: Fraser of Lisuland*, by Mrs. Howard Taylor, China Inland Mission.

why he laid down the rule that Lisu heathen should be evangelized by Lisu Christians, the white man staying in the background to inspire forward movement, to pray, and to teach the churches when established.

Five years passed, and Fraser with his colleagues were still busy establishing the Flowery Lisu church and caring for a new movement southward. The Munition of Rocks is to the north of their original work, and continued in its darkness, but a yearning God once more brought them to the pioneer missionary's attention. In 1919 Fraser wrote, "Last market day I met some Lisu from the Upper Salween. They were carrying tremendously heavy loads of betel-nut to sell. 'Come up to our village and teach us,' one of them said—his village is about sixteen days' journey away. 'We will give you food—rice and pork—as much as ever you want.' Though he meant it sincerely, he was too busy to do more than just invite me. That district *must* be evangelized, but I want to find suitable natives to go first."

Such were not easy to find. There were many dear Christians capable of being sent, but it was a tremendous thing to ask of any. The Upper Salween was at that time almost unknown; it was fourteen or more days' journey away from the mother church. It was peopled by Black Lisu, which meant difference in dialect, food, and customs. The postal system in the canyon is so negligible (only one post office in a six-day stretch, and that post office received mail only one in ten days) as to reckon none at all in Lisu eyes. There was no medical aid to be had anywhere, and those who had accompanied Mr. Fraser on his exploration trip, in addition to calling it "a wild, inhospitable region," must have added stories of its famous fevers. A scholar's recent book declares it "The most malarial spot in the world", and quotes this U.S. Army account of it: "Apparently well men, trudging along the mountain passes, would suddenly flush, complain of the fire in their heads, then die." The author's own trip to the Salween he calls "flirting with death," and he would have entered with pack mules of medicine, comforts, and protectives. Lisu evangelists take only what they can carry on their own backs. And with the easier southern field just opened up to the gospel and calling for volunteer preachers, it is not surprising that by 1922 (when Mr. Fraser had to go home on furlough, never again, as unexpected events proved, to be free to give all his time just to Lisu work) the Munition of Rocks was still Satan's unchallenged stronghold.

Yes, God had written their faces on a loving faithful heart which never forgot "the people waiting, accessible, and in desperate need," which his trip of 1914 had revealed to Mr. Fraser. In leaving for the homelands, he must have referred this burden to Carl Gowman, who, with Mr. and Mrs. Allyn Cooke, were his successors in the work. The Cookes were vitally linked up with the evangelistic spread southward, and so we find Carl Gowman taking up the burden of the Upper Salween thousands, with a valiance of faith and passion of vision that would not be defeated.

How long he tried to get an opening, I do not know; but about 1927 Mr. Gowman was writing to the Lisu church, "We need preachers for the Upper Salween!" One young heart felt that call. He who had been the missionary's goatherd, small in stature, badly disfigured with pockmarks; he who had been the most stupid student in the class learning Chinese—this one wrote to Mr. Gowman and offered. "I know that originally I am a Black Lisu, and that my forefathers came down the canyon from up there, and God has given me a sign that He wants me to go for Him."

I wonder how Carl Gowman felt, when, in mind's eye, he saw his first candidate for the Munition of Rocks! Had I been there, I know I would have been disappointed. I would have been hoping for a big fellow, "a man of presence," a walking photograph of Great Heart! It is a land of giants—giant peaks, giant winds, giant disease, giant spiritual forces. But, "God looketh not on the outward appearance," and Mr. Gowman accepted the goatherd. He accepted that first one but he wisely waited for the Christmas festival to present the challenge.

A day or so before the birthday of Christ, every Christian Lisu village is making its preparations to send a contingent, young and old, everyone who can go, to the Christmas celebration. The poorer women are washing their clothes in the approved Lisu manner, treading them with bare feet under the flow of some nearby stream. But if at all possible, new garments are prepared, so the needles too are flying busily. Then each person must bring a certain amount of grain, salt and pork for the feast, so the foot mills are busy pounding out the corn, and the early morning hears many a pig give its final squeal, as abundance of pork is what makes a Lisu meal into a feast!

Then, early on the appointed day, all over the mountains, a delegation from each village set out. Merry holiday laughter and teasing ring out as they file out along the trails, all converging gradually toward the missionary's home of Stockade Hill. Before they have come in sight of the village, *Bang! Bang!* goes a gun over their heads, and the long file all turn to nod and smile at one another, knowing that the lookout party has spied them, and that the gun's reverberations are to wake up the welcoming committee! So up the hill they toil (or down the mountains, for at Stockade Hill many guests would be descending from the top of the mountain range) and as soon as the village slope is sighted, they come upon a floral arch with smiling faces peeking at them from underneath. Here they must halt while the other side tunes up.

"One-three-five (doh-me-soh)," sings out the leader of the reception committee, "Let it come!" And voices in four parts rise up from behind the flowers.

> Christmas guests are at the door!
> Let them in.
> It is duty to receive them,
> Let them in.
>
> That of Jesus we may think,
> His Great Day that we may keep;
> Praise to God, we come to greet.
> Let them in!

Then through the arch they come, shaking hands with each of the long line of singers, after which they are free to check their food supplies and seek out a place to sleep. Singing groups and sports fill in the time until the big evening service.

It was at one of these evening meetings that Carl Gowman gave out his challenge. Jesus' birthday! A chance to give to Him who gave us so much. On winter days, Lisu farmers are free, and the Lord's harvest is waiting to be reaped. "Over thirty men are needed to volunteer for evangelistic work." Mr. Gowman said, "and of these, four men are wanted to go for Christ to the Upper Salween! One of those four has already offered; three more are needed to go with him!"

After that service, around the different home-fires, there was much discussion of that challenge.

"I'd like to go to the Upper Salween," says one fine-looking young fellow of about twenty-one years of age, hands clasped around his legs, chin on knees, eyes brooding into the flames.

"Go on with you!" anxiously thrusts in his mother. "That's no job for a married man! And you've a child, besides a wife. Volunteer, if you must, for the south country! Mr. and Mrs. Cooke are there; they'd look after you, give you medicine if you get sick, send your letters on to us. Pastor needs more men for the south than he does for the north—he said he wanted some thirty!"

"That's because he had no hope of getting so many for the north," comes the quiet answer. "He'll get thirty for the south— that's not very hard. But he may not get four for the north, that's why I'd like to go there. Thousands of Lisu are there," he said. And again the dark eyes brooded into the fire with a gleam in them that set his mother crying.

"A-eh! A-eh! He's going to volunteer for the Upper Salween and I'll never see him again. He'll die there of those awful fevers! A-eh. We'll never hear what's happened to him, for there's no mail up there. A-eh."

"Be quiet!" orders her husband. "Son, be careful what you do. Don't throw your life away. Remember you don't know the customs of the Black Lisu. They might not receive the gospel like we did. And if what your mother says is true——"

"It's not all true. Pastor Payne at the city of Paoshan has promised to keep an eye on us, and forward mail and supplies to us; and besides, there can be no harvest for Christ in those parts until someone takes a risk. Job, the goatherd, is going; he needs a partner. I'm going to volunteer." Then started the wails of the women and expostulations of relatives. Job told me, years afterwards, that not one of the four found it easy to say yes. The above arguments and more were anxiously poured upon them. But on the last night when Carl Gowman gave the final call, three more men stood up one by one: Andrew, Wa-si, and twenty-one year old La-ma-wu. I am sure the eyes of the Christian men shone with pride as they looked up into those four determined young faces, and I am sure their mothers swayed back and forth on the benches, weeping. Never had four Lisu evangelists faced such an unknown, distant and bleak parish. "You may get sick and die!" cried more than one anxious-faced relative, and not without ground for their fears, for of the four that went, only three returned. But more of that anon.

Our next picture of the little band with beautiful feet is after seven days' travel over strange country into Chinaland. One day they appeared, dusty and bewildered, in the courtyard of Mr. and Mrs. Talmadge Payne, who were living at that time in the Chinese city of Paoshan. The thrill of their adventure would once more be brought back to them in the joyous welcome the missionaries accorded them. Seven days of tramping through unfamiliar and indifferent country can take the glow off any enthusiasm. You don't realize how long is the road from home to your destination until you go over it foot by foot, money diminishing each day. I wonder if their faces, as they came in the courtyard that day, were not a little woebegone and anxious. One thing I am sure of—they did not look like "heroes of the faith" about to push into one of Satan's most impregnable strongholds. Maybe they looked more like children who have wandered away from home, dazed and wistful, yet determined not to cry. Having seen other such Lisu missionary parties arriving in Chinaland, I know they appeared poverty-stricken and ill-at-ease, suddenly conscious of bare feet and mountain manners. I heard one such boy say something like this, "When I saw the fine houses of the Chinese and how they live, I felt myself to be like a monkey just dropped down from the tree-tops."

But those dear, devoted missionaries saw them as they were in the spirit—God's beautiful feet, sent to carry the news of salvation to His lost ones, and they welcomed them as such. And I would like to say here (for these days some are emphasizing the use of national workers to a degree that outrules the white missionary) these four would never have accomplished their mission, if it had not been for the earnest, loving backing of Mr. and Mrs. Talmadge Payne. As you will hear soon, again and yet again, the little band fell back fainting in spirit, to be caught up in the strong arms of Mr. and Mrs. Payne's faith and almost thrust into the canyon afresh.

Their second encouragement (the first would be a season of sweet fellowship at Jesus' feet) was to hear Mr. Payne say, "I have supplies for you. From now on, I am your base of supplies. When you need money just come to me." A few dollars to buy some rice for present need clinking merrily in their pockets, the four start out for the town, and the excitement of a Chinese market. In their lonely hillside hamlets was nothing comparable to this rendezvous from the point of wares, numbers of people, or noise. It is like a mountaineer walking down Fifth Avenue or Piccadilly with the roar of a big city around him. Everything glitters and looks wonderful; the things you cannot afford to buy are as much fun to look at as the choosing of a bit of pork for dinner.

And then the people! To some Lisu the throngs of human beings were more fascinating than the tables of merchandise. Mostly Chinese farmers attended Paoshan Market, but frequently Lisu from the Munition of Rocks and even Tibetans brightened the spectacle with their varied costumes. On one such occasion, the four, hearing a Lisu sentence behind them, turned around to see a band of Black Lisu closely grouped together and talking to one another. Excitedly La-ma-wu and his friends accosted them and the Chinese farmers turned to stare at this large circle, blocking the traffic and babbling in a strange tongue—but only for a moment. "Earth people!" they say contemptuously, lose interest and press on.

"Where are you staying? Can you understand us? We're Flowery Lisu from the Burma border. We want to come to your parts. We'd like to talk to you—where are you staying?"

"Oh," with a wild boisterous laugh, "where do Lisu stay

when they come to town? You'll find us out on the city wall to-night after the stars appear."

The writer remembers meeting just such a group at the very same market; and then that night, searching for them on the wall. Too poor to pay inn-fare, and children of the open always, there they were, cosily encircling a wood-fire; the flames leaping up brought their turbaned heads, beaded necklaces, and strong handsome faces into the light. Above their heads the stars shone brilliantly, and behind them in dark shadow, stretched out the almost unlit streets of the Chinese city. A Lisu campfire? La-ma-wu would be entirely at home, and pulling a loose stone over for a seat, the band of four would soon be lost in thrilling conversation.

"Yes, I can understand you, though your talk is funny," says one big fellow with a loud laugh, shifting his long knife to a more comfortable position at his side. "We're Black Lisu, but we don't come from the Salween canyon, we come from the Mekong. Eh?——" . . . "Oh, the Mekong river runs parallel to the Salween—you can cross over to the Salween from our parts, one good long day's journey. But there are lots of Black Lisu in the Mekong. Why not come back with us? We'd like to hear your story. We're going back to-morrow, I think. We brought coffin boards down to trade for blankets—see?" pulling a new scarlet one around his shoulders with evident satisfaction. "Can't get such things up in the mountains."

They talked well on into the night. Lisu love to chat around the fire, and knowing no such thing as "hours," it is often very late before they retire. Going to bed is a simple thing to the Lisu traveller. He simply buries his fire for breakfast's use, curls up in his blanket and—he's asleep.

The four consulted Mr. Payne, for it was the Salween Lisu they had been asked to evangelize (and for whom there had been years of prayer) but might not God want them to go to the Mekong first? Here were guides all ready to take them! So it was decided to go back with these Mekong Lisu.

Money for food along the way was supplied by Mr. Payne, but Lisuland is different from Chinaland. The magnificently beautiful mountain giants are cold and indifferent to the human speck who tried to live along their sides, so the human specks, recognizing a common struggle for existence, are banded together in necessary loyalty. No Lisu of the Munition of Rocks, heathen or otherwise, charges a traveller for lodging or food. Free hospitality is a point of honour among them, so money for food after they reached Lisuland had not been given to the four.

This produced a difficult situation, for the Mekong Lisu turned out to have a different custom. Their guides were good to them in a way, but too full of thoughts of displaying their market spoils to the home folk to care about the message of the cross. When the party arrived, La-ma-wu and his companions were shown into the home of one of their guides. Almost immediately they sensed a different atmosphere. Their welcome was not very cordial. Their southern dialect was openly laughed at. When at length the market chatter finally wore out and they were given a hearing, it was not a friendly one.

"It's a strange story; we've never heard it before. It wouldn't be convenient," with a yawn, "for us to change our customs. Why don't you try going over to the Salween canyon? Maybe they'd like to be Christians over there."

Clearly there was no response of faith and no interest was shown. Remember that there had been no special prayer preparation for this field. La-ma-wu would easily discern, moreover, that extended hospitality was not going to be given cheerfully; so one morning, with courteous "Thank you's" (which the Black Lisu just gaped and laughed at—it not being the custom to say thank you up there), the little band started off into the unknown—down, down the mountainside until, a little knoll affording a resting place, they stopped for a word of prayer and to encourage each other.

"Should we try going to the Salween?" questioned Andrew.

"I hear there are no villages anywhere the whole journey across—it would be easy to get lost," said Wa-si.

"And we know the way back now, from here, but we would have no notion of the way out of the Salween canyon," offered La-ma-wu.

"I think so too," put in Job. "Look, you can see Lisu villages all over these mountains. We've tried only one village in this canyon so far. Let's go on, I say. Folks are praying for us, don't forget."

"Don't know about you fellows," piped up La-ma-wu, "But I'm still hungry. *Eh-eh*, I wish we could buy some rice. I just can't eat enough of this corn to get filled. But can't the Black Lisu stow it away, though! I counted nine bowls one of those chaps ate this morning. By the time I'd got four down I felt stuffed to the eyebrows—yet I didn't feel satisfied."

"Me too," said Andrew. "I've felt hungry ever since I've been here. They didn't serve us rice once, not once. I do hope some of those other places have rice!"

But no. In those northern reaches, corn is the staple diet. All the four were accustomed to eating rice, just like the Chinese, and it takes a considerable period to get adjusted, so they were hungry all the time, Job told me. Heartache was added to hunger pangs. Village after village did they climb to, only to be laughed at, argued with, and sometimes shown the door.

"We'd drop in at the first house of the village," they related later, "and not only the gospel was refused, but lodging and food also. 'Try the house above,' they'd say. We'd climb up there, only to be pointed to the house above that. Sometimes we'd go through the whole village, and arriving at the highest house, have them point us back to the bottom house which had already shown us the door. It was heart-sickening.

"Once we missed the road, and for a day and a half had nothing at all to eat. I'll tell you, that was tough," and there was a silent pause, as memory brought back the horrors and spiritual testings of that experience. "You'll never come back alive——" that wail of heart-anxious loved ones must have recurred often during those thirty-six hours without food, lost on the strange, wild, inhospitable mountains. When at length a village and a road were sighted, it is no wonder that the courage of one of the four faltered.

"I've had enough," said Andrew. "I'm going home. It's no use. These folk up here don't want the gospel. We don't know the country nor the trails and—I think we'd better wait until someone who knows more about the place can come with us.

A white man could hire guides. Mr. Fraser didn't get lost. I think we're wasting our days to stay on."

"Go back with not a single soul won for Christ? That's not satisfying to me. And we've never even been to the place we started out for—the Salween Canyon!"

The four argued back and forth. Lonely, heart-sick, discouraged and hungry, they finally decided to go back to the missionary at least. He stood to them for fellowship, comfort, counsel and—not one would dare to mention it, but each would think of it!—a square meal of rice! But all the way back to Paoshan the hearts of three of them were unhappy. *Volunteers for the Upper Salween!* They could hear Mr. Gowman's stirring call, could see the faces of their fellows glow with joy and pride as they four stood up to volunteer; and now—sneaking back *empty.* Thank God, there was a white missionary near to cast strong loving arms of courage and faith around them at that time! And like the true "Big Brother," as they called him, he went a second mile.

"I'll take you into the Upper Salween myself," he said earnestly. "Not even Andrew is going back home now, not until you've been where you were *called!*"

That is how, after a few days of rest and refreshment, the beautiful feet started out again, this time on a new road in every sense. The Lisu tribes people are simple and childlike in disposition. Through God-given wisdom, Mr. Fraser established an indigenous church—self-supporting, self-governing and self-propagating; but all the Lisu I have ever known, never work so happily as when there is a white "Big Brother" somewhere near for fellowship and counsel. I'm sure Mr. Payne's escorting them into the canyon played no small part in the harvest which ensued. Like a mother's hand smoothing the brow of a child in feverish sleep, it just did something to the four.

Through twisting ravine and over mountain-top the beautiful feet of God's messengers came nearer and nearer the Munition of Rocks. Late afternoon of the fourth day as they came on to a little mountain promontory, the panorama of the Salween canyon lay before them. Giant twisted convulsions of rock lie, contortion upon contortion, in every shape and form as far as eye can see; with a green ribbon of "the river-without-a-bottom" crawling in and out at their feet. Right before them the mountainside sloped in grassy sward to the river's brink, and across the river on another velvet slope lay the little fortified hamlet called Six Treasuries, glistening white against the green grass and trees.

Feudalism still reigned in the Munition of Rocks. The owner of one of those white castles told me he had purchased a whole mountain for six hundred Chinese dollars, and automatically all the Lisu on that mountain became his serfs. His personal servants (that is, those who "ate his rice" every day) numbered one hundred, and he showed us the huge pillars of his courtyard, each a whole tree trunk, felled from his own land by Lisu servitors. He also took us upstairs and showed us the fortifications of his castle. Brigands had attacked and destroyed the hamlet some years previously, and when he rebuilt he had gun-turrets made, and could now hold it against several hundred attackers, so he believed. He also showed us a roll-top desk, an organ and many other beautiful pieces of civilized, hand-carved furniture, made by the carpenters which he had brought all the way from Shanghai for that purpose.

Doubtless all this was shown to Mr. Payne also, for this feudal laird liked to entertain strangers, and was the only enterprising laird I ever met. And thus the gate to the Canyon was entered.

"Are there many Lisu in these parts?" received the answer, "Many? Thousands. Everywhere, both sides of the river!" So, using the laird's home as a base, the four were sent out. Horse-Grass-Level was the place first visited. As Mr. Payne was with them, we may be sure there was much prayer made unitedly before they set forth, but even so the Lisu encountered were slow to accept the message. Hospitality, however, was generously offered, and some said they would believe "when the wine was all drunk up." When the time came for Mr. Payne to return to his wife at Paoshan, he could sense the four were losing courage.

"Andrew, you go up the canyon a way. Try a few more places and I'll wait until you come back." Then, at what seemed the eleventh hour, God gave the increase. On a steep mountainside, in the little hamlet of Falling Timbers, fifteen families accepted Christ, and promised to throw out their demon altars. One other family, where there was a young girl named Homay, nearer to the Chinese laird, had also promised to turn, so Andrew hastened back with his glad news and sent for the other three.

With what a thankful heart the white missionary and the four yellow-skinned ones gathered in that first little home (Homay's) to tear down the demon altar and proclaimed Christ as Saviour and Lord! He had not failed their faith. He had not wasted their sacrifice. A great harvest was awaiting them, urged Mr. Payne, and they must be bold in faith and push on. But homesickness must have been written on the faces of the four, for Mr. Payne did a very wise and strategic thing.

"It's not time for all to go home now with victory just beginning. You stay here and cover as many villages as you can, and in one month I'll be back. I'll return myself, after a month, and we can then see what God has done, and again consult together."

Andrew, though, had reached the end of his endurance. "If you're going back, Pastor, I'm going with you," he said; and no pleadings could shake him. But the other three were willing to stay. *Stop, when the first fruit had just been gleaned?* They would never be satisfied all their lives if they did that. No, it must be a month's more hardship, a month's more eating corn (for corn is the staple food of the Salween too) and toiling up these mountainsides much more precipitous than in their home mountain country. Andrew would take word back of how difficult the task was, the mother church would pray, and they could send letters by Andrew, and—send for help! Maybe some other of the young fellows would come in and relieve them, now that a way in was cleared. Yes, hope shone a little brighter, and when Mr. Payne and Andrew said goodbye, the three watched them go with happier hearts.

> Give me the love that leads the way,
> The faith that nothing can dismay,
> The hope no disappointments tire,
> The passion that will burn like fire.
> Let me not sink to be a clod,
> Make me thy fuel, Flame of God.
> *Amy Carmichael.*

Now up the canyon go the beautiful feet—not flying with winged sandals, but plodding painfully in the hot and weary dust. The new believers were not stable—that is, not all of them; but here and there an earnest young face gladdened their hearts—that girl Homay, for instance. And up past Homay's house, on a high promontory commanding a magnificent view of the canyon, was a village called Deer Pool, where the most promising group of all had already built a chapel. In fact, Mr. Payne said that he and his wife were going to move in and live for a while right at Deer Pool, which news created much joy and excitement. Almost unnoticed among the worshippers on Sunday was a young girl of about fifteen, the Leah of the following pages.

And up the canyon by the main road (a trail too narrow for an automobile) the village of Pine Mountain impressed them as large and important. The harvest reaped there seemed large at first, though in reality it proved shallow. Nevertheless, Old Big, whose story is told in our last chapter, was one of the firstfruits of that village.

Higher up the same mountain to an altitude of some eight thousand feet is the village of Plum Tree Flat: you will hear of little Amos after a while; that is his village. So the work spread.

North of Pine Mountain the message was not received so easily at first, but across the river on the west bank of the Salween Squirrel's Grave, Sandalwood Flat, and Village-of-the-Olives yielded fruit that was to remain. Gad, of whom you will read, was from Squirrel's Grave.

But as the three travelled up and down mountainsides they kept hearing of Luda Village and Shangpa, said to be six or seven days' journey up the head of the canyon. The Lisu up there were quite different in dialect. Another tribe, called Nosu, was to be found there also. Eagerly Job laid before Mr. Payne the need to push farther on, to carry the Good News as far as human foot could take it.

By this time the Paynes were in residence at Deer Pool (a pioneering effort whose hardships and suffering were to tell on his dear wife, and was one reason they could not continue on in Lisu work), and Andrew's return to the mother church had produced the hoped-for results. Reinforcements arrived. As soon as possible (for the work in Oak Flat district badly required teachers) Mr. Payne gave the longed-for approval, and suggested that one of the new volunteers, Luke, should go northward with Job.

That trail up the canyon has been described by an experienced pioneer as "the hardest travel in China." Certainly that was true of it in the old heathen days. A considerable section of it we call "The Robber District," for obvious reasons, and those hold-up men kill to rob. But it was not only fear of evil men; those inner parts of the canyon afford a bare living and food was scarce. Often the boys were hungry and had to tighten their belts as they pushed on, but the passion of conquest was on them.

> Then with a rush the intolerable craving
> Shivers throughout me like a trumpet call,
> Oh, to save some! . . .

You can imagine, then, their feelings as one day, five days north of Deer Pool, they came upon an old man on the road.

"Boys, are you travellers in these parts?" he addressed them, eyeing their Flowery Lisu costumes and book bags.

"Yes, we are teachers, come to tell you of a life after death," replied Job. He said he always preached the resurrection everywhere he went.

"A-bo! Isn't that wonderful!" exclaimed the old man, sitting down on the earth bank of the trail. "We'd heard rumours that teachers who could tell you of those things had come into the canyon, lower down! And I've been longing to hear; I have been on the point of sending my two sons to find you! A-egh! A-egh! This is a wonderful day for me. You'll stay at my house to-night, of course! Come, let's go there now. You will be thirsty and hungry." So, talking excitedly, he led the way up a near trail to his village.

"I just knew my urge to come to these parts was not an idle one!" cried out Job ecstatically as they followed the old man. And that night saw the beginning of a new harvest, that of the Luda District Church, numbering to-day some two thousand Christians.

By 1932 missionaries of other missions had entered the canyon north of Luda; still farther beyond them, in later years, the Tibetan-Border Mission opened a station; so that the Munition of Rocks was at last invaded.

That stronghold of Satan, for so many centuries even unchallenged, has not "fallen"—oh, don't think that! Nor is the fight for it ended. A keen price of suffering and lives has been paid. Three white missionaries and one Lisu home missionary lie buried in the Luda district alone; and two Lisu home missionary graves keep solemn watch in the Oak Flat (Deer Pool) district.

Job and Luke were a month teaching the new converts when a call from Mr. Payne brought them back. On hearing the grand results they had witnessed, Mr. Payne suggested that Luke return, with La-ma-wu as companion, Job being needed elsewhere.

It was many long months now since Job and La-ma-wu had left home, but both were still pressing the battle to the gates. Several months in the Luda district brought in more families won to Christ; then the two young evangelists started back for Deer Pool, La-ma-wu hoping to go all the way home to his little family in Stockade Hill.

As they approached Oak Flat, La-ma-wu said he was not feeling well. But Deer Pool was only a day away, and then they would see their beloved white missionaries and get some medicine. So the two lads pressed on. It is a long and stiff climb, up from the Oak Flat ravine; over two thousand feet they had to ascend. Unknown to them, the virulent fever of the Salween had laid its death fingers on dear young La-ma-wu, for, as they reached the high level where the trail crosses that mountain, with the village of Deer Pool almost in view, La-ma-wu fell, like a shock of corn under the sickle.

He was only twenty-three years old: and what bitter grief to the comrade who had to bury him there by the roadside, away from wife, child, and even human habitation, the wild mountain trees and grasses waving over him while the Salween River moaned nearly eight thousand feet below.

It was Easter, 1938, before I learned the above story. My first Easter in Lisuland, it was, and we wanted to teach the growing church the importance and wonder of that celebration.

"Has the church no dead around here?" I asked Job, who happened to be back in the canyon, ministering again. It was then Job told me about La-ma-wu. My heart was stirred within me.

"Has there never been any monument put up there, Job?" I asked earnestly.

"Lisu don't use monuments, Ma-Ma," he replied, "But there isn't even a proper grave. It is sunken into the mountainside and in a few more years even I won't be able to find it. Guess I'm the only one around who knows where it is. I've thought more than once, as I passed, that we ought to do something, but we're all so busy——"

"No, not too busy to reclaim the resting place of God's corn of wheat, who gave his young life that the gospel might enter the canyon! The Lisu church ought never to forget La-ma-wu! And it will be grand and fitting that their first Easter service should be held at his grave."

And so it was planned. Easter morning found us in the village of Border Mountain, which is the nearest Christian village to La-ma-wu's grave. Four o'clock in the morning found Job, his wife Rhoda, Dorcas (a Nosu girl) and I, slipping out through the shadows of the sleeping village to stand on a rock there, and awaken them all with singing *Christ the Lord is Risen To-day!* At first all was cold and dark, the surrounding mountain peaks dim and black against the breaking dawn of the sky. But as we sang on, the light came over an eastern ridge and lit up deep ravine, towering rock, shaggy pine trees and flimsy Lisu shanties. Just so had our dear Corn of Wheat preached the resurrection message among the cold darkness of heathenism; just so had he seen light begin to break through, thrusting back the shadow of heathendom and bringing into clear view souls here and there who were destined to yield fully to its warm life-giving glow, and who were to carry on his work after he fell.

As we went on to sing *I Know That My Redeemer Liveth*, dim forms, hastily buttoning on jackets, stole out from the various sleeping huts and joined us. It was a great thrill, a great parabolic picture of how just that same thing, spiritually, had happened to La-ma-wu. By the time he died, Homay, Me-do-me-pa, Leah, and many others had turned to Christ—had joined him, so to speak, on the Rock, and were singing with him the *song of the redeemed*, bathed in that light which was breaking over the mountainsides in every part of the canyon. Hallelujah!

At the close of our song we were fourteen, and all went into the little rustic chapel, knelt together and had a worship-prayer service, then dispersed for breakfast.

After the morning meal, another Easter service was held, to which a greater number came, when we announced our purpose of honouring him who had given his life that the gospel might be brought to them; and we invited as many as were able to join with us in building him a good grave.

So noon found us trailing over the mountainside single file, as is habitual in the canyon, while the younger ones darted up or down the mountain to pluck scarlet and white rhododendrons, which were still in bloom.

By the side of a very high trail, skirting the banks of the Salween, Job stopped and began to look around. "It's somewhere near this pine tree," he said. Then he found it, quietly sunken into the wild grass so as to be almost obscured. Immediately our party dispersed to look for rocks and started to build it up in the common Chinese fashion. After the little mound was pronounced finished, we women took our lovely scarlet rhododendron blossoms and placed them upright in the centre, in the form of a cross, symbolic of the cross he died to proclaim; then all around it by the sides of the grave, we stuck in the lily-shaped and delicately fragrant white rhododendrons. It looked lovely. As Job had been La-ma-wu's comrade, I asked him to give the message as we reverently gathered in a circle. A copy of the Lisu New Testament in manuscript had just reached us, and so Job chose his text from 1 Cor. xv. 53: "For this corruptible must put on incorruption."

When he finished we sang the Lisu hymn for those who have gone on before us, *Sleep on, Beloved*—

> Although we Christians die,
> There will be an awaking from sleep:
> Because the Saviour died for our sins,
> When Jesus returns we shall meet again.

And as we left to go home, the strains of the chorus drifted back over the mountain trail to that lonely grave,

When Jesus returns we shall meet again.

In September 1944, as my husband, baby son and I left for our furlough, we had to come out over that high trail; and as we came to the one little mound under the pine tree, I stopped to look back, and say goodbye to Lisuland. It was a sunny day, the blue heavens flecked with white clouds which curled lovingly around the necks of the tall peaks, and cast little shadows on the mountain sward beneath. A more wonderfully beautiful spectacle could not be seen, and everywhere I looked—at the opposite bank of the canyon, or where both banks became indistinguishable in the winding, tortuous gorge of mountain knees, ridges, shoulders, peaks—everywhere I looked, I could see little villages clinging to ridge or shoulder, little "nests" above the abysmal ravines, nests that I knew were now Christian. We were leaving a church roll of some twelve hundred, not including catechists, and I turned to the lonely grave beside the road and whispered "Goodbye, laddie! *Already* it is, not a hundredfold, but a *thousandfold*."

3

A Tree Beside the Waters

A DARK little shanty that looks like a junk shop, dusty cupboards, two big iron pots unwashed pushed up against them, a low bed by the central fire which pours forth smoke and soot over everything, and a group of anxious-faced Lisu squatting around the fire and poking it occasionally. From the low bed a moan pierces through the smoke, and a restless, feverish turning of the figure stretched on it, tell its own tale.

"It's no use, Dad," says one of the young men. "It's because we turned Christian. The demons are angry with us. Why, even the white man was in the party of teachers who cast out the demons! If this Jesus they talked about is so powerful, why did He let the demons bite mother? She was in good health until that happened. I say—throw it all over and go back quickly to our old ways. Sacrifice to the demons, call in the village wizard, before it is too late and mother dies!"

A young girl of seventeen years, sitting among them, looks anxiously from face to face, then dares to put in a word: "The teachers said that Jesus healed sick people when He was on earth. They say sickness is *not* from the bite of a demon, and that if we got sick we were to pray to God in Jesus' name!"

"Well," says the older brother, turning angrily upon her, "you *did* pray, didn't you? I saw you kneel by mother's bed a while ago. A lot we know how to pray! And where's the teacher to tell us? The white man has gone back to Paoshan, and the three Lisu have gone up the canyon—who knows where they are!" Another series of moans piercing the dark makes all turn to the restless figure on the bed. "Dad, make up your mind! She's very sick."

The old father shifts his position uneasily. "It wouldn't look nice to backslide. We were the *first* family to turn Christian; and the white man is coming back, he said. He is to move into Deer Pool village just up the road. He'll bring lots of medicines, he said."

"That won't be for a few months yet," puts in the second son. "Ma will be gone if you wait that long. Everyone in the village is talking about you for not calling in the wizard. If she dies——"

"All right," cries out the old man, pushed to extremity and fearing public opinion. "We'll have to backslide, then. But you boys call the wizard. I won't."

At that word one of the sons arose quickly with a "Sure. I'll go!" and disappeared while the young girl buried her face in her hands and waited there, motionless.

Blessed is the man that trusteth in the Lord, and whose hope the Lord is. For he shall be as a tree planted by the waters, and that spreadeth out her roots by the river, and shall not see when heat cometh, but her leaf shall be green; and shall not be careful in the year of drought, neither shall cease from yielding fruit (Jer. xvii. 7, 8).

On the outside a quiet little figure; on the inside a raging, scorching fire.

Was it all going to be lost now—this new found joy and freedom? She had thrilled to the resurrection story, but even more (we must be truthful) to the answer that the Lisu teacher had given her. "Yes, it is for women too. Women learn to read and write just as much as the men." Blessed Christ, who brings emancipation to women of all lands! How her heart had surged with hope. Only seventeen years old, but she had chafed inwardly at all the checking which her bright mind had received. "Go to school and learn Chinese? Oh, no! That is for the men. Don't hanker for what you can't have. Women's part is to farm, weave cloth, bear children, serve the men. You'll get into trouble if you try for anything more than that!" Always restrained, held down, pressed into the old female mould, reminded that she was mere chattel belonging to the men.

Face buried in her hands, her hot heart communed with itself, with her past, trying to reach out to the future, but every direction was dark, hopeless. When the roots of our inward being reach no farther than our own thoughts, they find but dry ground. *"That spreadeth out her roots by the river."* She was not yet aware that the Fount of Living Water was already within. She had not learned to "spread out her roots," to reach forth in the spirit and touch the throne of grace. Poor little sapling! So newly planted. Many another has been uprooted, when the same sharp Wind blew. But searching within her own heart she found a ray of hope. Mr. Payne had said he would move in with his wife, and live, perhaps, at Deer Pool! That was only some four miles away! She could steal up there and learn. No. She wasn't going to backslide. The vision of a new and wonderful life had opened up before her. *Go back into dark heathenism, with its virtual slavery? No. Better die first.* Her underlip set firmly and she raised her head, for the wizard was being ushered in the door.

I do not know how she escaped taking part in the incantation which followed. A chicken, or pig, or cow (depending on how important the sickness was) would be killed, its blood offered with incantations, its meat cooked, and a big meal prepared. She would be called upon to cook that. Her only chance of escape would be—absence. If she were not home and did not return until all was over, she would be free. But she might have to take a beating for neglect of such an important occasion. I have seen women who had been beaten—saw one so bruised that she could not stand on her feet for several days afterward; and I saw another who had been hit on the head, and suffered periodically all the rest of her life from frightful headaches.

Years later when the young girl of this story had become one of the best readers and writers in the Lisu church (men included) I asked her, "Homay, how did you do it?"

"They punished me if they found me going to chapel at Deer Pool," she said simply, "so I used to reckon the days and make my firewood hunting on Saturday evenings and Sundays." (Of course the heathen do not count time by weeks so they would lose track of the Christian worship day). "Then I'd hunt it on Deer Pool mountain! Slip in and enjoy the Saturday night prayer meeting, and the three services on Sunday. Of course now and again they'd find out and I'd have to pay for it, but on the whole it worked fine! I'd go back with a big load of firewood on my back."

Her application for baptism, however, was turned down. Do not blame the Lisu teachers too much. Remember their disappointment when they heard that the very first family to turn Christian in the canyon had gone back. Of course no one paid much attention to the carelessly added, "except the oldest daughter." What does a girl reckon anyway, in oriental thinking? And who was near to see whether Homay partook with the family or not? In the beginning of a work it is good to be very careful whom you baptize—they set the standard forever after. And so this young Sapling felt the keen Wind of Humiliation. She was up for catechizing with the other candidates for baptism. She could answer all the questions, better and quicker than most, yet they would be accepted and she told "to wait till her affairs were clear." She endured that for two and a half years.

Even more than her family were involved—she was married. A few months before the gospel feet reached the canyon, her parents had held a drinking-wine affair, which is the Lisu heathen name for wedding, and her husband was supposed to enter her family as son. He was just a chit of a lad and Homay never liked him, and would not go near him (that is why I do not include him when speaking of her "family"). He did not seem to mind, for he was not at all faithful in staying with her parents. The marriage had been arranged for by the two fathers, and though the bridegroom would be consulted to some extent, he did not need to be enthusiastic over it. He also had turned Christian, with the coming of Andrew, but just as easily backslid when the others did. Homay never lived with him, and at length, when he eloped with another girl, she was secretly praising the Lord for such a deliverance. But her family were insulted and very angry. They had paid a big price to his parents for the privilege of having him enter their family (and do their farm work) and now that money was lost; at least, it would take a lawsuit to get it back, as his family excused his conduct on the grounds that he had not bargained for a "Christian" wife. Bitter words were her portion day and night; very bitter they could be, for her mother had died, and the wizard said it was because they had called him too late, so that also was added to the abuse poured on her head. A divorce had been obtained, however, and once more she was free. "We'll marry her to a heathen who will knock this nonsense out of her" was a threat which toned down her exaltation; earnestly and quietly she strove to win her father's pity by faithful work at home and obedience to him in all but that one thing.

Now she was learning to use her "roots." Up there at Deer Pool, Mr. and Mrs. Payne had lived for many months, and during that time she had the privilege of hearing them preach in chapel. She learned that she had "roots"—that she had the power, in the secret chamber of her spirit, to reach out and communicate with God. Her roots had "sensed" the river, and though outward conditions remained dry, and even antagonistic, down in the secret place her roots were reaching out thirstily, eagerly for the *living water*! She found that God answered her prayers in Jesus' name. Why He had allowed her mother to die, she could not understand. She discovered too that her prayers were not always answered immediately, and very frequently not in the way she had expected, but always sooner or later there *was* an answer. What an elation was hers! That she had a secret power with which she could overcome, and often change adverse circumstances, a power which her father and brothers were helpless to combat. She felt free, liberated! Gratitude made her decide to be His slave, for love's sake. As she went quietly about her work her heart talked with itself. When she saw the other heathen girls angered with injustice, chafing at their bondage, she said to herself, "I am different from them. I have eternal life. I have it now, within me, and it *works*!" Gently she would try to tell them about it, too.

At this time two big things were uppermost in her prayers. The matter of her marriage, and the longing to be free to worship. Daily she slipped up her secret stairway and laid these two matters before her new Father. Then one day a man from Deer Pool came into their shanty with a smirk on his face and asked for her parent. When the latter came, this man opened up the subject of Homay's marriage to a Deer Pool boy (whose name, later, was Philip). I do not know all the details of that transaction.

Christian Lisu do not pay money (called a dowry) for their wives. The dowry was a heavy bondage in heathendom. Young men often cannot afford to marry because of it, or are all their lives burdened with the heavy interest and unable to get it paid off. The Lisu church has decided to give its daughters free of charge, and of course no Christian may marry a heathen with the church's consent. Philip paid some money for Homay. Whether it was the costs of her divorce, or whether he had not yet publicly turned Christian, I do not know; but it seemed like God's answer to her prayers. True, Philip was not particularly attractive to her, but he planned they both should be Christians, so once again it seemed that she had conquered her family by remaining quiet and submissive on the surface, but warring valiantly and earnestly in the spirit. The marriage was delayed, however, so she still had to pray on for freedom to worship.

The answer to this was unexpected. She had been blessed and filled with joy at a visit from another white woman missionary. The Paynes had gone on furlough, and Mr. and Mrs. A. B. Cooke (successors to Mr. Fraser in the Lisu work) had volunteered for the Upper Salween. All Lisu loved Leila Cooke. Her kindly radiant spirit shone through her face, and just to be with her was a blessing. I once heard one of their servants say, "No wind ever blows under the Cooke wing." Although on this occasion Leila was just passing through on her way to Pine Mountain village, a long day's journey north, Homay felt the comfort of that "wing." After some months had passed, a note came for her from Mrs. Cooke, and she was all prepared to obey whatever it said. It told her that the Cooke family were again on the move, but that Mr. and Mrs. John Kuhn were coming in to the Oak Flat district. Leila Cooke ended with, "Mrs. Kuhn will have no servants to help her and I am sure she would be grateful if you would cook for her. Do you think you could?"

Cook to the missionary? I am sure she giggled at first and said, "Ma srghe!" (meaning "I don't know"), for they all do. No Lisu likes to be a servant. Poor as they are (and we always try to house and feed them better than they would get at home) they love independence. But the more Homay thought of the new proposition, the more attractive it became. To work with a

white woman might not be too bad; certainly not with Mrs.
Payne and Mrs. Cooke. And then there would be the freedom
to go to chapel services any time she liked. And every evening
there would be a service, probably, where she could learn more.
Learn to sing! How she loved to sing the hymns, and she had
discovered she could learn even the men's parts, tenor or bass,
quite as accurately as they themselves! And the missionary's
home was the centre of activity, with the evangelists coming and
going, and all that. It would be fun. Would her father allow it?
Well, there was the oriental way of doing that. Luckily it was
December, the slack time of the year. Farm work had ended.
The women were spinning and weaving cloth for the family
clothes. Weave a bit later at night, and a bit earlier in the
morning, and she would get it all finished. Then just tell her
father, "I'm going up to Pine Mountain to help the new Ma-Ma
for a few days" and—off she'd go. As the "days" lengthened out
—well, a nice gift out of her salary would be the most potent
argument to silence Dad! So again she was victor over her
circumstances through prayer and faith alone. What a good
God to plan this wonderful salvation, a saving grace that is
useful every day of one's life, let alone its consummation at
death! And so this young Sapling was drinking deeply of the
river of life, and shooting up straight and strong.

I was perfectly unconscious of the good things God was
planning for me, when, on our entrance into the Munition of
Rocks, my husband stopped our carriers before a sprawling
little Lisu village. "Belle," John said to me, "there's a nice
Christian girl in one of these huts and we're going to have
lunch with her. Be nice to her; she stands alone and needs comfort. She can speak a bit of Chinese too, so you can talk to her"
(I had not yet learned any Lisu). Mrs. Cooke had written to me,
"It is hard to get Lisu servants and in this mountain land you
cannot live without help. Pray for some, even before you come
in." But as I curiously picked my way past the pigsty, trying to
manœuvre my three-year-old daughter into the Lisu shanty,
servants were nowhere in my thoughts. The little Lisu girl who
needed comfort, and lunch (clean, if possible, please?) were
uppermost. There she was—a short, plump little person running

out to greet us; face slightly "dour" when in repose, but now lit up with a joyous smile as she cried, "Ma-Pa! Ma-Ma!" Then remembering that I had not yet had time to learn Lisu she changed it demurely to the Chinese greeting, "*Yang-si-mu, ping an?*"

I liked her the moment I saw her, I noted her tidy dress, how carefully she was washing her rice, and the air of ability which was hers, despite slow movements. I had not had a chance to inspect many Lisu girls, and she noticed my careful observation and laughed with embarrassment; so I said, "Don't be afraid if I look too hard. I haven't seen many Lisu girls before!" I never dreamed that she thought I was inspecting my new cook! She was so lovely with Little Daughter, too—saw that she had the softest rice to eat, washed out her bowl again, even though it was already clean, supplied her with a warm seat beside the fire, and so on. It was a happy meal, but we had to push on.

I thought I had said goodbye to her, when, the next day at noon, didn't our little hostess of the day before appear at our lunch stop, a roll of bedding on her back and all prepared, apparently, to go on with us!

"Do you think she is going to come with us?" I asked John. He too, was puzzled, but came nearer guessing it. "Wonder if she is not planning to be your helper?" he suggested. Hardly able to believe such good news I essayed a question, "Are you going to come with us and—stay?" Whereupon she laughed and said, "If you want me!"

The story of our arrival that night is told elsewhere.[1] But thus she became one of us, and from now on, our little Sapling was free to deepen her roots, and drink in her living water, with nothing to hinder. I think maybe you would like to get glimpses of her from our circular letters, because they were written down, not in the light of what happened afterwards, but "uncoloured," just little home things, but very revealing. They will incidentally give you glimpses of what composed the white missionary's life during those early days. In our first circular, dated December, 1934, we wrote:

[1] *Precious Things of the Lasting Hills*, China Inland Mission.

I will lift up mine eyes to the hills
For my help comes down from the height,
Lord, Thy strength is the strength of the hill
And I cradle my heart in its might.

Here we are at last—in the mountain fastnesses of West Yunnan, with the stillness of God's country all around us, broken only by the surly roar of the rough Salween River hundreds of feet beneath us, or the musical tones of Lisu voices drifting over from some unseen place on the steep mountain side.

Come with us on our evening walk along this narrow path that skirts the edge of Pine Mountain. Let's stand beneath this old tree for a moment and lift up our eyes to the hills. Did you ever see such a chaos of mountain peaks? There is the highest topmost range, a jagged line piercing the blue, and thrown against it to right and left as far as the eye can reach are masses of sharp crests, precipitous pinnacles, queer knobs, slim pine-wooded ridges, round dumpy foothills, and at their base, the Salween River cutting its snake-like path through and around the solid rock. Wonder and awe fills the heart at first, and then joy comes; joy that the Creator of all this has said, "And I will walk among you, and will be your God, and ye shall be my people."

One evening as I was walking here with Homay, I heard a voice that sounded very near. I looked up and down (there is only up and down here, no level spot) but could see no one. Then Homay smiled, and pulling my sleeve, pointed way, way down, a hundred feet or more beneath us where a second path crawls along the hillside. "It's Pu-fu-si-pa praying," she said simply. My unaccustomed eyes gradually made out a figure in the middle of the dusty road. This dear man had been trying to carry a heavy load up to his home, and being weary, he had set it down by the roadside and he himself was kneeling in the dust of the path, talking to his Lord. The mountain wind had brought his voice up the slope until it sounded quite near. Yes, you may pray in Lisuland—wherever you like; and if anyone does happen to meet you, they accept the fact simply and pass on.

Now we must go back. See! the sun is finally withdrawing from those highest peaks, the cold grey-blue mantle of winter twilight is falling around them, and we must hurry back home.

Home? Oh, you don't see anything like a home on this wild mountain side. Look keenly—clinging to the hill in front of us, can't you see three or four little brown shanties? Here we are!—walk in.

Our Lisu house has only braided bamboo mats for a floor over the earth, so we live much like kittens in a basket. The roof is formed of

wooden stakes laid on the beams and held down by logs. There are no
nails used in the building, everything being tied together with bark.

It's true, the walls are rather porous and, as a matter of necessity,
the weather is a member of the family, coming in and going out at
will. One morning at breakfast, a little white cloud walked in our
door! It vanished the next second—guess we scared it away! The
clouds up here are a continual marvel of beauty. I have seen them go
coasting down the mountain side like gleeful children or fairy beings.
Sometimes they coax and cuddle around the shoulders of the great
smiling peaks or tumble merrily down their sides, or rise in still soft
beauty from their feet, as the sun draws them with his hot magnetic rays.
The human children of these mountain fastnesses are much like them—
clinging with tender hearts to those who love them, but delighting too
in a good romp, play, or something to laugh at! However, they also
have their still moments, when the heart of them reaches out yearningly
toward Him they call their "Sun of Righteousness."

The Christian festival engaged our thoughts for the next
month, but after that it was decided that the white missionaries
should change their place of residence from Pine Mountain
Village to Oak Flat Village. The Christians at Pine Mountain
had proved shallow and the deacon body felt they were un-
worthy of the presence of a missionary. Mr. Cooke had heartily
approved the change, so our next letter describes it.

January, 1935.

And now for our "flitting"! About three miles crawling up the
southern trail, and still on the Pine Mountain range, the path comes to
a kind of huge knoll, dotted with old gnarled oak trees. The rock cliffs,
with here and there a lacy pine tree to add colour, lift abruptly above
this high little tableland, and scrub-tree covered mountain sides sweep
steeply down from its edge. Here is the village of Oak Flat where
Me-do-me-pa, "The Shepherd," lives and where Pade-John has a log
cabin home. The latter also owned a large field at the lower edge of the
knoll, but when he learned that Ma-Pa Cooke thought Oak Flat a
desirable centre for the white missionary, Pade-John came forward
with his sunny smile, and said that he would like to give this piece of
ground for Ma-Pa to use free of charge, as long as he wished. So in
January we moved to Oak Flat Village.

About this time an incident occurred which changed Homay's
life. One late afternoon I was about to give Little Daughter her

evening bath, when Homay came running into the room, flushed in face and excited. She was followed by the laundress who laughed and said, "Homay's fiancé has arrived!"

I had not known she was engaged to be married, so, hastily leaving Kathryn in the tub to be washed by Homay, I went to the back door, and saw Philip for the first time. I did not like him—at least not for my beloved little cook. I thought he looked shallow and mercenary, and indeed since then he has justified those doubts. I returned and looked at her.

"Homay, you are not engaged to him?"

She flushed and giggled nervously.

"My child, you must not marry that fellow! Don't you know that if you marry a man who is not as spiritually minded as yourself that *he* will pull *you* down? 'Be not unequally yoked together' means spiritually, as well as Christian to unbeliever."

"I have already said yes to him, Ma-Ma," she answered quietly. "We are engaged; what can be done about it?"

"Oh, break your engagement!" I cried hastily. I did not know then that a Lisu engagement is like the old Hebrew engagement, almost as binding as marriage. "If you marry that fellow you will wreck your service for God! Anything but that!"

She was silent, and I said no more. Later I was afraid I had said too much, as indeed I had, so I never mentioned the matter again. But I had sown a seed, and I believe it was of God. Outwardly she was the same, but the secret roots were reaching out in question to her *Fount of Living Water*. One day she asked me for permission to go home. She was gone for several weeks. I had forgotten about Philip, but when she returned to us, others told me that she was now free, the engagement had been broken. I asked her about it, but she was not inclined to talk. Yes, she was free; her father was furious—money must be paid back to Philip's family.

"Father always calls me—introduces me, now, to others as his 'Dry Daughter,'" she said to me, so quietly that I was not conscious of how deeply the reproach stung her. "A dry tree" is a barren woman; in the Lisu mind it is a stigma much more dreaded than actual deformity, I think. "A dry tree"—for

Christ's sake? The little Sapling's roots must have clung desperately when that hurricane Wind of Temptation struck. To her dying day she never ceased to wince inwardly at the sting of that name, even after its use was impossible.

Now for more extracts from the old circulars.

June, 1935.

Homay is developing. She has twice brought messages at our local services, quite a departure for a woman. I asked Lisu teacher John what was the hindrance to there being Lisu Bible-women as well as men teachers, and he said, "None, except there is no woman fit for it." Let us pray Homay into fitness.

One day Ah-sah-me-pa came to ask Ma-Ma for help. A deacon of Spirea Flat Village had had his leg torn open to the bone by the kick of an animal. There was only one thing to do—summon Homay (always delighted to go trotting along behind), pack some medicines and go. (My husband remained with Little Daughter.) Despite its pretty name this village leaves the impression of just steepness and gravel. It is in a fold of the mountain, and its only view is the other side of the "fold"; although lower than Plum Tree Flat it is even steeper.

Arrived, I cleansed the wound (with a houseful of people watching me of course), and then asked where we were to sleep. Ma-fa-tsai-ma looked around the little hut. There was the bed her sick husband lay on, and opposite was the one her children slept on; at the head of this latter stood two square wooden cupboards. "Oh, you and Homay can sleep on top of the cupboards!" she said. Well—I looked at Homay's short fatness, and she looked at my long thinness, and our vote was unanimous. *Us for the chapel:* Our rejection of the proffered sleeping quarters gave no offence, and when we went to service that evening, we found two big planks already set on the benches in preparation for our night's repose; so I had the unique experience of participating in Sunday evening service, sitting on the top of my bed!

On the way home, travelling on a high trail, whom did we stumble over, resting in the middle of the path, but Pu-gia-me! (She was the third of the three servants who came to help us at the first, but her conduct did not approve itself to the Lisu church, so they had asked us to dismiss her and then word came that she had really left the Lord and this was the first time we had met her since.) Now here she was, all togged out with the big silver earrings and ornaments of a heathen girl. She looked abashed at seeing us, but there was no escape. As my Lisu is insufficient I left her with Homay and the last I saw, Homay had taken her in her arms and was weeping over her—but Pu-gia-me remains obdurate.

However, those tears were not wasted, for the very next circular records this:

Some weeks later Pu-gia-me unexpectedly returned and announced that she wished to come back to the fold. As she gave due warning, they were ready for her. That was a time when I was ill, but John said that it was splendidly arranged. She was made to confess to all the church, and then in audible prayer to the Lord. They put her through a kind, but very firm cross-questioning. (The Lisu believe in apostolic discipline and offenders have no easy time. But Pu-gia-me took it as if she really was sorry and meant her repentance.)

Homay was my dear companion in trips among the villages. She looked after Little Daughter (who loved her devotedly) when I was occupied with preaching and ministering to the Lisu, and my heart could rest about it, for she was chaste and dependable and I knew little Kathryn would be safe.

In July, 1935, we went as a family on a tour of some of the northern villages. We had some blessed experiences, but little Kathryn became infected with malaria. From then on John and I felt that we must be willing for separation. It was a pale-faced, thin little girl whom we brought home, so we decided travelling in that country was not suitable for white children, and that while one of us went, the other must stay at home with Kathryn. John always has declared that the Munition of Rocks is not a woman's country, so the one to itinerate was mostly himself.

However, more than Little Daughter had found the above trip too much physically. We learned from this experience never to try to itinerate in the Rainy Season. It takes such a toll of health that it is not worth while, unless God definitely leads to put aside this rule. This was one of the reasons which led us to hold our long Bible schools in the summer, when rain made itineration impossible for the white man.

John's next trip was to Goo-moo, the story of which will be related later on; but it was while he was away in Burma that I became sick with a disease unknown to me, later diagnosed as erysipelas. The circular of this time records that Homay was

called back to her own home because of the sickness of her
father. He died, and she returned to me just a day before I was
compelled to go to bed. I was six days' journey from the nearest
white person, many days away from a doctor, and my husband
"somewhere in Burma," beyond communication. So you can
know what it meant to me to have Homay back. She, like all
Lisu, knew nothing of caring for the sick. It was that experience
which taught me what the Lisu suffer when they are ill. I had
high fever, felt sticky and dirty and longed so for a bath. Day
after day passed in that condition—I was much too weak to
wash myself. At last I asked Homay if she would not try to wash
me. She was all love and pity, but when I asked her to bathe me
she looked completely baffled. She went and got a basin of hot
water, dipped her hands in it and rubbed her wet hands over
me—that is all she knew how to do, and I was too weak to
direct her, though the tears came with disappointment. How
much enlightened countries owe to Christ! He is the origin of
those studies which bring alleviation to the suffering; in every
land the first hospital is always founded by Christ's messengers,
the missionaries. We ought to think how much we owe Him,
and to those who brought Him to us and be willing to share our
knowledge! "We are debtors."

The Lisu came every night to sing and pray for me, but as
I was obviously getting worse, Job (again evangelist in those
parts) decided to go for help to the distant Chinese city of
Paoshan. In two weeks time he was back with Nurse Kathleen
Davies and Miss Winifred Embery, and from then on I was
properly cared for. But medical orders were adamant—I must
go out to Chinaland for a while, where I could get better food.

I asked Homay if she would go with me and stay with me,
so I could continue my Lisu studies with her. She gladly consented. The circular of October, 1935, says:

Homay's father has died. Legally now she becomes the chattel of her
heathen brother, and we are told he intends to get money for her. He
has the power to sell her as a bride into a heathen family or even sell
her as a slave; pray for her. We would like to buy her ourselves and
let her work out her redemption gradually by serving us, but there are
difficulties.

So all was not easy for our dear little cook. But I remember on the way out, as all of us were gathered about an inn fire one evening, our Lisu carriers started to sing hymns. I heard one young evangelist whisper to Homay who squatted next to him, "Sister, sing bass with me!" She could sing it better than he, and he wanted to learn the bass from her!

We were out in Chinaland for three months, and I tried to have prayer in Lisu with Homay each day; first to practise my Lisu and secondly to encourage her to pray daily for the other members of the Lisu church. One evening as we were kneeling together at my bed I felt urged to pray for a dear deacon at Small Hemp. But I could not remember his name exactly and, hunting through my mind for it, I was praying something like this, "And bless dear old *A-va-ni*—no. *A-va-tse?* No. Oh, *Va-chi-kya-pa!*" Whereupon Homay fell back upon the floor, opened her mouth and simply howled with laughter. I felt she was too excessively merry when I was merely reaching around in my mind for his name, when I was brought to remember what his name *meant*. All their names have meanings even as we have Mr. White, Mr. Baker, etc. And Lisu use their names without thinking of their meanings. However, my feeling around for this man's name had brought its full meaning back to Homay. In her ears I had said, "And bless dear old *Pig-Dirt*, no—*Pig-Grease?*—no. Oh, *Expel Pig-Dung-Man!*" And it had broken up our prayer meeting!

I might say here that the heathen Lisu give their children these horrible names in order to deceive the evil spirits into thinking the child is refuse, like its name, and thus they will not "steal" it; in other words, that it might not die. But such names are so repugnant that we often give Bible names in their place, if the Christian proves earnest. Homay was given the name "Phœbe," but almost no one used it; because we had come to love her as Homay, I believe, and Homay means simply Ho-girl.

Those days in Chinaland, Homay watched over Little Daughter, did our laundry and was by no means idle, so at the end of the month I handed her the salary of five Chinese dollars, as usual. She stood looking at it in her hand as if dissatisfied; at last she picked out half of it and returned it to me. "Take this back, Ma-Ma, please. I am not doing a full day's work and my conscience would not be happy if I took money for full time labour."

I record this little incident so that you may see what lovely fruit was growing on this little Tree. I know of no keener test for any Christian, white man or yellow, than his reaction to the greed for money. I would like to testify that Homay is not the only Lisu Christian we have found to be pure from this taint, but let us not pass over it lightly. Those days she went on the Chinese market where she beheld hundreds of useful pretty nicknacks she would have loved to own, but could not afford to buy. "A conscience void of offence toward God and toward men"; White man or woman, do *you* prize that above all else?

Another little incident from old letters gives a picture of the tenderness of this young Lisu heart. We were able to get back into Lisuland in time for Christmas.

January, 1936.

Going into the kitchen last Sunday morning I was brought to a halt by the sight of Samuel, head between his knees, sobbing; Job at his right hand weeping audibly; Homay at his left crying into her dishpan; and Me-do-me-pa trying to look as if he were not going to be next.

"What are you crying for?" I whispered to Homay.

"Because Job is crying over Sam's affair," sobs Sister Sympathy.

Sam's affair (of which you will hear more later) is this. He was married to a girl, Philip's sister she was, whom he said he did not love, had not lived with, and so wished to get rid of; he had intended to reveal this by flying off to Luda, as a sort of ultimatum. That morning Job had gone to him and told him that this might not be, and the big young fellow took it so hard that all in the kitchen were dissolved in tears with him. As one knelt beside the lad and sensed the furious tide of hot youth, one felt utterly impotent to stem it, and could only cry in one's heart, "Oh God, Thou alone art sufficient to bend this strong young neck to the yoke!" And it was an hour or so before the gentle Lord of Calvary got possession of that vigorously resisting young nature. But as he arose to his feet quieted, we tried to prepare him for the loneliness of cross-bearing—no one can help us bear our cross but Jesus; it is one thing to surrender among tender sympathetic friends, but quite another to go back alone to the hut and its unwelcome presence. Homay knew so well what that struggle was. Knew how she herself had felt tied to a heathen; remembered her bondage to Philip, and though she had experienced God's power of deliverance, her tears flowed for the agony of this struggle. It was not always the missionaries in their study room that helped the church. The kitchen, where there was a Lisu Tree-Beside-the-Waters, was felt, somehow to be a place of power; and what the mistress sometimes might not be able to accomplish, the cook had ability to perform!

During these days Homay was sharing with us another experience. The little old Lisu shanty in which we had now lived for a year or so was considered unhealthy, and it was suggested that we build a better home. All had to be done from the standing tree on the mountainside, and the February, 1936, circular tells a bit of it.

There is a bare spot on Sunset Ridge where some thirty noble and beautiful trees have given up their lives that the missionary might have a safe dwelling in Lisuland. Day after day it was—

Anon a sound appalling,
As a hundred years of pride
Crashed, in the silence falling,
And the shadowy pine trees sighed.

Day after day, "out of the copse the stroke of the iron axe," accompanied by the *chip-chip* of long Lisu knives that had to hack off the bark, and turn the round trunk into square beams, with the nasal *sizz-sizz* of the great saw which further converted them into joists or beams. Noontide brought Ma-Ma, Kathryn and Homay down the hillsides with baskets, and soon beside a pine-chip fire a picnic lunch was spread out. Then a long, hard afternoon; and dusk saw Daddy wearily climbing the trail homeward, perfumed like a pine forest and covered with shavings!

After three weeks of such preparatory work, we were told that the day had arrived when we must flit. Up behind the Shanty was a rickety, black-sooted little log cabin, the only empty house in the village. So we attacked it with brooms, hung up some cheery texts and pictures, brightened it with our old but still gay travelling rugs, tucked into it those indispensable comrades, the baby organ and our dear books (arranged on cretonne-curtained shelves hastily shaped out of packing cases!) and the cabin looked so cosy that we quite fell in love with it.

It was a sad day when the beloved though leaky old Shanty had to be torn down, but joy returned when a solid, sturdy framework began to rise in its place.

But before the walls were up, the February rains descended on us black and relentless. Allyn and Leila Cooke were scheduled to arrive on a certain date and we were all to hold a Bible school for the Lisu. As the day approached we had only a wall-less but roofed-over house, no kitchen, and rain still descending. John was laid low with a very bad tooth, his face terribly swollen, and too ill to stand on his feet, let alone superintend the weaving and nailing up of the bamboo walls. Homay had to cook meals with only a lean-to roof over her mud stove, and the ground beneath her feet a constant puddle. How she ever did it I never knew, but she was so sweet and serene with it all that she was a benediction to us. I quote from the March circular:

"They will never be able to make it, Ma-Ma. It's been raining for days, you know, and the roads are too bad in such stormy weather. You need not expect them this week." The little group of Lisu women, shivering in the cold drizzle, nodded their heads to confirm Ah-be-pa's words.

"Well, but they said in their letter that they would arrive to-night or to-morrow, and we cannot but prepare for them, can we? Let's get the bedroom completed anyway, and as much of the dining room as we can accomplish, and let the rest of the house go."

Lisu do not usually work in such weather, but the faithful little group agreed, and despite their thin garments, and the penetrating damp chill, they threw themselves into valiant effort, Homay cheering them on, occasionally with cups of hot tea, or steaming honey water. And by Saturday night the two rooms were walled and ready for occupation. Then, as we were in the midst of finishing touches, a cry came echoing over the knoll—"They're coming!" and John (now better) came running in upon me, "Belle! Cookes are here! Cookes are here! Just climbing the hill now!" The next moment we parted as if a bomb had burst us asunder—he to the right to welcome our guests, and I to the left to the bedroom to pull out dresser scarfs and linen that had been packed away from the building dust.

Up through the thin drizzle, our beloved friends plodded. "Why, none of us thought you'd *ever* get here to-day!" we cried, as we shook hands. "Well, we had promised we would," was the simple answer that covered the two nights they had had to sleep with insufficient bedding, for they had become separated from their coolies, and the hard bitter day, up before daybreak, pushing on through biting cold and wet, not even stopping for lunch, and all because they had "promised." Allyn and

Leila Cooke are a never-ending inspiration to us, a joy and comfort for which we continually thank God. Before going on to Luda they had said they would join us in holding a short term Bible school for the Oak Flat district Lisu, and God rewarded their faithful sacrifices by pouring out unusual blessing during the week's session.

But all through those hard days, the little cook, so serene and thoughtful of others on the outside, was carrying a secret heartache. Her brothers were threatening her, anxious to turn her into money whether it be by selling her to a heathen for wife or as a slave. So once more the little Tree was shaken by the Sharp Wind from the Bitter Heights. And once again her only strength was to send down her roots, secretly, deeply to draw on her Living Water.

> There is a viewless, cloistered room,
> As high as heaven, as fair as day,
> Where, though my feet may join the throng,
> My soul can enter in, and pray.
>
> One hearkening even, cannot know
> When I have crossed the threshold o'er,
> For He alone who hears my prayers
> Had heard the shutting of the door.
>   *Amy Carmichael.*

And once more there came an answer. Evangelist Joseph proposed to her and was accepted. That story is told in *Precious Things of the Lasting Hills* and Homay is the girl there called "Heart's Desire." How her brothers were prevailed upon to give her to him, I do not know.

And now we were called upon to separate, for the Kuhn family was needing to go on furlough. John had been out ten years and I, eight.

Before we left, however, Leila Cooke had written to me, "Would you be willing to lend Homay to me until you come back? I do not know her equal and I would like to have her with me in Luda so as to be an example to the other Lisu girls up here, who are far from attaining to Homay's spiritual position." Of course both Homay and I were delighted that she should be under such a safe wing until the day of her marriage to Joseph, and so we parted.

Furlough brought us the new delight of Lisu letters, and among others was this one from Homay herself.

You-who-have-gone-back-to-the-foreign-country—
Ma-Pa, Ma-Ma, and Kathryn,
Ma-Pa, Ma-Ma and Kathryn whom I love, whom I never can forget, whom I deeply regard in Christ Jesus, whom I long to see. Oh dear. I think of you three and send you a handshake on paper. After we parted I wanted to see you, loved you, and many tears came out. When we came to Luda from Oak Flat, Sunday we paused at Lu-mu-teh and were there three days. The following Wednesday we went to Luda. The (Chinese) laird at Lu-mu-teh wants to hinder the building of the chapel and put two of the villagers in jail; Saturday they were imprisoned and Tuesday they were freed. Sunday early, Mr. and Mrs. Cooke, the villagers and many others of us before breakfast prayed (for them) and God answered our prayers. Tuesday, toward evening, they were released, thank God!

By God's help I was enabled to walk all the way from Oak Flat to Luda in peace. Ma-Pa, Ma-Ma, you three, I would like to know if you arrived safely at the foreign country. Oh dear. Ma-Pa, Ma-Ma and Kathryn I thank you; we lived together over a year and by God's grace (during that time) there was nothing happened to be regretted. I thank you. I learned how to study a little, while I was with you, and learned how to do a few things. I am so glad. Oh dear. Ma-Pa, Ma-Ma and Kathryn I can't tell you how I long to see you and touch your hands a little, and take you, Kathryn, around a little. I can't forget your faces; it's as if I hear your voices in my sleep. Oh dear. When you get to your foreign country, don't forget us but pray for us all the time, thank you— please forgive any mistakes I've made in writing this; thank you. The writer Homay Phoebe who loves you and will never forget you.

Her letter was enclosed in one from Mrs. Cooke which tells that Homay's engagement may have to be broken. She says, "We are sorry to hear that Homay's younger brother wants to make trouble. Homay feels that it is not so much that he wants a bridal price, as that he wants her to marry the blue blood instead of an ordinary Lisu. She says the folks in her village like to claim they are not Lisu but Chinese, and they want her to marry one of the same class. They all think her brothers would be satisfied if she decided to remain single all her life, and she is quite willing. But Job does not feel that she had better tell her brother that as yet, and Moses feels the same. It is difficult to know what to say about it. I am sure you are praying. I feel sorry for Joseph, for she is the second one he has sought for a wife."

Always the dread fear of the "dry tree" life following her! But it caused her roots to go all the deeper; and by fall (1936) her third hope of a husband and family were gone—but in a most unlooked-for way.

While we were at Orcas Island, a letter came from Andrew (sorry I cannot find it or I would translate) giving the heart-breaking news that our dear Joseph is with his Lord. He was returning from Goo-moo, where he had been teaching, and was on his way home to get his bride, dear Homay, when he was drowned. The day was hot and he and his companions decided to have a bath; Joseph could not swim and got out of his depth. Samuel and Lysias were with him at the time, and they buried him and carried his things back home for him.

When John first read this out to me, it just seemed as if I could not allow it to be true. It was so hard to have lost one beloved teacher the year before, and Joseph was one of our priceless ones—a pure spirit, absolutely devoted to his Lord. He could have been a farmer like the rest, but he left it all to carry the gospel message to others of his own race. For a year's labour he received merely his board and lodging and fifteen local dollars for clothes. Poorest of the poor, he was rich in another kind of goods—"as poor, yet making many rich."

One of my last memories of Joseph is of the testimony meeting one Christmas. The testimonies were a blessing to us all and Joseph kept quiet as long, doubtless, as he could; then he sprang to his feet, and with his face so radiant it was almost glorified he cried out, "I haven't anything to give to God, but all that I am and all that I have, I give back to Him." And now God has gathered in the complete offering.

Our hearts wondered about dear Homay, and how she would receive this sad solution to her problems. A letter from Mr. Cooke (also mislaid, so sorry) told us she received it bravely.

After a while they heard her singing softly in the kitchen, *Have Thine Own Way, Lord,* and *Looking This Way.* Then after a time she went out into the little house where Miss Ward had died, and had prayer. Brave little Lisu sister, what are God's plans for your life now? Back to the old place where she is, humanly speaking, unprotected.

Lisu-like, her next letter never mentions it:

Ma-Pa, Ma-Ma, you three—
Whom I love and can never forget, whom in the name of the Holy Spirit of the Trinity I behold in my heart all the time, I send you a hand-shake and greetings on paper. Oh dear. Are you happy now in your own country? We love you and long to see you beyond expression. Oh dear. Ma-Pa, the letter you wrote to me has come, and I received it October 15, and my happiness knew no bounds. Oh dear. Ma-Pa, thank you for that letter. You said you had arrived at Grandpa Miller's home, and we thank God. Are you now also in peace? You said you had been to a summer conference where you received much spiritual food, and I thank God. You had received three letters from me; now Ma-Pa, did you really and truly cry when you read them? Oh dear. I truly long to see you more than I can express. Since I have been at Luda my physical strength has grown, pray for me that my spiritual strength may increase also. Oh dear Ma-Pa, I am in much prayer that you will come back to us; we at Oak Flat would be delighted if that were God's will. Now Mr. Fraser arrived at Luda on November 5, we do thank God.
Oh Kathryn [I had guided the little girlie's hand in writing Homay a note, and also stuck in a part of the snap on which Kathryn appears and apparently one of my own feet], So happy I was to get your letter, and also for the picture. Ma-Ma, I can see your foot but not your head; this is not satisfying! Oh dear. Ma-Ma, have you forgotten Lisu words? Please write me a Lisu letter, I long to read one from you. When I think of you I weep and love you very much. Oh dear. Ma-Ma, the writer is the one who wants to see you, thinks of you, and to whom you gave the name of (Homay) Phœbe. Oh dear. Ma-Pa, Ma-Ma, and Kathryn, dwell in peace!

But we see by this that now the pioneer of the Lisu work, our provincial superintendent, Mr. J. O. Fraser, had arrived at Luda where Homay was staying. He and the Cookes were working on the revision of the Lisu New Testament. Inevitably he got

to know Homay. In that northern district where the tribes
are farther away from the Chinese civilization, and so are cruder
in the living, Homay's neat capable cleverness must have shone
like a diamond among rough pebbles. Her fiancé's death having
been noised abroad, proposals of marriage began to flow in!
The great, brilliant superintendent at the translator's desk, and
the little Lisu housemaid . . . what connection could there ever
be between such? But it was part of his greatness that he always
had time and loving sympathy for the humblest life near him.
He heard of those proposals and was greatly amused. As they
began to mount up in numbers and passed the fifty mark (if I
remember rightly) he suggested jocularly to the Cookes that
they have refusals of marriage printed for Homay—it would
save her so much time and letter-writing! But he was pondering
what he knew of the strange movings of Providence in this
young life, and one day he called her to him.

"Homay, have you ever thought that perhaps God is calling
you to a single life, in order that you may serve Him in a sphere
new to Lisuland? You know the Lisu church has few Bible-
women. All its evangelists and teachers are men. Yet men cannot
reach women like a woman could. Would you consider giving
yourself to the Lord for His ministry?"

With all his spiritual penetration I do not think that Mr.
Fraser knew what a knife he had plunged into Homay's heart.
Outwardly she was always serene and quiet—she had schooled
herself for so many years to keep her inner thoughts from showing on the surface, that she had wonderful control of herself. She
would not appear to have been "stabbed," and he of course
did not know of the stigma-name of "Dry Tree," and that it
had been a horror to her all these years. Even if he had known,
he would have put the question, for he never feared to face-up
any soul to God's highest demands; and I have often wondered,
would Homay's story have had a different ending if she had
accepted his advice? But Homay had never seen a woman single
for Christ's sake—her Lisu white missionaries were married,
why couldn't God use her, married? I do not say she was un-
willing; but her answer was, "If God asked me to remain single
I would do so; but I cannot now promise never to marry."

She must have left his presence with a hurricane in her heart. Was it necessary to be a "dry tree" physically, to bring forth spiritually? And there was such a handsome, consecrated young evangelist now casting eyes upon her. Mrs. Cooke had written to us of this boy, Daniel:

Daniel has given his life to the Lord's work. Please thank the friends at home who have been praying for him. God has answered prayer in the breaking of his engagement to the heathen woman to whom he was betrothed in childhood. It was a real fight with the powers of darkness, but God made Daniel victorious. Daniel's heathen brother said he would kill Daniel rather than let him free from the engagement. Daniel ought to have had plenty to pay back the bridal price but the father and brother refused to let him use his share of the property. For one year's wages as evangelist David received twenty-five dollars. When the father saw Daniel would not be forced to marry the girl, he asked Daniel to give him twenty dollars to get rid of her. Daniel gave it to him and of the five dollars left of the whole year's wages he handed me fifty cents to help pay the coolies to carry (Teacher) Moses when Moses was too sick to walk.

But a new and exciting page of experience was about to be turned for Homay. Cookes were asked to go on a long journey south to investigate the field of Bana, which had been offered to the China Inland Mission. And they had invited her to go with them! What fun! A long trek through beautiful Lisuland. Then (thrill of thrills) a motor bus ride into Burma, along the Burma Road. Homay had never seen an automobile in her life. After that a train ride—and she had never seen a train before! Then an exciting day in the city of Mandalay—her first glimpse of modern civilization. Then once more familiar trail-trekking, and the mission station of Bana was reached, where several other tribes beside the Lisu were being evangelized. But amidst all these thrills, in the Secret Place she was wondering about the bearing of fruit for God. In her next letter Mrs. Cooke wrote:

Homay is here with us and is a constant joy to us. The other day I found her out in the kitchen counting the kernels on one ear of corn. She asked me to help her and we found 538 kernels on one ear. She wanted to know the number so that she could glorify God for His power in making so much out of one grain of corn. Then another day she was looking at some caterpillars, and when I came along she said, "Isn't it wonderful that these can all turn into butterflies?" And then another day I was telling her about the verse in Hosea where it says, "I will be as the dew unto Israel" and she said Teacher John (the Lisu evangelist who died in 1935) said, in preaching, "We must not feel that God forgets us, for He does not even forget the little leaves, but sends a portion of dew for every little leaf." I often find Homay off in a quiet place with her portion of the New Testament and a pencil. And at night after she is in bed I hear her softly repeating scripture verses before she goes to sleep. As you think of Homay you will pray that God will provide His own escort to take her home from here when we leave for furlough. She is about thirty days' journey from home. Her sister and three Lisu men are here to return with her, but as it is necessary to sleep out in the open while travelling, we feel it would be more to the glory of God if she had an older man or a missionary to escort the party.

Into these thoughts walked the postman, with a bunch of Lisu letters from Luda. Among them was one from Daniel to Homay! Evidently she had been expecting this proposal, and had made up her mind, for the return mail to Luda took her acceptance of his offer of marriage. Mrs. Cooke said that Homay's reply to him was very sweet, and that she had said, "I am sure that I love you, but wait until there are no doubts in your own mind about your love for me." That, of course, was just a bit of coy teasing!

However, the happy little acceptance note arrived in Luda station where Mr. Charles Peterson was living alone at the time. As he read it, he sat filled with grief and bewilderment. For he had just been bowled over in spirit to hear that Daniel, their shining splendid Daniel, had fallen into sin. A period of idleness at home had brought temptation. Laziness, even if under the guise of "rest," is no preparation for overcoming, and Daniel had fallen. Of course, had Homay known this, she would never have said yes; so what should he do? Thinking it might touch and revive Daniel, Mr. Peterson took it to him, but Daniel read it with darkening face. He knew of course, that he now was not worthy of her, and that his fall had cancelled this sweet little answer. And so ended *this* engagement of Homay's also. Of Daniel's reclamation, largely due to the earnest intercession of a faithful prayer partner in Seattle, you will hear later. But when Homay and we met again, she was still single and free.

We were back in Lisuland (from furlough) four months and then, on April 21, in the afternoon, a cry came, "The Bana party is arriving! They are coming up the hill now!" How we dropped everything and ran. There being neither telegraph nor telephone and almost no postal service in the canyon, expected loved ones could not announce their arrival beforehand. Yes, there was my dear Homay, not seen for two years now, but she was plump as usual, and her laugh and hug were as warm as ever. Along with her came Luke, A-che, another Luda Lisu unknown to me, and her sister Ruth. We took their picture to let others see the Bana party almost as we saw them.

You can imagine how Homay and I hugged one another, each of us conscious of the absence of a little form who had never swerved in her devotion to "Big Sister Homay," and who remained always, as Homay's precious white baby (Kathryn had gone to school at Chefoo). Almost immediately, with tears flooding her eyes she asked, "What is the latest word of Kathryn, Ma-Ma?" And so I shared with her the latest letters from Little Daughter.

And now we found that our Homay was too advanced for her old position as cook. She had learned to use the Lisu typewriter, and of the three Lisu whom the Cookes tried out in typing the manuscript of the Lisu New Testament, Homay was the most accurate. So she became a sort of secretary to us. She oversaw the housekeeping, the buying in and measuring of the year's supply of grain, charcoal, salt, potatoes, etc., but she gave half of each day to typing out copies of the various New Testament Books for the Bible students, of whom you will be hearing anon. (It was half a year before the printed New Testament reached us.) At the month's end, when we went to give her her small salary, she again handed half of it back to us saying. "Ma-Pa, Ma-Ma, I would like to contribute the half of each day to working for the Lisu church by typing, as my gift to God. I will do that for nothing. The other half of each day, we will reckon as working for you, and for that I will take wages, if this is agreeable to you!"

It touched us very deeply—as you may imagine, but we have long learned the truth that God is no man's debtor. To be rich toward God is to be rich eternally; and so we accepted her offer.

And now we faced the coming true of a vision given to us while on furlough, but before I mention that, I want to quote from the circulars again, so that our station personnel, when referred to, will be intelligible to you.

A New Missionary

We had brought a Christmas gift to the Lisu on our return in December 1937, in the. person of a new missionary, Victor Christianson. He worked with Earl Carlson among the Chinese over a year ago, and when he heard of the latter's death he felt that God had asked him to take up the fallen torch, among the Lisu. I think I can best describe our new comrade to you by a picture. Our first day out was very long, and dark overtook us while we were still on wild mountain tops. The end of the stage was a very long steep and rocky descent, the last miles of which were made by feeble moonlight. Indeed three of the Lisu carriers did not reach the village at all, but had to spend the December night, huddled supperless, in the middle of the road. Those of us who managed to get to the inn were very weary, and I was not slow in getting to bed. Victor had to sleep in the main room, a very public place. As he was having his devotions, an old (Chinese) lady in the house asked him about the Book he was reading, and tired as he was he started to teach her. As I lay there on the other side of the thin partition I heard the kindly voice going on and on patiently explaining the way of salvation, regardless of his personal fatigue and a waiting bed—she had never heard before and very probably might not again, so it was told her in full before he slept. And in my heart, as I lay and listened, I praised God for His missionary in lonely mountain places.

Then another worker was brought to us, but before I quote concerning that, reference should be made to a young missionary hero who laid down his life while serving the Lisu in the northern field of Luda. While the Cookes were at Bana, and later when they went on furlough, the Luda station was in charge of two white men—Mr. Charles B. Peterson and Mr. Earl Carlson. This book is about Lisu "Nests" and so I do not feel free to interject missionary biographies, but one might well be written about the noble young life which Earl Carlson laid down in that far-distant corner of the mission field. He was smitten with typhus fever (we think it was), taken while toiling unremittingly among the Lisu villages. There was no doctor to tend him. One was sent for, but he arrived too late. And so Mr. Peterson had to see his chum laid to rest on the little knoll outside his kitchen door. Mr. Peterson continued on alone, but the Mission felt it was too precarious, so the following quotation will explain itself.

OUR FAMILY ENLARGES

On January 15 we had the glad privilege of welcoming Charles Peterson to Oak Flat. Charles is one of "our own" boys; we use that designation only of those young missionaries who spent their initial days in Yunnan in our home, as language students, in years past. So Charles is no new friend. If I had to describe him in one word I think I would choose "faithful." No matter how trying his post, you cannot tempt Charlie away from it until he feels the Lord has said, "Go." Both the superintendent and fellow missionaries urged him to take a holiday after Earl's death, and "come out," but he quietly refused.

However, it has been decided to vacate Luda temporarily as a main station, and work it by visits, as an outstation of Oak Flat. Under such advice Charlie moved, and so we are the wealthy possessors of two other workers, Charles and Victor.

To go back to our "vision"; it was that of holding a Rainy Season Bible School for three months, June through August, of each year. The main purpose was to teach the Bible to the Lisu evangelists. We had soon discovered that these dear zealous young fellows were really ignorant of the scriptures—much too ignorant for their work. Of course they had never read the whole New Testament, and they had done the best they could with the four Gospels and Acts, which they possessed. To win heathen to Christ, one does not require much more knowledge than the plan of salvation and John iii. 16. But to *build up a church* after they are won is a different matter. There were now many babes in Christ waiting to be shown the next step, and since the Lisu New Testament was available in manuscript form at least, we felt the need for a prolonged session over the Word. Mr. Fraser was delighted, and urged us on. A full-time Bible school was an impossibility; we had the oversight of a field four days' journey in length, and more if you counted the outstations. The Luda district, just committed to our oversight, was six days' journey away. The pastoring of hundreds of believers, steadily increasing in number, demanded visitation. And we were the only medical help anybody had within the radius of three or more weeks' travel, at that time. We could not possibly spend all our time at a Bible school.

We chose the Rainy Season for this purpose as our experience, related in previous pages, had taught us that it was dangerous for us to travel at that time of the year. Also, the summer being the farmers' busiest time, the Lisu teachers had then much less to do. People lived in their fields to protect the growing grain from birds and animals, and the villages were partly empty. So we chose June to August for Bible study. Of this work I hope to devote a whole chapter later on. Just now, its effect on Homay is all I will relate.

We began that first school (R.S.B.S., we called it, standing for Rainy Season Bible School) with a session of heart-searching and cleansing. Although it was mainly for men, a few girls attended it at first, and Homay always took in as many classes as she had time for.

One of those first days, John and I were seated at our table, deep in work when Homay came slowly up to us and stopped, waiting for an invitation to speak. Her face was so grave that John said immediately, "What is it, Homay?"

"Ma-Pa, I have a confession I must make to you." As she spoke tears began to well up in her eyes.

"All right, don't be afraid," her pastor answered kindly.

"Before your furlough, when we were building the house here, I—I lied to you once, Ma-Pa," and at that word the flood gates broke and the tears streamed so that it was hard to get the rest of the story.

"I found a penpoint on the ground, after everything was torn up, and I did not ask if I might have it, but just took it—I knew you'd give it if I asked; and I found a twig and made a stem for it, and it worked as a pen quite nicely. But one day when I was using it, you came by and said, 'Where did you get the pen, Homay?' and I was scared and before I thought I had answered, 'Mr. Cooke gave it to me,' and then you walked away. I was not happy afterwards, but I was always too ashamed to confess it to you. You might have thought I was in the habit of telling you lies and I've never lied to you in anything else." By this time she was shaking so with sobs that we tried to stop her. But she had more to say.

"Then you left for furlough, and we went to Bana; but always in the services, when sin was mentioned, that penpoint came up before me. I confessed it to the Cookes, but still I got no relief. Then I told Teacher Luke, and he thought it was too small a matter to worry about, but still I was not happy.

"And then on the way back from Bana, we stopped at Paoshan where Miss Anna Christensen was holding meetings, you remember, and she spoke of unconfessed sins, and said even little things might keep us from God, and so I made up my mind to tell you about the penpoint."

By this time all of us were weeping, but I hope this little story will speak to some reader, who has been told by the Holy Spirit to confess a sin, perhaps a seemingly unimportant one, and you are not obeying, because Satan tells you it is too small a matter. There is no path to peace or blessing until you confess. Confessing to other people than the ones involved, like Homay tried, is the devil's own snare to keep you in bondage. And the fear of confession is his delusion also. After confession was all over, and the tears dried, what joy and lightness of heart! And her Ma-Pa against whom she had offended, and whom she deeply loved, only cherished her all the more because of her obedience to the Spirit in the little thing, and her great desire to be a clean vessel for God to use.

And now we have a surprise for you. The circular of August, 1938, recording the end of our first R.S.B.S., has this paragraph.

WEDDING BELLS
That busy day before closing day, about four in the afternoon, Job performed a ceremony which made Thomas and Homay man and wife for life. I do not know how it came about, but feel it was more of a comfort marriage than a hot love affair. She is the best to be had in Lisuland, as Thomas well knew, and Homay was conscious that she could not say yes to a more faithful or finer Christian, so I think that was how it happened; but happiness seems to increase in their hearts every day. Homay was dressed in a combination of orange silk and

dark blue cotton. Rhoda was her bridesmaid (and a very pretty one) and Luda-Peter was best man.

I played Lohengrin's *Bridal March* as they entered and left the chapel, and the whole ceremony was holy and quiet—a lovely memory. Thomas is to be kept in this district for a while at least, and they live in a little house right next to ours, for Homay continues to help us in typing and in the house work. (Dorcas has gone home to her family in Luda.)

Thomas is a Stockade Hill boy. A deep sorrow in his life (one that need never have happened if he had not obeyed his conscience before the promptings of his heart) made an evangelistic trip away from home seem attractive to him. And so he was sent to the Munition of Rocks, and worked most of his time in the Luda district. As a strange providence had it, he paid one evangelistic trip to Goo-moo, and while there heard of dear Joseph's drowning and was asked to conduct Joseph's funeral. So as it turned out in the end, the one to bury Homay's fiancé was the one who married her! As the Luda district was temporarily under the Oak Flat district, the Luda evangelists were all summoned to R.S.B.S. and thus Homay and Thomas met.

Both were very nervous. Thomas lost ten pounds between the date of the engagement and that of the marriage. And our usually serene Homay, when asked by Job (at the wedding ceremony), "Are you pleased to take this man as your husband?" opened her mouth to answer, "Pleased," but only a wheeze came out! Her mouth was so dry with nervousness that she could not get her voice to work. Astounded, Job said, "What?" whereupon, her eyes beseeching him in agony, again her mouth opened, and again only a wheeze emerging, Job was loyal. "Oh yes, she says, *Pleased!*" he announced to everybody, and proceeded.

Then when the bridegroom was to put the ring on her finger, his hand shook so, that he could not pick up the ring; so again Job silently came to the rescue, and put the ring on her finger in lieu of the bridegroom. But these are small matters—the Lisu consider it went off very nicely.

Their honeymoon (which Lisu do not take) was a trip to Goo-moo, Burma, which will be recorded in the story of Goo-moo. The Goo-moo Christians loved the pair of them so much, however, that when the time for our departure came (Homay and Thomas had gone with us) they begged us to leave the newly-weds with them to teach them the Bible for six months; and we gladly consented. They were given the little house which the Goo-moo Christians had built for us, and six happy and useful months were spent over there in Burma.

In the beginning of 1939 a shadow passed over their sunshine. The February circular has a note—

Thomas has been incapacitated for work by a strange illness giving him acute pain. It sounds like a serious hernia, but we really do not know. His valuable ministry is being hindered—pray.

And now 1939 R.S.B.S. was coming upon us. During the time that the Cookes were on furlough, the Luda teachers came down to study with us, and this time, to our joy, Daniel appeared with them. He had returned to the Lord, and felt the need of studying the Word. His deacons had recommended him, so were glad to receive him along with the other students from Luda. Their arrival is told in the following circular:

And another delightful reunion was the following Monday night—a cry from the kitchen sent me flying through the doorway. It said, "Teacher Job has returned!" As I came up to his humble doorway I asked, "Didn't Rhoda come too?" and a meek "Yes" from the direction of the garden revealed the lassie herself, braids hanging down her bosom, coming from the vegetable patch with something for supper. She got a kiss on the spot and then Homay pulled my hand and whispered with a meaning smile, "Daniel's in there!" thrusting her chin (native fashion) in the direction of the hut. She did not seem the least embarrassed, in fact I think she was secretly pleased that she could now show the one who had been faithless to her, just what a fine husband God had eventually given her. I hurried into the crowded shanty (for everybody was there to welcome them) and was happy to see Job's face once more, and sure enough, there in the corner, hanging back as if ashamed, was Daniel—he has come for the Rainy Season Bible School and is doing odd jobs before it begins. He is paying his own way for these three months of study. He listens to the messages very earnestly and one can see why the Cookes loved him so much. The next evening, when a little group of them including Homay were present, Daniel apologized to her in front of them all—she herself told me so with shining eyes—

and once more I thought how God works out all things, even the heart-break of unfaithfulness to the one who loves and cleaves unto Him. "You must learn, you must let God teach you, that the only way to get rid of your past is to get a future out of it. God will waste nothing."—*Phillips Brooks.*

But Thomas's trouble did not clear up. He was a good student usually; in fact in 1940 he led the whole student body. But this year of 1939 seemed to be going to be a failure. The August circular says:

I had no sooner spoken of Thomas' glowing face in last month's issue, than the Enemy put a blight upon it. Praise God he could only touch the outside, but he did hit hard. Thomas got severe pain in his head and around the left eye, and then after about a week of suffering, the pain passed, but left the sight impaired. The right eye has now become affected. Do pray for him—he is only twenty-six years old and he and Homay are expecting a little gift from God in December.

I remember well those days. We could not diagnose his trouble; as a matter of fact, it was double hernia, but at the time the whole pain was in his eyes and he seemed to be going blind. Now blindness in a mountain land, where everything is perpendicular, is an awful affliction. Well that Homay had learned to send her roots out to the Living Water! Yet even so, when such a storm hits a young tree, the upper part of it can be badly shaken. And one morning I shall never forget. I was called to see Thomas again—he could see out of neither eye and was in severe pain. I could do nothing for him, and felt my uselessness. So I just put my arms around the anxious little wife and whispered, "Don't worry, dear. God is faithful and remember you are like a daughter to us. You and Thomas will always have a place in our home." She broke down and wept, which was most unusual for her, who had such wonderful outward control.

In answer to prayer, Thomas was healed sufficiently that he was able to finish R.S.B.S., but at the end of the school, it was plain that he must seek medical help. In Burma there was a mission hospital where they were very kind to the Lisu, and Thomas knew that if he could only get to that faraway place he would receive attention free of charge. That autumn and winter we itinerated a lot and were seldom home, so I do not remember when Thomas left. I only know that later I discovered that his little wife had given all her savings to pay his expenses there and back. Here I would like to say what a good wife Homay was. She was a very nimble seamstress and I think she had secretly made up her mind that her husband was to be the best dressed and best cared-for of all the evangelists. Living still in our home, she was at the source of supplies; when cloth or books came in, to be sold to the students, she made the first selection and bought the very best for Thomas. I once teased him, "Don't you know what a lucky man you are, to have such a wife?"

"I sure do," he replied with such a happy laugh that I felt he was not being spoiled, and I was glad that happiness had come to them both.

It was a regret to me that I could not be present when her first-born arrived. No longer a Dry Tree! God knows how to lighten our loads. How joyfully she prepared for that baby. Lisu do not usually make any preparation for a coming child, except, perhaps, to sew it a hat! "Why, you can't tell whether it is going to live or not!" they will say when you suggest a few garments to welcome the wee newcomer. Such a thought shows how high infant mortality is, and is expected to be. Over half their babies die. But Homay had lived with missionaries and had learned some hygiene; so an array of knitted bonnets and small clothes were carefully being added to as the months rolled on.

Baby was to come in December. Thomas was still away and no letters were possible. The Kuhn family had to leave on a long three months' trip to Village of the Three Clans, but fellow workers were present to carry on the work of Oak Flat district. Mr. Peterson was on furlough, but Mr. Christianson had married Miss Cath Galpin, and she promised me to do all in her power to help Homay when her time came. I knew she would, but at the same time, she was a stranger to the lonely little mother. But my duty called me north and I had to go.

When I learned that Homay and Thomas were expecting a little one I wrote and told Kathryn that God had promised to give Homay a baby for Christmas, but had not said whether

He would give a boy or a girl. Her reaction was the following letter to Homay which so amused us that I copy it here.

                                                    Chefoo.
                                            October 31, 1939.
My dearest Homay:
    I think of you a lot and pray for you too.
    I cannot speak Lisu now except yes. I hope you will teach me some Lisu when I see you again, because it is fun learning other languages.
    Mummy has told the secret that God told you, and I think it is a very nice secret. I will love the baby. I will tell you a name if it is a girl—Kathryn—not because its my name because it is the gift of God, and if it is a boy—John—that is only to help you.
    I love you very much.
    I am having a good time at school am learning very much it is only twenty-eight more days till the holidays.
                                            With love from,
                                                KATHRYN K.

Homay was thrilled that her "white baby" should want to name her own real baby, so when a son appeared she named him John. Though that was his legal title, she herself always referred to him as "Oldest Hemp" (Thomas' surname is Hemp). I could not understand it, until I "thought Lisu" and saw that she was looking forward to many more little Hemps; and then I realized how the name "Dry Tree" had stung, all through the years. Always she referred to her baby as "Oldest Hemp" with a smile which spoke of the secret hope that there would be many others.

When we returned in March, 1940, baby John was already quite big and very cute, but cried a great deal. He just cried night and day, and Homay was exhausted long before he was. Germs of a serious illness were already working her body, but this we did not know. Homay had been the healthiest Lisu I have ever met. Every other helper had periodic hours in bed with malarial headaches at least, often more serious diseases, but not Homay. Plump and flourishing, she seemed immune to everything, so when we came back and Cath Christianson told me that Homay had moved out of our house and was living in a room off the Lisu church kitchen, and that she never seemed to have time to do anything but look after little John, I was worried. A baby takes a lot of time and young mothers can easily fall into the habit of letting the baby steal their quiet time with God—and that is fatal spiritually. I sought out the little mother and watched her for some days. She seemed lazy—so unusual for the energetic girl of the past; she disliked to haul water to wash John's baby clothes and would sit by until our laundry girl had finished and then beg for the wash water.

Then in April, one evening as the Infant Brigade (of whom you will hear later) were in the midst of their singing lesson, a gunshot rang out through the dark. Immediately we were all out of the room and into the night. Pushing up the trail, I could just discern other villagers emerging from their huts. A white horse was coming with someone leading it! Job! and behind him Luke, Andrew, their wives, and—Thomas! I believe that was our first word that he was even alive, after the hospital treatment. Here he was, cured—and anxious to behold the baby he had never yet seen.

After joyful greetings we all hurried back to Luke's house where, snug and cosy by the fire, we felt at leisure to ask questions. Thomas was entirely healed! How we thanked the Lord and how mystified we were to hear that an operation for hernia was what fixed him up, eyes and everything!

Of course little John was hauled on to his Daddy's lap for much inspection and hugging. There were the other teachers who also had stories to tell, so that Thomas and his little family were able to slip away to the privacy of their own room next door.

Events followed one another and it was R.S.B.S., 1940, before my attention was drawn particularly to Homay again. Thomas appeared one evening and said, "Ma-Ma, I'm concerned about John's mother" (the Oriental way of mentioning one's wife). "She has had no appetite for a long time, and her legs are swelling. Do you think you have any medicine that would help her?" He looked very anxious about symptoms that seemed unimportant to me. Homay had always had fat ankles. I examined one medical book, but none of the diseases attendant on swollen ankles seemed to fit. From then on I watched the little mother as closely as possible in a busy life that did not often, now, touch hers. She looked all right, but was so lethargic and sluggish that I began to think that maybe it was a spiritual problem and wrote the American prayer helpers to pray for her. I had her in for an interview, too.

"Homay, are you reading the Word and praying, like you used to?"

"No, Ma-Ma," she answered immediately. "There isn't time now and I have not the strength. Baby cries so at night that I am too tired in the day." She had a sort of "What's the use" attitude, that it made me anxious for her. Never having known her to be sick, I did not dream that a dread disease had already laid fast hold upon the still plump little form. She knew herself to be ill, yet she was not in actual pain, so that no one but Thomas took it seriously. I myself thought it was a spiritual matter and exhorted her to remember that the spirit needs food as much as the body. Poor little Nest; it was a sad wind blowing upon it.

At the end of each R.S.B.S. the Lisu teachers are reappointed to districts where they usually remain for the following twelve months. Thomas was sent to Village of the Olives, across the river from us, and the Christians there had prepared a nice little house for him and his family. Homay was reluctant to leave us, although no medicines we had given her had helped her. I urged her to go, thinking that some active testimony for the Lord might be her greatest help. So we parted rather sadly on each side.

For the next few months I had many important things to take my mind off Homay's "lethargy," as I thought of it. Mrs. Christianson had become seriously ill, her life was in danger, she had to be taken out to a hospital, and eventually she and her husband had to return to America. We ourselves were called upon to make a long trip south to Stockade Hill district, there with the parent church to hold one of the first Bible studies since the New Testament came into their hands—for they had had no missionary for many years, and at present writing still have none. This was important work.

So it was Christmas before we returned to Oak Flat and I found a lot of Lisu letters awaiting me, among them one from

Thomas which said something like this: "I hope you will forgive me for not travelling around my field here. Homay is so ill that I cannot leave her. I fear it is a destroying sickness. But I teach every night in this village."

Then it was I became alarmed, and as Leila and Allyn Cooke were expected back from their furlough, to arrive soon after Christmas, we sent one of our mules to Village of Olives for Homay to ride, and urged Thomas to bring her that Leila Cooke might try to diagnose her case. Homay came, outwardly a little thinner, but that was all that was apparent. Inwardly she seemed back at the place of victory. Her face had once more that quiet peace upon it.

> Perhaps thy way is weary oft,
>   Thy feet grow tired and lame;
> I wearied when I reached the well,
>   I suffered just the same:
> And when I bore the heavy cross
>   I fainted 'neath the load;
> And so I've promised rest to all
>   Who walk the weary road.
>   *S. C. U.*

I had no opportunity to talk with Homay personally that time, so I do not know when it was that the Little Tree awoke to the fact that the *one thing needful* is to spread out our roots unto the *river*. Then, "it shall not fear when heat cometh, but its leaf shall be green."

Homay's "leaf" was so green that neither Leila Cooke nor I thought it was "a destroying sickness." We proposed her going out to a Chinese hospital and offered her our mule to ride, but as I remember it, she refused, saying she had not the strength to make such a trip. "I always thought that horseback riding was restful," she said with a smile, "I never imagined that it can be as tiring as walking, until I had this trip over from Village of the Olives." And I laughed too, recollecting the many bone-aches of a whole day in the saddle through such a country—and how the Lisu expect you to be quite rested after "sitting all day," at the end of such a trip!

So back they went and we prayed for her daily, but with no

special concern until February, when Orville Carlson (who had now joined us, to take his dead brother's place in the Lisu work) made a trip to Village of the Olives to conduct a Bible school. He brought back an enthusiastic report of the growing little church there, but added that he was burdened for Homay. "She does not complain of pain, but seems to have no strength to do anything. Just crawls out into the sunshine in the morning and lies there hour after hour. It is pitiful. We ought to pray for her."

From then on, we did, very earnestly, and yet a faith to claim healing never came to us. I was really alarmed now, and the next month, after conducting Bible school in a neighbouring village, I came over and spent a week-end at Village of the Olives. I was shocked at the sight of Homay. She had simply wasted away. She said she had no pain, but daily diarrhœa (medicines for this had long ago been given her without effect); and it was plain to see that death was stamped upon the thin, wan face.

Deeply moved at her obvious condition, I probed for the most important thing—the health of the spirit. And I can still see the light that sprang on to her wasted features as she smiled and answered, "The Lord's will be done, Ma-Ma; I'm happy to accept His will." Tears came with the smile, but did not overflow. Neither of us mentioned what we knew caused them— namely, the question, "What will happen to Baby John?" I did not dare offer to take him, for I was committed to a life in which travelling occupied most of the year. And at that time we had no dependable woman working in our home, only three irresponsible boys, The Infant Brigade, of whom you may hear later. So the question had to remain unanswered.

As the earthly vessel was wearing thin, the treasure within was shining out. All of her Christian life one of Homay's favourite hymns was, *Have Thine Own Way, Lord*, and now that the supreme test was being put to her, those words were always her answer. The Christians there told me that Homay was simply a marvel to the heathen women of the village. They used to come just to see and talk with the young teacher who was not afraid to die, nor even rebellious. The Tree Planted by the Waters . . . "shall not be careful in the year of drought, neither shall cease from yielding fruit." The little group culled out of the heathen-ism during that year of dying were among the choicest of the Munition of Rocks.

As for ourselves—we had work calling for us, and could not stay to see her through the Valley of the Shadow, except in spirit. Our circular letter, telling of the gathering of R.S.B.S. students for 1941, has this paragraph:

THE DISTANT TRIUMPH SONG

Among all our wonderful forty we missed Thomas' face. "Homay is too ill for me to leave her," he wrote, "and I can hardly bear to look at her" (she was so wasted). "My heart is breaking to see the others going off to school and I must stay behind, but there is no help for it."

Then one night after those weeks of heavy rain, as I was about to open the evening service, someone said to me, "Thomas has come! He came in just now, carrying his little son on his back." The news, though long expected, pierced with the sharpness which only the last enemy to be destroyed can inflict. Thomas' coming meant only one thing. Hardly able to speak for tears, I asked, "When did Homay pass away?"

"Sixth of the sixth moon," was the answer. Then I had to go in to prepare for service.

The next day our Thomas was in class. He is very brave, but when opportunity afforded I asked him to tell me of Homay's last days. He said her faith was triumphant to the end. Spiritually she seemed to grow stronger as the body grew weaker. There was never a murmur against this decree of her Father's, although she was only about thirty years old. Fellow villagers say her patience under suffering made the heathen marvel. But when it came to telling her last words, which were ones of pity for himself and little eighteen-months-old John, Thomas broke down; so I said, "Write to me." With no one to care for baby, Thomas had at first said he would go back to his relatives and his own old home, but the pleadings of the flock in Village of the Olives made him hesitate. Here is his note:

"Ma-Ma, I want to answer you now. I wanted to answer you when we were talking together, but I couldn't, because of grief. First I said I was going back to my home, but that was for sorrow of heart. Now I would like to say this, if God shows me the way, I will go back to Village of the Olives. The brothers and sisters there were not satisfied that I should not, and neither am I. For they are more to me than my own people—all in that district are. But I cannot forget Homay; before

R.S.B.S. I cried all day—not for her, but for myself and for Baby John. Homay's last words were, 'I cannot eat. If God is going to take me I will go, but it will be hard for you and baby.' After that her speech was not clear; she felt so sorry for Baby John."

Asked to speak at the Sunday main service, Thomas chose 1 Thess. iv. 13-18 and used it as a testimony to his faith in the resurrection. "We sorrow not as others who have no hope," he quoted. Then we held a memorial service for her who is rejoicing in her Saviour's presence. Since turning to Him, Homay's life among her fellows was without reproach. She went to Him having no cause to be ashamed—what a glorious finale!

Thou wast their rock, their fortress and their might;
Thou, Lord, their Captain in the well-fought fight;
Thou, in the darkness drear, their one true Light.
Alleluia!

And up in Heaven, her old friend, Mr. J. O. Fraser, pioneer missionary to her tribe, he who had given up a brilliant career in the homelands that these poor despised "earth people" might know the way of salvation, was already there to greet her. I would like to ask you, dear reader, what of the many other tribes' girls, just like Homay (for there are many more) who would love to accept and follow this Saviour, *if only they knew how*! What of the many other little Wind-blown Nests, who seek desperately for a Cleft in a Rock to shelter them, but cannot find Him, if you and I do not go and point out the Way?

What of the thousands of young Saplings who wither up and perish under the scorching fires of Life, because no one has told them of the River, and the secret path their roots may take, to drink of its coolness?

Friends, let us live and work for eternity.

4

Nest for Singing Bird

What a God, who, out of shade,
Nest for singing bird hath made.
                    AMY CARMICHAEL.

WHEN Homay was just a new believer, struggling to
worship God at Deer Pool chapel under the cover of fuel-
hunting, another young girl was also entering into the joy and
emancipation of Christ's salvation.

Deer Pool Village is one of the most magnificently beautiful
village sites in the canyon. The trail climbs gently up from a deep
ravine until it reaches that face of the mountain which banks the
Salween, and there, some eight thousand feet high, it runs on the
level around the neck of the mountain until it has to curve back
into another abyssal drop. And below this level pine-needle-
carpeted path are the tiers of little Lisu shanties. There are two
mountain knolls side by side on the trail which make a natural
divide, so that the village is in two parts, and in between, by the
side of the level trail, a little chapel has been built. I wonder if
Homay and Leah first met there? I know that the heathen Lisu
women do not usually travel; many of them never visit even
neighbouring villages until they become Christian. So it is quite
possible that as Homay left her wood basket at the door and
slipped in on to one of the women's benches, she often found
herself beside Leah, who was only a year younger than Homay.

But such a contrast the two young lives presented! Both girls
were in earnest and both became outstanding Christians; both
loved to sing and became good singers. But the one had to
believe in secret, surrounded every day by heathen talk and
heathen habits; and the other was one of a fine Christian family,

F

free to go to the uttermost for God. Leah, as she sits in chapel beside Homay, can reach out and touch her mother, one of the most devoted Christians in the community, and two dear little sisters are sitting beside her eagerly trying to learn. Across the aisle is her father, partially blind but with a light from heaven on his face, and in his arms is a baby boy who grew up to be a sturdy little Christian. Lucky Leah, easy to be a Christian under such circumstances, isn't it? Yes, but wait. This little family Nest is already built well into the Cleft of the Rock, it is true, but the Evil Spirit, so long ruler of the Munition of Rocks, has plans laid to dislodge that Nest.

In the meantime let us share the joys of those early days. The Lisu teachers told us that the first Christians in the canyon were not stable, except those at Deer Pool, who became a joy and inspiration so sweet that it gave courage and hope to push farther in. "God is a rewarder of those who diligently seek him," . . . so to Deer Pool Village was given the honour of becoming the first mission station in those parts. Mr. Talmadge Payne and his wife moved in from Chinaland, and made their home in one of the Lisu huts, with a tent pitched at the side. I wonder what were the feelings of the first white woman to enter the canyon of the Upper Salween! I can but record my own impressions when, some years later, I followed in her footsteps.

By the time we had climbed the long trail the sun had set, and we were ushered into a tribal shanty where we were to spend the night. But I had caught a glimpse of the breath-taking scenic beauty of this village site, so, setting down my hat and things, I hastily went outside to view the panorama before darkness hid it from me. The back of the shanty rested on the ground; the floor, to make it level, was supported in front on stilts, and as Lisu have no nails the floor boards were just laid loosely on the stilts. I stepped gingerly on the warped planks which wobbled at each of my steps, for underneath me was just air—the ground beneath was a steep cornfield which dropped away from under the house like a gigantic toboggan slide of some seven thousand feet, to the Salween river, unseen, far below. I crouched there nervously afraid to look down again at that disappearing slope, but enthralled with the beauty around and above. I seemed on top of the world. The high peaks opposite appeared to be just on my own level, while beneath us many lower peaks and ridges spread themselves north and south; in either direction one could see the twisting canyon for many, many miles—in fact for two or three days' journey—and all was sinking gradually into the black shadows of night. Such beauty I have never seen surpassed. Up there close to the heavens God seemed very near, and worship was an unhindered joy.

But one cannot live on scenic grandeur, so I had to turn at length and find my way back into the shanty, where around the crackling cosy fire a hot meal was ready for us. They had cooked rice, meat, and vegetables Chinese style, which was really enjoyable; then after supper a copper gong's mellow *boom! boom!* drifted through the night air, calling the village to chapel service. Our Lisu host led us over the pine-scented trail, and other forms, each holding a flaring pine-torch to light his way, loomed out of the darkness. The chapel was of their own building—earth floor, backless benches, and a huge elevated flat stone, up at the front, on which burning pine chips were piled to give light. Men sat on one side, women on the other, all peering at the new Ma-Pa and Ma-Ma, and smiling happily, if self-consciously, as their look was returned. I could not understand Lisu then, but we were all on common ground when the singing commenced. They in Lisu and we in English together could sing—

> I'm tired of sin and straying, Lord,
>   Now I'm coming Home;
> I'll trust Thy love, believe Thy Word,
>   Lord, I'm coming Home.
>
> Coming Home, coming Home, never more to roam,
> Open now Thine arms of Love,
> Lord, I'm coming Home.

or perhaps it was—

> What a friend we have in Jesus
> All our sins and griefs to bear.

White skin or yellow skin, we all had the same testimony, the same experience. As the flames leaped up, every face stood out clear and shining with joy, and as it waned, shadows stole forth and framed their faces softly. Through the crevices of the crude wall a pine-scented mountain wind sighed gently in. I thought of how far we were from home and civilization. I thought of the bitterly rugged road we had come over, and I was filled with exaltation and joyous thanksgiving to God that He had allowed me to be one of His messengers to the ends of the earth.

I imagine Mrs. Payne's experience was much the same. And the Lisu, on their backless benches, gazing at the white woman, marvelling at the colour of her skin and the height of her nose, trying to picture her natural background but quite in vain—what were their thoughts? Grace Payne was the first white woman ever to enter the canyon, and as Leah and the others watched her that first evening of their arrival I wish we might enter their thoughts. Of one thing I know for sure—gratitude and love were uppermost. One of the questions in the Lisu catechism is, "Why should we be grateful to the foreign missionary?" and the answer tells clearly of the cost of leaving home and loved ones. And the Lisu do not forget it.

"You are the one who brought us salvation," they will exclaim, and pat your hand lovingly. And as Leah watched the white woman and remembered that she had left father and mother, brothers and sisters to come that long journey just to help earth people, a fount of love and gratitude sprang up in her heart that was never to die. In heaven they will see what it cost even more fully perhaps, and the love tie between us will be eternal.

"I'll pray for her every day," vowed the young heart, in all probability, for that is what our spiritual children do.

And then how enthralled they must have been to hear her sing! Grace Payne was a lovely soloist in the homelands, and the Lisu script, being based on our own English letters, is easy to master. We all can learn to read (and hence to sing, if the tune is familiar) long before we can talk.

"Isn't it funny?" whispers one of the girls to Leah. "When she sings I can understand what she says, but when she talks, I can't!" Not realizing that the "talk" was, as yet, English!

"Her voice is different from ours," says another. "When she sings it touches my heart and the tears come out!"

No wonder, through those precious months when Paynes were at Deer Pool, that lonely little Homay loved to slip in at the back of the chapel and listen. It was worth a scolding when she got home.

But to happy Leah they were the most wonderful days of her life. All day long while she herded the cattle on the wild mountain-side, or hoed corn with other villagers, or spun cotton for the family clothing, she would think and talk of nothing else.

"Did you hear of Ba-shia-nyio-pa?" someone would say to her. "He wants to be a Christian, you know, but he is so tied to his opium. And when he broke it off to believe, Ma-Ma gave him medicine to help when the craving comes on, and dandy stuff to drink that she calls *coffee*—I drank some; he let me have a sip. My, it was good! Just imagine anyone being so kind as she is! She pities us so."

Mrs. Payne is a trained nurse, and the village has never forgotten her loving ministry among them.

Mr. Payne could already speak some Lisu, and was quite eloquent in Chinese. Leah loved the evening services when the white man opened up the Word of God to them. He had the whole Bible, while at that time all the Lisu church had were the four Gospels, Acts, a catechism, hymn book, and a small book of abbreviated Old Testament stories. Mr. Payne felt that the catechism alone might give an impression of legalism, and so he preached ardently on the grace of God, on the uselessness of man's doing anything to save himself apart from accepting that grace, and one young heart at least caught the vision of our heavenly Father's marvellous love and condescension—caught it so vividly that all the storms and trials which were waiting on the path ahead of her were unable to shake her faith in God's kindness.

But the hard life of privations was telling on the white woman. I myself slept one night in the shanty that had been given to the Paynes for a home. The rats held carnival over my head and down the sides of the walls. Scared at their boldness, I wrapped myself tightly up in my bedding with only my nose sticking out in order to breathe, and part of my forehead. But there was no escape—a rat walked right over me—I could feel the coldness, on my forehead, of tiny feet sauntering across! But Grace Payne's trials were much greater than mere rats. The rainy season had begun. Day after day the tent and miserable hut were swept by torrents: clouds and drizzle veiled the grand scenery. All was just cold and mud and wet.

"From Sunday morning until Saturday night, I never had my galoshes off, except to go to bed," she told me.

But in addition to this, the work had spread so rapidly that Deer Pool was no longer the centre and so Mr. and Mrs. Payne felt the time had come to move on, to build a little shanty somewhere else that would be healthier and more central. The Village of Pine Mountain was chosen. How Deer Pool villagers lamented! Of course the missionaries would only be a day's journey away, but that is far when a loved one is sick and needs medicine.

And after they had gone? How empty the beautiful mountainside seemed! The shanty they had used was still there, but no loving forms to cheer and help them; and somehow in chapel even, everything seemed desolate; a cheeriness, a fellowship had gone.

"I don't want to go to chapel any more; it makes me cry," someone would say.

"But God is still with us," urged young Leah, "and He will hear if we pray in Jesus' Name. We must keep on worshipping." There she was always at service time, near the front seat, and her clear voice leading in the hymn singing cheered on many a disconsolate neighbour.

Loss of her missionaries was like a brisk breeze which foretells the coming of a storm. For some time now Leah's eyes had been itching. Knowing nothing of hygiene, she rubbed them, of course, when they itched, unconscious that her hand was not clean. Lisu homes are ventless, hence very smoky and sooty. In her person Leah was always remarkably clean and neat, but in cooking every Lisu has to handle sooty pots and hands cannot remain white. Little wonder, then, that dread trachoma had laid hold of her eyes. Her father was almost blind from it already, but, not understanding the danger of infection, Leah had not been careful in contacting him. Trachoma victims are everywhere in Lisuland.

Whenever anyone was going to Pine Mountain Leah would ask them to buy for her "a little eye medicine," and after using that, sight would be clearer for a few days, and so she was not alert to her danger.

My attention was first called to Leah when in 1935 I took sick, as mentioned in Homay's story, and Nurse Kathleen Davies came in to attend me. She and Miss Embery had stayed one night at Deer Pool, and Miss Davies was impressed with Leah.

"There is a young girl up here with eye trouble," she said. "Ingrowing eyelashes is a part of it, and she asked me to pull them out for her, but her eyes are really very bad. I noticed her at Deer Pool that time we stayed there. She was sitting in the sun, practically sightless, but *singing*—singing away like a little bird. Extraordinary, to be so happy under such an affliction."

> What a God, who, out of shade,
> Nest for singing bird hath made.

Life was to be an ever-deepening "shade" experience for Leah; yet through it all the testimony of those who knew her was that she was full of song, full of stout testimony as to the Lord's goodness. How could such a thing be? As mentioned above, the canyon contains many blind Lisu, but I never once, in all my ten years of travel there, saw a blind heathen with a song in her heart! They are the most wretched of the wretched unhappy ones. And lest you think that Leah's was just a chance case of a naturally cheerful temperament, let me testify that she was not the only blind Christian who had an inner joy that upheld.

I knew another woman, almost blind, eyes continually running pus, but who had light in her face. Her daughter, in the early twenties only, was really blind—could do no work. Her sister-in-law, who lived with them, was totally blind and totally deaf and dumb. She, with her suffering eyes, had to farm and work for these afflicted ones, yet it was a blessing to meet her. I once asked her what made her happy. She answered, "It is the thought of Heaven, Ma-Ma. The Lisu teachers have told me what a wonderful place Jesus is preparing for me. There is no sickness up there, no blindness, and things that even good eyes have never seen or can imagine for beauty and wonder are being kept for us. God is going to wipe away every tear from our eyes. I like to talk and think about it."

Yes, in the sad shade of blindness, God has made a nest for singing bird! He only can give songs in the night. When outward eyes fail, if the heart reaches out after Him, He will open the eyes of the spirit and lift the inner man from earth's drudgery to sit in heavenly places with Himself.

It was 1942 before I had much contact with Leah. I knew her only as the Blind Singing Girl of Deer Pool Village. But in February, 1942, we started a new venture: a month's Bible school for girls only. Lisu women were always the hardest to reach. Their husbands and brothers said with a laugh, "Oh, they can't learn!" so when a Bible study week was planned for a village, the audience was mainly men. At such a time the farm work was thrust upon the sex that "couldn't learn." And of those that did attend Bible classes, I must say that it looked as if the men had spoken the truth. At any attempt to make them recite scripture or study in the simplest form, they would dissolve into giggles and silliness; to try to get them to pray in public was to ruin your service hour. It seemed hopeless. Yet there were Homay, Leah, and as these pages proceed you will meet with others, here one and there one, who seemed an exception to the general rule, which made us hope that, with patience, work among the women also might be accomplished. When the Rainy Season Bible Schools began, a few girls also would come and sit on the back row—mention of them will be made later. But we gradually saw that the mixed education was attracting the wrong type of girl, and endangering our boy students, so we had to forbid their coming.

That is why we decided to try a school for girls only. But, if there were no boys present would any girls come? We did not know. The right kind would come, we hoped. Another serious question was, *when* could they come? Lisu were free as soon as the year's harvest was over. Lisu women were never free. When farming ends, spinning, weaving, and sewing the year's garments for all the family commenced. Even the deacons were not much in favour of trying for such a thing as a girls' school, but one young evangelist said, "Except at Chinese New Years'! Everybody is more or less free then. If the school were in February, and those who planned to come were to weave cloth a little later at night and a little earlier each morning during January, they could get it all done and be free to come for February!"

Some shook their heads dubiously; others agreed it was a possibility. None thought that teaching the girls would amount to much, but they hated to disappoint Ma-Ma! So at Christmas time, when the great crowd from all over the district was present, we gave notice that a girls' school would be held the next February, and asked the applicants to sign up for it. Not everybody was invited. We had rules of admission:

1. The girl student must be a saved Christian, not just a professing one.
2. She must have a recommendation from the deacon of her village that for the past year at least, her conduct has been irreproachable.
3. She must be able to read and write. (In later years this rule was cancelled.)
4. She must be at least seventeen years old; no limit after that.

A great deal of talking, girls heads bowed together in whispering circles, and of course giggling, followed the above announcement. Only about six signed up; but the Lisu evangelist mentioned above said to me, "Don't be discouraged, Ma-Ma. More than that are planning to come. They just don't know what 'sign up' involves and are afraid to sign lest later they are hindered from coming."

We had to make preparations for them in faith and prayer. You can imagine our joy on the day of assembling, when twenty-four students arrived and enrolled! Two had to be turned away because their deacons would not recommend them. But some of these girls came a day's journey from north in the canyon, south in the canyon and from across the river. And from the south came—Leah, with two other women from Deer Pool. Her chum Tabitha came forward, that afternoon, while Leah hung back shyly and nervously, and Tabitha said, "Ma-Ma, the rules are that every student must be able to read and write. Well

Leah used to be able to, but her eyes won't admit of it now. Still she'd like to come and listen; will you allow her?"

"We surely will!" I cried out most happily, reaching out for the blind girl's hand and patting it. "That rule is only to weed out girls that could not follow the meaning of the lectures, which does not apply to Leah. She is very welcome indeed." And how the sightless face beamed with happiness!

Then the little band of three went off cheerfully to find a dormitory where they could all be together. The Chinese school had kindly lent us their little dormitories, as it was New Year's holidays and their students had gone home. These dormitories are merely shacks with wooden planks for beds, earth for floor, and three rocks for a fireplace!

Before school commenced, it was the custom for the white teachers to interview each student personally and alone, as to their salvation. When Leah came into my study, we went through the usual procedure of questions, even though I knew she was an exceptional Christian.

"Well, Leah, here you are at our first girls' Bible school. I want to know just what each of you understand about God's Word, before we begin to teach you. So I have a few questions to put to you. Are you yourself a born-again Christian?"

"Yes, Ma-Ma. I am born again from above."

"What does 'born again' mean, Leah?"

"It means to have eternal life as well as physical life, doesn't it?"

"That's right. And when were you born again, Leah?"

"When I took Jesus as my Saviour, who died on the cross for my sins."

"Why do you want to study at this school, Leah?"

"Because I want to know the Holy Book better. I have not been able to read for some years now, Ma-Ma."

"How old are you, Leah?"

"About thirty years old. . . . I don't know exactly."

"Well, we are very glad to have you, Leah, and if I can help you in any matter, you just come to me."

A shy twisting of her hands betokened there was just such a matter right now.

"What is it, Leah?"

"I'm told that this girls' school is to be conducted just as nearly like the men's R.S.B.S. as possible."

"Yes, we are going to try and give you just what we give them."

"Then there will be week-end preaching assignments for the girls each week?"

"That is our plan, but . . ."

"Ma-Ma, I'd like to ask a favour. When you send me out, could you please send me with Tabitha and Abigail? I can see a wee bit, but I cannot walk quickly over strange trails. My friends are accustomed to that and don't mind it; but if I had to go with girls I do not know, they might not——"

Tears were in my eyes. I had no thought of sending a blind girl out over these high and perilous paths, but the stoutness of her courage shamed me. If she was willing to go, who was I to say it was too much?

"Leah, set your heart at rest. You will never be asked to go with strangers. I am delighted that you are willing to go, and I am sure God will use you. I will arrange that Tabitha, Abigail, and you will always be on the same team." Her smile of relief betokened that her one dread in coming to school had been allayed. Now all before her was one sweet enjoyment.

In the classroom, Leah was given a seat at the front, near the speaker, of course, and her quiet, attentive, sightless face was an inspiration. It was on the first morning that she, and most of the others, received their Bible names. Heathen names often have such a polluted meaning, as I have explained before, but it is mostly to help the praying friends at home that we give the Bible students a Bible name. *Leah*, for instance, is much easier to remember than *Sah-me-nyio*.

At that first year of girls' Bible school, each evening I gave a talk on one of the women of the Bible. Biographies of the saints are rich in practical application to all our lives, but especially to the lives of women in the East. When we came to Leah, I tried to point out (as does Dr. Edersheim) how God was Leah's ally all throughout.

As we told the story, outside the little shanty the night wind howled and moaned bitterly. But inside a radiance rested on the young faces uplifted to mine. God taught us all precious lessons in those evening hours together. And the blind girl saw things as they really are, and was comforted and strengthened to accept the trial which is but for a moment and which worketh a far more exceeding weight of glory.

Another evening stands out in memory. It was when the story of Abigail was told. Leah's chum, Abigail, was also going through deep waters those days. It was she who had married Philip, when Homay broke with him, and he had definitely backslidden, deserted her and their unborn babe for a heathen girl; and just before Abigail came to Bible school she was told that Philip had carried off her corn—her store of food for the winter. We named her Abigail purposely; for the Bible character of that name also was married to a churl, a son of Belial. The fact that the Abigail of old was very clever and beautiful only made her plight the more pitiful—and incidentally when that little matter of beauty was mentioned in class, there were many girlish grins and nods in Lisu Abigail's direction, which provoked a wan smile from the grim young face. Then the story unfolded; hopelessly tied to a man who did not deserve her and with whom there could never be any fellowship, Abigail must have faced the inevitable temptation of a woman in such a position—the temptation to take matters into her own hands, and run off with someone else more attractive. Lisu heathen readily do that. The only other alternative is to bank your all on God, and leave it for Him to work out. That Abigail did this latter is evidenced in the way she pleaded with David to do the very same thing, when the temptations to use force had swung David off his spiritual balance.

And then the wonderful "end of the Lord." When she proved that her own lesson was humbly and faithfully learned, God suddenly worked for her. Within a few weeks the *churl* had been removed, and she was wife of—a *king!* And of David, at that. Abigail ended her days as wife of a king. Someone had said it is not fair to judge a thing while it is in the making; wait until the product is finished, then we may pass judgment. And so we should never judge our lives and our trials, until God has completed in us what He is trying to do for us. When we see His finished product, we will be satisfied.

Friend, can you not see what balm the Word of God has for a torn young life which *longs* to do what is right, if it only knew the way? Can you feel the suffering of Abigail's little nest until the shelter of the Cleft Rock was pointed out to her? Can you know the gladness of the missionary, when at the end of that evening, at the close of the lesson, her hand was grasped and held, while two earnest young eyes looked into hers and said, "Thank you, Ma-Ma. That helped me so much!"

And yet, my friend, as we stood there with clasped hands, both of us safely out of the danger of the sharp blast that blew towards the Abyss, how many were, *and are*, battling hopelessly against that Wind and that Abyss, with no knowledge of the Rock, Christ Jesus, nor of His way of salvation, because no one has gone to them. Always it presses on my heart. . . . Those others that would so gladly take Him as Saviour, if only someone would go and tell them the way!

At the end of school, although it was only of a month's duration, to encourage the girls, we held closing exercises and gave out certificates to those who had passed. The results were good, considering not one of the girls had ever been to school before, and had never studied to take an examination in her life. But only one girl got first-class honours. And who do you suppose she was? The blind girl, Leah! She had had exactly the same examination questions as the other girls had, only we took hers orally. They had written down notes from which to review; she had none. Always part of every examination was the recitation of scripture passages, and Leah could not read, yet she alone passed with first-class honours. I asked her how she did it. Her face glowed with pleased embarrassment as she answered. "Well, I could hear the other girls in my hut going over their notes and scripture in preparation for the exams."

We were very proud of our twenty-two Lisu maidens as they marched into chapel to the music of the little portable organ, and separated in simple form to their designated seats. One of them conducted the singing for the whole service, and two of them gave valedictory addresses! One of them was chairman, and they had closing day songs and music just like the Rainy Season Bible Schools. Many of the boy students had come, some a day's journey, to "escort sister home" or some such excuse, but really to see what good the teaching of girls could ever accomplish. At the end of the service one such boy student exclaimed with beaming face, "Why, wasn't it nice! It was almost as good as ours." Complacent male! I thought it was quite as good.

After all was over and as the happy, excited girls were rolling up bedding and clothes to go home with their proud brothers and friends, I called the three from Deer Pool aside, and, little dreaming what the future was to hold for them or me, I said something like this:

"Now you girls are going back home, and for none of you is life easy. I want you to promise me not to forget the *power* of *prayer*. I want you to promise me to meet together regularly and *pray through* your problems. You know Deer Pool Village is not now what it used to be, spiritually. The craze to make money by trading has been used of the devil to cool off many, and some of the first believers who were so consecrated are now dead. Is that not so?"

"Yes, Ma-Ma," they answered sadly. They promised to pray and not to faint, and we parted.

I never saw Leah again. A severe toothache and other ills warned me that I had better go out to Chinaland to seek dental aid. John had been attending a conference in Chungking and as I had not seen him for three months I hoped we might be able to come back together. But in the spring of 1942 the Japanese were walking up Burma as with ten-league boots. By the time I was physically fit to return, they had already reached Lisuland, and I was evacuated out of the province by the British Consul. Six months elapsed before I was able to get back to the Munition of Rocks. When I did arrive, and had time to inquire into my dear girl student's affairs, this is what I was told of Leah.

Shortly after she got home from Bible school her young brother, the only son of the family and a fine Christian, died of tuberculosis of the leg bone. One of her younger sisters had died of a fever the year before. And within a few months, Leah herself was laid low of a fever, probably typhus. Up to that time she and

Tabitha and Abigail had been faithful in holding their prayer meetings. But not long after she took sick, Leah knew that God was going to call her Home. She asked the family (then only mother, father and one married sister) to gather around her bed, and they said the strength with which she was able to talk was wonderful. "I know I am going back to God," she told them. "And my one concern is for you folk, *lest your faith fail you.* You have been afflicted much this last year; we none of us can understand why these troubles come, but two things we know; that is, that *God loves us* and that *God is faithful.* Everything that happens to us is for our good and some day He will show us why it had to be. You must not wail for me—I am going to the land of Happiness and Light, and where Christ is. But what concerns me now is lest you dishonour Him by complaining, because He is taking me! Dad, promise me you won't! Promise that you will go on believing and not doubt God's goodness!" And they said that with her last strength she pleaded that God's honour should be defended by the ones she left behind. Who can account for a spirit like that, except it be, even as Christ said, "Born from above"?

So they laid their third child in the grave and, as tears flowed, they strove as a family to follow out her injunctions and not let other people suggest that God was too hard on them.

But still the Sharp Wind from the Bitter Height continued its onslaught. The mother, one of the most faithful of the Christians, was ill with an unknown and very painful disease. I think it was cancer. Within a year she too had gone to be with the Lord; so the old sightless father and the married sister were left alone. But the words of their dead Singing Bird were constantly with them. "Promise me that you will not complain! Promise me you will believe on!" And they followed in her faith. "The Lord gets His best soldiers from the Highlands of Affliction," someone has said. One little picture, as told me by a Lisu evangelist who was ministering at Deer Pool for a few weeks, will show the faith and trust which was their life.

"We had an exciting experience of fire while I was at Deer Pool," he said. "One or two of the huts were aflame, a keen wind was blowing and we were afraid the whole village would go. I was on top of David's house, spreading wet blankets over it to save the roof from flying sparks, and everyone was running around hauling water, etc., when I happened to look up, and there in the middle of the road was Leah's old blind father. His house was right in the path the flames were taking, but he had no one to help him now, of course. And there he was, lifting his sightless eyes up to the sky and *praying*. There he stood, and even as he prayed the wind began to veer around and his house was saved. He, a layman, old and afflicted, was *committing*, and I the preacher, was rushing around *working* to save the house in which I was guest. He surely taught me a lesson. I came down from off that roof and went on to my knees. And the wind carried the flames out toward the wild mountainside, and no other house was harmed."

Friends, there is a blessed shelter in the Cleft of the Rock for you and me. Blindness is a cruel Wind from a Bitter Height, but a blind girl had her inner eyes so opened that her vision of faith lived on and enlightened others, long after her physical voice was silenced.

5

A Rock in a Weary Land

(This scene goes back many years, perhaps to 1921)

A TALL young figure clattered over the loose boards of the narrow veranda and plunged into the semi-darkness of the Lisu hut.

"Mamma!" he called out, "Have you heard the news?"

An equally tall lean woman, sprawled on a bed near the fire, faced streaked with soot, a dirty turban wound around her head from which the hair had all been shaven off, sat up, pulled a long pipe out of her mouth, and answered, "What news? Ain't heard nothing."

"Well," answered her son, and as he talked he was hunting through the dim light of the shanty for his crossbow and arrow sheaf, "Dad's gone and run off with Nyio-Er-Me, curse her!" and a string of profanity filled the air.

Then it was the woman's turn to get excited. Every other sentence a filthy curse, she ranted on, working herself up into a passionate rage.

"What's he done that for? Haven't I been a good wife to him? I've given him sons! There isn't a pair of fellows on this mountain that can touch my two for stature or strength. And a daughter besides, have I given him. What's he want to run off with that ——" and more profanity.

By this time her tall son had found his bow and arrows and slung them over his shoulder. A dangerous knife, some three feet long, was fastened at his side. As he stretched himself up to adjust the weapons, he was a splendid-looking figure, despite uncombed hair and dirty face. About six feet tall, with broad shoulders, he was well-proportioned, and the comeliness of fine straight features was manifest in spite of dirt. His face was fierce with excitement.

"Give me a drink of wine, Ma!" he cried. "Don't you worry!" And with a turn and a fling, he was clattering back over the loose boards and on to the trail above the house. The old mother, left alone, cursed and wept alternately as the sore evil which all Lisu women dread and fear loomed up on her horizon.

Up through the mountainside plunged the four young men, talking excitedly and laying their plans. Somehow they had learned which was the village where the eloping pair had decided to spend the night, and which family was befriending them. Of the capture details, I do not know. Being only sons, they could not force a separation, and this the father knew well. But of the fierceness and cleverness of his eldest son he had reason to know also, and likely he did not dare bring home his second wife immediately. Their persuasion was impotent to change his mind: his passion had fastened on Nyio-Er-Me and she knew how to hold him her slave. She was truly an evil woman. So with what lying promises he held off the wrath of his two formidable sons we do not know, but return home alone, he did not. To run off to Burma for a year or so had often proved successful for others, but he had aroused a strong character against him, one who did not forget. That oldest son—well, everybody dreaded him when he got into a fury. Give him a present of opium? Yes, that probably was the most potent way to calm things. Opium will destroy any character, if taken over a sufficiently long period. And because it soothes pain it is greatly prized. His oldest boy was already an opium addict at the age of twenty.

But as the father and his evil companion were laying their plans, the oldest son was also laying his. It was time he was being married, anyway, and he had already started out to build his own house. When that was finished, and his bride brought home, his mother could come and live with him—and then her face would be saved and his father could do what he wanted.

In the deep ravine was another village named The Village of Tree Roots, and there he found a girl more or less to his liking.

She was not pure, but then, who was? That does not reckon as important in heathen thinking.

"What do Lisu look for in a wife?" I once asked one of them. "Oh, some want good looks," was the answer. "Others want to marry into a rich family; and still others want a wife who is hospitable. It's humiliating to a fellow if his wife does not want to entertain strangers, and some women don't."

One or other of these motives influenced Lao-Ta, and the engagement was made. He must pay a lot of money for her—perhaps two hundred dollars in silver. Her family reckon they have had the expense of bringing her up, feeding and clothing her, and once she is married she is lost to them as a farmhand, so they reckon that the ones who get the benefit of her abilities should pay for what she has cost. This is called "dowry money" and its various items are amusing. The mother will charge for having nursed her, i.e. a "milk bill" is sent in. Then sometimes there is a charge for *Jwa-jwa-chwa*, that is, the labour of pre-masticating her food for her when she was a baby! (The mother chews the corn or meat, and then with her own lips puts it into the baby's mouth.) And so on. To wed is expensive in Lisuland. For this reason the Lisu church in our parts has voted against the dowry, and no Christian may pay it. But we are discussing the days before the gospel arrived; for our hero was already married and a father, when he first heard of Christ.

Time heals all wounds. Ten years later we see Lao-Ta and Lao-Er both married and living in their own house, and tilling their separate farms in the Village of Oak Flat. The father and his second wife live in the original homestead, and now have a son, and a daughter, Susanna. Father and sons have long forgotten their anger, and work and help each other happily, but the two wives never forget. Bickering, jealous quarrels continually upset the peace. The first wife has been offered a home with her oldest son as he promised, but love for her husband probably drew her back to him after a few years. When the gospel came, and her husband wanted to become a Christian, however, a final break was made, and she came permanently into the home of her oldest boy.

That boy had now seen his first-born, a little girl, whom he named Me-do-me, and so his own name is changed for the rest of his life. Lisu practise teknonymy; that is, the father takes the oldest child's name with *pa* (man) added to it, and the mother takes the same name, only with *ma* (woman) added to it. So automatically the family is now Me-do-me-pa and Me-do-me-ma and little Me-do-me. From now on their fellow villagers must address them as such; to call them by their childhood name is to insult them.

Now we must go back in thought to 1932.

One evening, up the long winding two-thousand-foot ascent from the ravine stream, climb two or three Lisu men of a slightly different costume. They stop at Cha-Lao-San's shanty and ask if they may spend the night there. Welcomed cordially, they sit down on the big low bedboards which inevitably act as fireside seats in the daytime, and take out *books* from a small bag slung over their shoulder.

"Oh, you read Chinese?" asks Lao-San curiously.

"No," said the visitors, "these are Lisu books."

The effect is electric. Everyone in the shanty turns around and amazed attention is riveted on the speaker. He is, of course, Job, with that little band.

"Lisu books? Didn't know there were such! Do you mean to say that those leaves speak *our* language?"

"Well, I'll read some and you judge for yourself," says the speaker casually. Whereupon the Book is made to tell its own message. Job's favourite was the story of the resurrection of Lazarus, but sometimes the Catechism was used. Its first question, "Who made the earth and everything upon it?" is arresting.

Then the interest swung around from the books to the message and soon the shanty is filled with amazed questions and thrilling answers. Finally, someone says, "Better go call Me-do-me-pa!" for our hero had now become the political headman of his village, and it is not convenient to do anything "different" without consulting the headman. So Me-do-me-pa was summoned.

He enters, tall and matured now into young manhood, perhaps thirty-two years of age. But being a heathen he is still dirty, a wine-bibber and an opium-smoker. There is the gleam of a

keen mind in his eye, nevertheless, as he listens to the story of
Calvary.

As all wait for his verdict, he says, "I'd like to have eternal
life—who wouldn't? But it's never been followed in these parts
before. What do you do to get it? Could a Lisu receive it?"

"You must believe in God," was the Lisu evangelist's answer.
"Jesus died for your sins. You must cast out your demons and
turn to God. You must stop unclean sinning, and so forth."

This was shock. The only excitements and pleasures of a
heathen life are those just named! Immediately some voices
were raised against it. But not so Me-do-me-pa. While the others
clamoured that that was too much to expect of human mortal,
he was thinking. A glimpse of something that answered a long-
felt heart cry was holding him. Every now and again he shot a
keen question into the hubbub, and always it brought a silence
while all listened for the answer.

"Have *you* done all this?"

"Yes," was the sturdy reply. "We cast out our demons over
fifteen years ago; hundreds of Lisu have done so in our parts,
and nothing has happened to them. Jesus is stronger than the
demons. And as for worldly pleasures, God gives you other things
in their place. We have wonderful songs to sing; happy fellowship in worship services. Once a year we all gather from all over
the canyon and hold what we call the Christmas Festival. It is
lots of fun. I would not go back to heathen life for anything.
And in your own district here, the people of Deer Pool have
already cast out their demon altars and accepted Christ."

Long into the night the discussion waged. By that time most
of the men of Oak Flat Village would be in the crowded little
hut, listening to the new doctrine. At the close Me-do-me-pa
stood up.

"I want to believe. Come to my house to-morrow morning,
teacher, and cast out my demons. And have breakfast with me!"

Up stood Cha-Lao-San. "And you must cast out my demons
for me also," he cried. "I'm going to believe in God, too."

And so the work began at Oak Flat Village. Word soon spread
over the mountain. "Teachers have come with a strange doctrine.
They say we should not worship demons but should believe and

trust in God. The headman of Oak Flat and some others have cast out their demons!" And so as the teachers pushed on they found their way prepared for them. Joseph of Dried Fungus (later engaged to Homay) joined the little band of Christians. At Tree Roots Me-do-me-ma's brothers turned to God. At Pine Mountain, old Big and Pu-fu-si-pa. Plum Tree Flat turned as a village. At Spirea Flat a fine young man and his wife took their stand and became the nucleus of a church there, and so on.

Finally, word came to the Feudal Laird at Place-of-Action, and he was easy to stir up against the new movement. They whispered to him: "This new doctrine is not Chinese. It was brought by the white man. It is a ruse he is using to steal your land. Better stop it before all your people go over to the white man. Me-do-me-pa, of Oak Flat, has already joined them." Of course it was all lies—the devil is the father of lies—but the Laird thought it was true, so he sent forth word that his people were not to accept the new doctrine. Such messages are taken to the headman of each village, who, in turn, is responsible for conveying it to each member of his village. Undoubtedly it came to Me-do-me-pa.

What conflict must have waged in that Lisu heart! He was quite a favourite with the Laird. It meant much to be a favourite —no taxes, partiality in law suits, and innumerable other advantages. And to *disobey* him! Well, wealthy men who had done so had gradually been reduced to poverty. And some, who had wilfully disobeyed, had been tortured. He knew what the Laird could do, if he wanted to. I think it went this way.

Cha-Lao-San came running in the door.

"Oh, Me-do-me-pa! I hear that runners from the Yamen have come with orders that we are not to turn Christian. Is it so?"

"Guess so," was the grim reply.

"Well, are you going to send the notice around to all of us?"

"No." A gasp from all who were listening.

Cha-Lao-San asked slowly, "What will he do to you, if you don't?"

The tall Lisu lifted his head and looked the questioner in the eyes. "Whatever he does can only be done to the outside of me—he can't take away the eternal life God has given to me. This

morning I was reading Luke xii. 4, 5. 'And I say unto you my
friends, Be not afraid of them that kill the body, and after that
have no more that they can do. But I will forewarn you whom
ye shall fear: Fear him which after he hath killed hath power
to cast into hell; yea, I say unto you, Fear him.' "

Silence reigned in the little huts, now nearly full of villagers.
Then Cha-Lao-San spoke again softly. "It is like an answer,
isn't it? Well, I won't turn back either, then."

The word went around like wildfire, "Me-do-me-pa is not
going to turn back!"

It was a crucial moment in the forming of the little church.
Friends at home were praying that God would raise up a leader,
a Rock-man, to steady the weak little group of new believers
sure of persecution. We have known many other similar cases
where the villagers all turned back to heathenism because the
headman decided to backslide. It is a weary land where you
cannot do what you long to do, and believe is right to do. But
if there is *one man* who is willing to take the punishment on his
own head, many others will shelter under his shadow and stand
with him.

I would just like to ask the reader one question. *What made
that man* WILLING?

Willing to lose all his lands and physical comforts, perhaps.
At the same time he must give up all his popularity, his wine,
his opium—everything that had spelled pleasure to him before.
And gain what? A nebulous "eternal life?" This man was no
dabbler in philosophy; he was an illiterate farmer. Moreover,
he was unusually marked out by common sense. You would
never catch him making a poor bargain. Then *what* made him
gamble his all, for Christianity? The only answer is in Rom.
viii. 16, "The Spirit itself beareth witness with our spirit, that
we are the children of God." 1 John v. 10, "He that believeth
on the Son of God hath the witness in himself." This earth
person (as the Chinese slightingly call the Lisu) *knew*, though he
could not explain it, that he was contacting God through faith
in Christ. He *knew* that whole worlds of undreamed-of joys and
privileges were opening up to him. And he *knew* that he was
only at the weak ignorant beginning of new life, and he was so

thrilled that none of the old pleasures of the flesh could compare with it any more. They might go, but this new life with God, he *must have.* So he stood, and everybody waited to see what punishment would ensue.

Days passed without anything happening, but Me-do-me-pa was not deceived. He too was Oriental, and knew the ways of the Laird. One day he was driving pigs to market. He had to pass Place-of-Action; a retainer from the Yamen came out and laid his hand on Me-do-me-pa's shoulder, "The Laird wants you!"

Ah, it had come, then. All right. He followed quietly into the Chinese courtyard which began, likely, to fill up with onlookers. The Laird was standing there in a great rage, apparently.

"What are you doing, driving pigs to market when you had orders to be building the road?" he shouted. There was no use answering that there had been no orders. Everyone present knew it was but an excuse to hide the real reason. Legally China recognizes religious freedom.

"Tie him up to the whipping post and give it to him!" cried the Laird, and feudal hands reached out and grasped the strong frame which did not resist. It was done. Lash upon lash. What a beating that must have been! One of the strongest Lisu in the district, he was beaten so that he could not walk for three days. When the miserable punishment was over the tall form lay senseless on the ground. Word had gone as fast as human foot could take it to Oak Flat Village; his fellows dropped their work and with grim faces sped to the scene, knowing they would have to carry him home. They wondered if he would live—if he would ever be the same physically again, and the little group of Christians whispered together and trembled. Would it be done to each? Or was Me-do-me-pa, like his Master, only in a small way, to bear in his wounds "the chastisement of our peace?" Perhaps they had all better backslide? No, word came that the suffering man was recovering. He had spoken! He had said it was all right and that he was *going on in the faith!* Days passed and no other Christian was touched. "A man shall be as a rock in a weary land." Spoken of his Master, it was true in a sense of the followers. The anxious, frightened believers gradually rallied, and, as usually happens, others joined them! What was Me-do-me-pa getting from Christianity that he deemed it worth such a beating? It did the cause good.

Dr. Jowett has said, "The man who is sure and restful in the conscious companionship of his Lord has about him the strainlessness and inevitableness of the oceantide, and gives off bracing influence like God's fresh and wondrous sea."

And the Laird? He had beaten his loyal henchman in ignorant suspicion, and for some time tried by heavy taxation to discourage the new doctrine. But gradually he began to notice things. He noticed that the Christians were prospering in a material way. That they were well-behaved. That their obedience to him was just the same, if he did not step on their religious toes. And after some eight years, he ended up by proclaiming openly that the Christians were his best citizens; and as they gave up opium and became physically strong enough to work their fields properly, their tax returns were actually netting him money! (The taxes are a percentage of the harvest, so the more harvested, the more grain is given to the landowner.) This man never became a Christian, but like Felix of old, he used to call the deacons in and ask them to preach to him. Perhaps he planned to believe at the last hour, but it was not granted him. A sudden fever laid him unconscious and he passed away without repentance.

Now the church in Oak Flat district was an established thing, but evangelists to carry the Good News afar were few. La-ma-wu's partners went home to Stockade Hill; some others came in their place, but always too few to meet all the demand for teachers, so the responsibility of personal witness fell on the shoulders of the new believers. A long day's journey to the south and across the Salween River on the west bank was the Village of Horse Grass Level. Among the first to hear the gospel, they had been slow to receive it, but now they wanted teachers, so Me-do-me-pa volunteered to go down there and give his testimony.

"How did your wife take all this?" I asked him one day, as he was telling me this story. "Did she believe along with you from the very first?"

"No, she didn't, Ma-Ma," he said with a broad smile, "and she caused me no little trouble. She resented having to give up heathen pleasures, and made such stormy scenes that I just got sick at heart with it all."

"Well, she is certainly one with you now!" I replied. "What effected the change?"

"I got to my wit's end over her," he said, a twinkle of reminiscence in his eye, "so I decided to pray about her. For instance, she did not want me to leave home and go preaching, as I had volunteered to do, but I found that as I prayed regularly and faithfully for her, she began to change. She kept on changing as I kept on praying, until now she never objects to anything I want to do!"

I might say right here, that as long as he lived, Me-do-me-ma seemed the model deacon's wife. She was faithful at prayer meetings, testified and exhorted others until, a full day's journey away, I heard of her being the means of effecting peace between another headman and his wife! After her husband's death she lapsed into girlhood weaknesses, but that does not change, only heightens the fact that his prayers had made a different woman out of her.

At Horse Grass Level, Me-do-me-pa's quiet, common-sense witness bore much fruit, and a steady little church grew up there. Now we approach the days when my husband and I moved into Oak Flat Village, into a house just beneath Me-do-me-pa's and where we had many neighbourly touches. I would again like to quote from the circulars written during these years.

I first saw him in the spring of 1934 while we were visiting Mrs. Cooke at Pine Mountain Village, before we actually moved in as a family. It was Sunday and Mrs. Cooke was pointing out some of the main men of the church as they arrived for Sunday service. Pointing to Me-do-me-pa (easily discerned because of his height) she said, "That big Lisu I call The Shepherd because he has such a heart of love and care for the rest of the flock." Then in December, 1934, the Cookes moved up to the Luda district and we moved in as a family and took charge of the Oak Flat district. March, 1935, has two references to Me-do-me-pa.

One of the snares in our Lisu work is the matter of lawsuits, quarrels over land, etc., referred to the heathen Chinese Laird for settlement. We had a grave discussion about it on Sunday afternoon, for Pade-John

(Cha-Lao-San) and Me-do-me-pa were among the guilty parties; in the evening when the testimony meeting was thrown open, the dear "Shepherd" was the first to stand up, and he confessed his fault before the flock. His face was so shining and modest as he talked, that one could not but love him.

The Lisu church, being founded on indigenous lines, was self-governing. The missionary gave advice when asked, and likewise preached only when invited. In each Christian village there was one elected as service leader, and this one wrote down on the blackboard the names of those he wished to preach during the coming week. If the white missionary's name did not appear, he did not preach but sat in the audience while the selected native Christian officiated. In those early days, before I could speak Lisu, I was in the audience one night when Me-do-me-pa was the speaker. Not knowing much of the language, I could not follow his message, but I knew enough Lisu to find the text he had chosen. It was John xii. 1-9, the story of Mary's alabaster box of ointment poured forth at Jesus' feet. As I listened and saw the glow of inspiration on the Shepherd's face, and felt the hush in the audience, I wondered just what in that story had spoken to this farmer's heart. He had received very little Bible teaching up to that time, but he was gifted with keen spiritual insight, and Mary's costly offering ungrudgingly lavished on the Master had touched and blessed him. There was a kinship of feeling with that Hebrew maiden of old, on this Lisu man's face. "There is neither Jew nor Greek, there is neither bond nor free, there is neither male nor female: for ye are all one in Christ Jesus" (Gal. iii. 28).

From the circular of July, 1935, comes this paragraph demonstrating that although the foreign missionary was present, the matter of discipline was left in the hands of the local church.

That night in the evening service, Prodigal got up and said he wanted to return to the Lord, that he realized it meant salvation and happiness. When he sat down, teacher John grunted, "You didn't say enough!" And then, Me-do-me-pa and Pade-John went after him. "What about your sins? 'Return to the Lord' and not a word about repentance? God is not to be treated that way!"—it was good to hear them hot after their Lord's honour. No, once we forfeit His "well-pleased" there is no path of *self-complacency* back to it. The church has accepted Prodigal's confession and is giving him a second chance to believe, and allowing him to shake hands again—a sign, not of church membership, but of fellowship.

In September it became necessary for Little Daughter and me to go out to Chinaland for a few months' physical recuperation as has been told in Homay's story. We got back in time for Christmas, and the circular that month tells of our arrival.

We had a wonderful welcome back to Oak Flat on December 16. Half way down the mountain John met us, accompanied by Ye-Chia-me (Kathryn's playmate), Gu-fu-chee (banging the chapel gong) and Mark. The rest of the crowd was ordered to be in ceremonial line farther up the hill, but on hearing our voices Plum Tree Flat-ers could not contain themselves and came pelting down on us, led by Caleb with his big boyish laugh and gripping handshake. One old man said half to himself, "Thank God—He wouldn't allow us to be separated"—an involuntary little word that nestled down softly into the missionary's heart.

Farther up was the reception line—Job, Pade-John, Me-do-me-pa, Keh-gee-sen, and others. On our approach they began to sing, but in their excitement suddenly forgot the words and all came to a stop. There was a blank and awful silence for a second, and then Job said, "Oh, let it go! Let's shake hands."

Our dear Lord is a magnificent giver; He knows how to add the tiny little extras which make a pleasure perfect. Among those who ran forward most eagerly and shook hands most warmly were some we had long been praying for as "cold-hearted."

We had a happy three months with them before having to come home on furlough. I am glad that the furlough circulars contain a letter from Me-do-me-pa, because, although it is not a remarkable one, it is his own voice speaking.

Oak Flat Village.
March 14, 1937.

Big Brother and Sister:

Whom I yearn for, cannot forget and continually long to see, in the name of the Father, Son, and the Spirit I send you a handshake. Now Big Brother and family, are you dwelling in peace? There is nothing wrong with us and because of the help of the Lord we are all well. Won't you pray very much for me? Also pray much for the deacons of the surrounding districts. Thank you very much.

We are earnestly praying for you to come back and teach us. Won't you do so?

The photo you three had taken, came in the early part of March; we were unspeakably happy to get it. Now there is going to be another period for Oak Flat of "no missionary"—sheep without a shepherd once more! I am wondering whom God has for us in the future?

The writer is one who loves you, the servant of Jesus Christ.

ME-DO-ME-PA.

Reading it in this respect, one is struck by that simple little question, *I am wondering whom God has for us in the future?* because the answer to it involves the biggest storm that ever struck the Rock-man. He little knew what he was asking.

For some months after our departure, Oak Flat was without a white man missionary; and then one whom the Lisu named Brother Two volunteered to go in and help. It is not the policy of the China Inland Mission to put new workers on a station alone, without the counsel and help of experienced seniors, but sometimes in an exigency, when no senior has been available, this has been done. And the following story is the result of such an emergency.

Brother Two was a very zealous and devout young missionary, and one with brilliant gifts. He picked up the Lisu language quickly, and his indifference to personal hardship and suffering was a blessing to us all. His arrival was heralded with joy and satisfaction by Me-do-me-pa and everyone else, and his quickness in learning their tongue elicited their admiration.

However, the Lisu language is a very ambiguous one, which even an experienced missionary can misunderstand. And later, the Lisu told us, "There were times when Brother Two thought he had understood us and he had not; we could tell by his answers." Let us keep this in mind as the story unfolds.

With no experienced senior missionary present to explain matters as they cropped up, and full of zeal to see the Word spread and multiply unhampered, Brother Two gradually began to take exception to the way the Lisu church conducted certain things. Mr. Fraser had given them a catechism, which long experience with various tribal attempts at catechisms has made us value because its simplicity makes it easy for the beginner to master, and thus encourages him to further study. But Brother Two felt that the catechism, with its simple question and direct answer, had a tendency to produce a "do-this-and-thou-shalt-be-saved" effect on the Lisu mind. In other words he feared legalism for the Lisu church. He was much strengthened in these misgivings to hear that Mr. Payne had feared the very same thing.

Brother Two decided to step out and combat legalism, and began to take exception to the way the church was handling cases of church discipline. This of course, brought him up against Me-do-me-pa, who was the head deacon and in charge of all such decisions. Hitherto the missionary, as already pointed out, had let the church do its own disciplining in its own way, only giving the word of advice now and again, the purpose being to strengthen them as an indigenous church; but here was a white man who wished to sit in on their consultations, seemed to want to take charge, and was insisting that methods taught them by the mother Lisu church were wrong. Me-do-me-pa objected to such an abrupt change, without being able to consult Mr. Fraser or Mr. Cooke who were experienced in all the districts of the Lisu work. Brother Two was a newcomer; Mr. Fraser and Mr. Cooke had long ago proved and approved themselves to the Lisu mind and heart, and both had sanctioned the methods Me-do-me-pa was using. It was very painful, very upsetting and very bewildering, for Brother Two held to his opinions and pressed them with all the zeal of youth and the inexperience of a novice in Oriental matters.

Samuel Rutherford in a mellow old age said, "Satan has a Friend-at-Court in the heart of youth," and commenting on his own past added sadly, "Often my zeal was mixed with my own wildfire." This was a case in point, but neither side was able, as yet, to discern it as such.

Matters came to a head, finally, over young Samuel of Deer Pool, whose dislike for his wife had made Homay weep.[1] In order that the case might be more clear to the reader we must go back and see what happened to Samuel.

[1] See p. 55.

The exhortation by Job and Me-do-me-pa to take up his cross and accept his wife had held Samuel to the Narrow Way for a few months. But Sam was never one to "spread out his roots by the river" as Homay did. He just would not take time to read his Gospel portions and pray, so when the Sharp Wind from the Bitter Height struck him he was easily upset. After we had left for furlough, Samuel had met with a crisis and definitely, wilfully left the Lord and had gone into sin. There was nothing bad that he had not done, they said. His old father, believing it to be because of the unloved wife, took her to the heathen laird at Six Treasuries and bought a divorce. Now Samuel was a very attractive young Lisu, tall, broad, open-faced, and with a sunny smile; we all liked him. Moreover, Brother Two had misunderstood part of his case—thought that his wife had been married, without himself being consulted, in the heathen days; whereas in truth Sam had had a Christian wedding. It was noticeable that none of the deacons was making any effort to get Sam back; Brother Two evidently did not know that Me-do-me-pa had spent much time and loving exhortation in trying to keep the boy from going into sin. "You do not even try to reclaim sinners!" said Brother Two with heat, and went after Samuel himself, prayed with him and earnestly urged him to return to God. Much flattered by the white man's personal interest, Samuel at length confessed his sin and consented to return. Brother Two was naturally overjoyed, and expected everybody else also to open wide their arms and receive the young sinner jubilantly. But it was not so.

"We are glad he has confessed his sin and wants to come back," said the Lisu deacons. "He went into sin wilfully—it is not our custom to receive such back immediately to the Lord's table. We would like him to be suspended from handshaking and the Communion Table for a period, that he may prove his repentance is sincere."

Again, Brother Two gave out opium as medicine, and when told that Lisu Christians were not allowed to have anything to do with opium, replied hotly that "there is nothing in the New Testament which says that one may not use opium! Nothing to say you may not smoke tobacco or drink wine either!" This was an awful shock; and some of the weak Christians made his words an excuse to go back to old sins. And always Brother Two quoted the New Testament—a book which Me-do-me-pa and the others had heard of, but never been able to read, as the translation was not yet finished. Mr. and Mrs. Cooke were working on it at the time.

And so a definite schism broke the Lisu church. One need not go into the details, but some followed Brother Two and the others stood by Me-do-me-pa. Never had such a Sharp Wind ever blown upon the Shepherd or the little flock. The beating from the Laird was nothing to this; that had been from the outside but this was from the inside of the body of Christ! Fearfully and weakly they talked together in the desolate chapel. Was there any use in going on?

Then it was that Me-do-me-pa again became a Rock-in-a-weary-land. "I know what we must do," he said sadly. "We must write to Mr. Fraser, and ask him if we are wrong, ask him what to do. If we should have let Brother Two rule us, we can confess it—God knows we only want to do His will. But Sam never looked sorry for his sin as far as I could see. He confessed it to please Brother Two, to my mind. What will happen to the church if they are allowed to drink, smoke, handle opium? . . ." Everyone groaned thinking of the misconstructions already put upon Brother Two's words by some. And so that letter was written and mailed. But it would take some three months to get an answer from the superintendent who was away off in the east of the province. In the meantime there was the split church to face every day, and the jeers of the heathen.

One day this came out from Brother Two's followers. "Brother and Sister Kuhn are back in China, but they are not coming back here. They are to work at Paoshan. If you don't accept Brother Two he will leave, and you will have no missionary ever!"

This was a hard blow. It was true that we were back from furlough and had been designated to Paoshan city; our own letters gradually arrived and ratified it. Then the Wind blew its fiercest. "We had better write to the China Inland Mission Headquarters to leave Brother Two here," said some of the deacons anxiously. "We can do as he says! It is better to do that, than to have no missionary!" And they drew up a letter to the Shanghai Council asking that Brother Two be left with them. Only Me-do-me-pa refused to sign.

"I did not refuse lightly, Ma-Pa," he said to us, in relating it afterwards. "Keh-teh-seh-pa and I stayed up all one night praying; all night we cried to God to show us what to do. But I could not sign."

His refusal shook the deacon body. But finally, after they had swayed back and forth, now going to send it without his signature, now not daring so to treat one who had always proved wise and loving to them; finally, they rallied around the Rockman—"All right, then we won't sign either," they said sadly. And at that point, help came.

A letter from Mr. Fraser arrived, expressing tender sympathy and telling them to stand their ground; that Brother Two had misunderstood some things, and that he, Mr. Fraser, was coming in to discuss these matters with Brother Two himself; then all would be talked through and cleared up. "You have not been wrong in your stand," he had written. Oh, how those words comforted! "God has answered our prayers!" Me-do-me-pa cried, almost weeping for gratitude.

After that it was easier to wait with patience. Finally, word came that Mr. Fraser was too busy to come so far, but that he was coming to Paoshan, and that Brother Two was to go out and meet him there; and in the meantime, Mr. and Mrs. Kuhn were being sent in to visit them and, he trusted, "comfort their hearts." Joy and sadness!

Joy to think of seeing the missionaries who had lived among them in 1935-6; sadness to see Brother Two packing up, still maintaining he was right, and saying that he would never return to them—for the Lisu love their missionaries more than they do their own parents, and although Brother Two was vexed with them, they remembered that he had come all that long way from his own country, had parted with his loved ones, and had made many sacrifices in order to bring the gospel to them, despised earth people that they were. So it was grief to see him go without a reconciliation.

In about a week's time, a runner arrived to say that Brother and Sister Kuhn were coming up the hill that afternoon probably. As Me-do-me-pa waited behind the Welcome Arch a few hours later and saw his loved missionary coming towards him, something within him seemed to crack; all that weight of decision as to what was wrong and what was right, might be shifted now on to familiar shoulders. It was too much for the dear Shepherd; when he saw my husband he just threw his arms about John's neck and let the tears run. It was a moving sight, for he said nothing at all, he criticized no one, just clung and wept silently. And in the long interview which followed, I never heard Me-do-me-pa say one word about Brother Two that was angry or "nasty." All was just grief.

That very night the Shepherd had a severe attack of pain. It was the beginning of strange seizures, which finally settled down into the constant pain and symptoms of cancer. But for over a year, though the loved deacon would have one of these attacks every now and again, we never dreamed he was in danger.

We must say a word of the meeting of Mr. Fraser and Brother Two. The latter had told the Lisu before he left, that he was severing his connection with the China Inland Mission; so sure was he that he was right, and that Mr. Fraser could never convince him of anything but that. Truth to tell, none of us had much hope that the meeting could result in anything satisfactory, but we prayed anyway. December 31 of each year the members of the China Inland Mission set aside for prayer and fasting; and as the year was drawing to a close John invited the Lisu to join in keeping the last day thus. Me-do-me-pa and some ten others gathered with us that afternoon on the open hillside. Of course the matter of the meeting in Paoshan city was uppermost in the minds of all of us. As my husband led, in a little preliminary talk, he said something like this: "Now in our prayers, I do not want to hear anyone telling the Lord about the faults of Brother Two. God knows them already. This prayer time is to confess *our* sins, and get *our* hearts right with God. After doing that, we can ask Him to help Mr. Fraser and Brother Two get reconciled."

The prayers that followed were among the most precious
I have ever heard. The dear Lisu did just what their Big Brother
had asked. Not a word that was not loving was said of Brother
Two, but many confessions as to anger, hardness of heart, etc.,
went up to the Throne of Grace.

> And if your hand or foot offend you,
> Cut it off, lad, and be whole;
> But play the man, stand up and end you,
> When your sickness is your soul.

There was "cutting off" that day in Lisuland, and way off
down in Chinaland, God worked beyond thought and expecta-
tion. The result was, gradually, a letter from Brother Two to the
Lisu church came; it asked forgiveness for disrupting them and
for anything done or said wrongly. He did not say that he had
been entirely wrong. To the end he believed the Lisu church
discipline was wrong; but Mr. Fraser was too big a man to ask
a sincere opinion or conviction to be changed. All the superintendent wanted was that *unity of heart* be restored. So although
their individual convictions regarding church discipline and the
catechism continued unchanged, their fellowship as members
of the same Body was re-established. The same mail brought a
letter from Mr. Fraser, one of the sweetest I have ever read, in
which he told us that they had been reconciled as brothers in
the Lord; and he added, "Now I never want to hear Brother
Two's mistakes mentioned again by anybody! As regards myself,
they are already forgotten—he is a brother beloved. And I
order and exhort you also to receive him as such, and urge the
Lisu Christians to do the same! 'Love covereth.' " And I believe
it did.

Years later, Old Big (of the following pages) was watching me
open some mail. "Ma-Ma," he said, "where is Brother Two
now? I know there were some things happened when he was
here," with a twinkle in his eye, "but he healed my foot when it
was badly cut, once, and I can never cease to be grateful to him.
I love-long after him!" Brother Two was sent to another part
where the China Inland Mission was working; and the last I heard,
he was in the British Army, and winning many souls to Christ.

And now to our joy, permission was given to us to stay on in

Oak Flat, and in addition to ourselves, the two fellow-workers previously mentioned were granted to us. Then, as summer approached, the dream and vision of our furlough was laid before the Lisu church—a three months' Bible school (the R.S.B.S.) for Lisu evangelists and laymen whom the Lord might choose to send.

The deacons were pleased with the idea, but when John told them that the expenses (food of the students, chiefly) were to be paid for by the Lisu church (indigenous principles), they were in consternation.

"Ma-Pa"—They approached the objection anxiously—"food for fifteen or so for three months takes a lot of corn! Where can the church find so much? It's never been done before in Lisuland, has it? Not for such a long period? Not even in the parent church of Stockade Hill? To feed fifteen students for three months!"

Me-do-me-pa was church treasurer. He, the man of ingenuity, also looked grave. "Ma-Pa, I think it would be fine, but I do not know how it would work out. There are many difficulties——"

"Well, Me-do-me-pa," answered John, "suppose we start out and try to feed them and teach them for three months. I'm sure God will supply the corn, but suppose we just say we will hold the school for as long as He does supply corn?" On that basis the deacons were comforted and plans were made. The story of the R.S.B.S. will be told in a later chapter, but suffice it to say here that the results gratified all so much that a vote was taken to continue the same thing the next year, and it was unanimous. Thus it became a yearly institution.

As told before, we began that first school (and subsequent ones) with a time of heart searching, and I notice from the circulars of those days that it touched more than the students— I quote from June, 1938:

THERE ARISETH A LITTLE CLOUD

In looking over prayer partner letters I came upon this sentence— "We are led of the Spirit to pray for a general revival among the Lisu Christians." We rejoice that the Lisu have people praying for them who are led of the Spirit. Like Elijah's servant on Mt. Carmel, sent up to look for the prayed-for showers, we would like to tell you that "there ariseth a little cloud . . . like a man's hand." From the first days of our arrival there have been individual confessions of sin—some every month—and in a few cases the ones who sought cleansing were touched directly by the Spirit Himself; that is, not through a human medium. It is always a peculiar joy to see God work all by Himself. He uses us to give us that pleasure, but He does not have to use us.

Sunday, May 1, was the day the little cloud arose. The first Sunday of the month is always communion here, and that day John led the service. He spoke on "Go, and sin no more," then before administering the sacrament, he asked if there were not some who wished to make things right before partaking. Immediately Me-do-me-pa was on his feet. He is church treasurer among other things, and some time ago in making up accounts he found $1.50 more than was necessary, so he decided it must be his own money and pocketed it. During prayer in his own home, thinking of something quite different, the Holy Spirit brought that $1.50 to his mind and told him he should have given the church the benefit of the doubt. Me-do-me-pa had already confessed it to Job, but now wished to tell the church. His lead made it easy for others. I cannot relate all here, but will pick out some I think might interest you most.

Va-ci-me-pa is the brother of our Joseph who is asleep in Jesus. This boy has had further affliction; their father died a few months ago, and by the way, on his death-bed he said he saw Joseph in heaven leading the singing! Then just lately Va-ci-me-pa's house burned to the ground through his wife's carelessly leaving the flax too near the fire. They lost everything, and in his shock and grief Va-ci-me-pa beat his wife. He arose that day to confess to all and publicly shook her hand before us. Dear boy—he seems to have the same tender heart that Joseph had, for he broke down and cried and cried.

Rhoda, Job's wife, had a quarrel with Pade-John and the two of them were not on speaking terms. They both confessed and shook hands.

Then Pade-Peter came forward. First he confessed to having stolen a pencil from us three years ago; then to having ill-treated his old parents. At this point Me-do-me-pa, from his own seat on the penitent form, looked up and ejaculated grimly, "Yes, you had better say that!" Both old people were in the audience and both broke down and cried and started to flood us with miserable details of how unfilial the boy had been, so that the Spirit was quenched and no more confessions followed. Job closed with prayer saying, "Father, there must be many more and greater sins in our midst. Please cleanse us." Altogether we were four hours in chapel that Sunday.

One of the rare qualities in a Rock-man is the ability to say *no*. Many a leader has spoiled his career, and failed to attain greatness, when he met this seemingly simple test. But Me-do-me-pa had that ability to be upright at any cost.

As spring of 1939 advanced, the Kuhn household began to run low in corn. We often bought the corn which the Christians had donated to the church, and which had to be sold. We paid the regular market price, of course, but it was convenient to get it from next-door, instead of having to have it hauled from a distance. So John asked Me-do-me-pa, as church treasurer, to sell him some of the church corn. To his surprise Me-do-me-pa refused! He did it very graciously and explained his position thus, "If I sold any of the corn which is in this village now, Ma-Pa, there would not be enough left to feed the Bible students through R.S.B.S., and the church should not pay to have corn hauled, when there has been enough stored here, to start with."

My husband was slightly nettled at first, then we saw that properly we should rejoice, "Just think how he has shouldered the responsibility of feeding the students! He is thinking and planning carefully that the school may be run without hindrance. If anyone is to be bothered with hauling corn, it should be private people like ourselves. After all we can afford it. What a gift, to have a man who cares about the interests of the church whether it makes him popular with his neighbour or not!" And truly after Me-do-me-pa was gone, we had a succession of worries over that very thing. The Lisu who later took charge of the corn (a true Christian himself, but unable to say "No" to friends and relatives who want to "borrow" or otherwise use church corn) was embarrassed by many a shortage which should never have been. It was not due to dishonesty, but merely to that lack of courage in not daring to become unpopular.

As R.S.B.S. (1939) was approaching, Pade-John presented himself as a candidate for entrance. He applied to Me-do-me-pa, saying that he now intended to do the Lord's work, and so expected the church to feed him free. But Me-do-me-pa refused him free board, saying it was against the rules. Now Pade-John is a relative of Me-do-me-pa's, and in the East it is customary to wink at rules if the applicant is your blood relative. But the dear deacon knew that there was just enough corn for the teachers, and to admit a layman free would be to run short for the evangelists. Pade-John certainly never expected to be refused, and he was quite upset. The kind Shepherd looked at the disconsolate young fellow, and said, "John, have you no money of your own to buy corn?"

"Yes, about three dollars; but the cost of three months' food is five dollars."

"Well," said Me-do-me-pa, "you use that three dollars and I'll add a fourth!" Whereupon a guest in the home piped up, "And I'll give the fifth!" and so the boy got his study expenses and the church did not suffer. This is a small incident, but it is revealing. For the good of the majority, Me-do-me-pa had to stay by "the law"; but he tempered it with "grace" out of his own pocket! That is why his reputation for integrity and yet for kindness and ingenuity, spread for many days' journey up and down the canyon.

It was now becoming clear that an incurable disease had laid hold of our beloved Rock-man. We sent him to a Chinese doctor at Paoshan city, but though they put him through many tests, some very painful ones, they could not diagnose the trouble. Perhaps if they operated they could find out, they said. But at that he refused and elected to come back to his beloved mountain home.

A little incident stands out in my memory, but I cannot place its date. However, I give it here. Charlie Peterson had just returned from the district of Luda, where he evidently had spent some time. It was Sunday morning at breakfast.

"Who is slated to speak this noon?" he asked.

"Me-do-me-pa's name is up," I replied.

"Me-do-me-pa!" he exclaimed, sitting back in his chair. "So I am going to see and hear the celebrated Me-do-me-pa! Well I tell you frankly, *I am prejudiced against that fellow!* What a time I have had with the deacons up there at Luda! No matter could be brought to a decision. Just as it seemed to arrive there, someone was sure to say, 'Well, let's wait awhile and see what Me-do-me-pa will say about it.' Me-do-me-pa, six days' journey away, and who does not belong to their district at all! What has he got to do with Luda affairs, anyway? What is he? A Lisu pope?"

At that time I did not know of the Shepherd's reputation for godly wisdom and I was alarmed lest something had been going on which I did not know. So I just answered, "I don't think he is like that. But, anyway, you will hear him yourself this noon. You can ask him anything you like then."

That noon service as the dear Shepherd stood up to break the Word of God to us, his face aglow with the light so often there, I soon forgot the suggested accusation, in listening to his humble, sweet message. It touched my heart and I did not think of the matter again until at the close of the service I suddenly saw Charlie Peterson rise from his seat, and go forward with both arms outstretched as if he would embrace the Shepherd. But he planted those hands on the big Lisu's shoulders and said, "Thank you, Brother. That message was a blessing to my own heart." And the Lisu deacon blushed with pleasure like a schoolgirl. Charlie Peterson was one of his faithful friends from that hour onward.

Our next circular said:

Our beloved Shepherd Me-do-me-pa is likely dying of cancer. Pray that he may end triumphantly. He has had to resign from all church work and the church is in a flutter. In fact I am so grateful for the privilege of being here at so critical a time—if there were no missionary here I don't know what would happen—likely there would be difficulty in having any Rainy Season Bible School at all. As it is, the deacons insist that there is food for only one month's supply. Perhaps they are to have a lesson in faith. Perhaps God has other plans for this summer, but pray that if the R.S.B.S. is God's will for these months that Satan may not be allowed to hinder supplies getting through.

But though he "resigned," Me-do-me-pa was not allowed to lay his burdens down. People flocked to his sick bed with their problems. The following extract will be a sample:

May 23, 1940.

THE VALLEY OF THE SHADOW

It was Sunday evening, May 12; the sun had just set quietly behind the opposite mountains. No glorious streamers of gold and crimson has he displayed for a long time now; he merely wraps himself in a

mantle of grey cloud and silently drops over the edge. Was he trying
to match the grey tenor of my days, I wondered? Or was he also
grieving for the emaciated suffering one, up there in the little shanty
in Oak Flat Village, whose feet are painfully threading the unlightened
path of the valley of the shadow? Me-do-me-pa is not far from any
of our thoughts, as the following little story will tell.

Dusk in Lisuland. Although I was still alone and the days still heat-
misty I rejoiced in this hour. Everything then is settling down for the
night's rest; grey though the sky is, it is peaceful and serene; twitter of
drowsy bird and happy hum of contented cricket or cicada, the quiet of
God's holy places seems to brood over earth and sky. I was strolling
back and forth over the rock platform which made our shanty home
level, drinking in all the stillness and the nearness of the Other Land,
when my solitude was interrupted by Papa Peter coming jauntily down
the hill and seating himself near the edge of the stone foundation work
evidently intent on having a conversation. After a while it burst out.

"Ma-Ma, there is a wind-word has reached my ear"—with many
grimaces and gesticulations without which Papa Peter would be as
unable to talk as a Frenchman.

"And what did it say?" I asked, smiling and stopping in front of him.

"It is said that when Me-do-me-pa goes up to heaven the Big Fellow
is going to leave too."

I was puzzled. Lisu is a most ambiguous language which often leaves
much to the imagination. Other Lisu had appeared and were grouping
themselves around us. "He means," said La-fu-si-ma with a smile,
"that when Me-do-me-pa dies you white folk will go away too."
"Yes-s," groaned Papa Peter expressively; "and that is why everybody's
heart is cold. Oh, when Me-do-me-pa goes I won't dare to live on the
earth any longer, for when evil men abound and try to steal my fields,
what shall I do? Even sick as he is now, he always has some plan or
idea to help me out of a trouble. I'm a fool; I have no ideas to combat
anybody. I'll just be a helpless victim when he is gone!"

His woebegone face made me smile, but the tears were very near
the surface. Memory flew back to a Sunday years ago when Papa Peter
had brought some iron to church (he is the village blacksmith) in order
to bargain for the coming week's work with a certain heathen or some
such thing. The heathen came before the service was over and called
Papa Peter in the middle of the meeting. When Me-do-me-pa saw that
the old man had actually brought the iron to chapel and was hiding it
under his bench, he seized it and threw it outside. Whereupon there
was a hot argument afterwards, and the Shepherd said, on our trying
to make peace, "I was wrong to get angry, but there is no one gives me

more trouble than that old man. He is a continual trial to me!" And
here was Me-do-me-pa's "Continual Trial" sitting before me with a
gloomy countenance telling me that he would not dare to live after the
Shepherd dies!

But I saw in a trice that Papa Peter was the voice of the ignorant
part of Lisu church. So I pointed the obvious lesson. "But, Papa Peter,
the Lord is not going to leave us, nor is your white pastor." (How
grateful I was at that moment that I had stayed behind. My very presence
was a living testimony that the wind-words were not true and need not
be feared.) "Don't you suppose the Lord Jesus has ideas too, and can
defend His own from evil? Is your trust in Me-do-me-pa or in Christ?
Perhaps this is the reason that Jesus is taking Me-do-me-pa from us, so
that His children will learn that He is their true Leaning-Place. Haven't
you heard Mr. Yang's story of how the Lord took care of him some
months ago? He was on his way to Luku market when his horse ran
away at the top of the mountain as they were about to descend. He had
to chase back after it, but when he caught it and finally reached the river
bank he found a heathen fellow bleeding and wounded. Robbers had
been waiting there, and because Mr. Yang's horse ran away the heathen
man reached the robbers first, lost all that he had with him, and had his
arms badly cut, or perhaps broken, besides. Could Me-do-me-pa have
done that? Isn't the Lord Jesus a safer trusting place?"

Papa Peter was impressed—he had not heard that story. "That's so.
You've comforted my heart, Ma-Ma. Thank you," he said slowly.
Then . . . does it ever fail? . . . "the fowls of the air devoured it"; the
"fowl" this time being Abel who said with a light laugh, "Oh, but
Mr. Yang is a preacher; you and I could not expect such attention!"
Do not the devil's lies make you angry? But aren't there some Abels
at home who say just the same thing? "Oh, that life of faith is all right
for the missionaries. God has a special love for them"—and so on.
Yet all the time the Word says, "Then Peter opened his mouth and
said, Of a truth I perceive that God is no respecter of persons; but in
every nation *he that feareth him and worketh righteousness* is accepted with
him." The only conditions to such acceptance with God are faith, the
love that fears to sin against Him, and the life that in no point has been
consciously disobedient to Him. But I do not know whether "the seed"
was wholly devoured or not; the group broke up and the conversation
ended.

But I have told you this so that you may see how to pray. In every
church there are spiritual and carnal Christians, and in every church
practically the same class predominate. Are you harshly judging Papa
Peter and his crowd? Listen. My mother died when I was twenty-two

years old—old enough to stand on my own feet—but I can never forget that awful sense of desolation. I had never known this world without mother to run to when in trouble, I did not know that God had a dear husband all planned for me. Well the Oak Flat church has *never known Christian life without Me-do-me-pa* to run to when in trouble. They are shaking and trembling; that is, the carnal ones are—our spiritual Christians are not afraid. But I sympathize with Papa Peter. I have had experience of the Lord's love and power. I know He can raise up some one, something to make life livable again—in my case it was my husband, but always it is something. Those who live after the flesh have no such experience to bolster them and they are needlessly afraid. But we are not told to cast them out because their faith is not enough ... "him that is weak in the faith *receive* ye." Put your loving arms of prayer about these doubting ones, that they may *see*, later on, the glory of God.

Amy Carmichael says that the words, "No one is indispensable. God will give you another Me-do-me-pa" are not true. She says, "No it is not *by giving us back what He has taken* that our God teaches us His deepest lessons, but by patiently waiting beside us till we can say, 'I accept the will of my God as good and acceptable and perfect of loss or gain.' "

> When is the time to trust?
> Is it some future day,
> When you have tried your way,
> And learned to trust and pray,
> By bitter woe?
>
> Nay; but the time to trust
> Is in the moment's need,
> Poor, broken, bruised reed!
> Poor troubled soul make speed
> To trust thy God.

And now the Wind of Death was blowing bitterly upon the dear Shepherd. It was his "time to trust." At first when he realized recovery was hopeless, the "why" of it bothered him. One afternoon as I was sitting with him, he turned to me almost weeping and said, "Ma-Ma, I have searched and searched my heart and I cannot find any sin big enough to have brought this upon me!" And then, as I went over the story of Job and showed him how suffering is not always caused by sin, is not always a punishment, he was comforted, and from then on he seemed to enter into peace of heart, although bodily pain was on the increase.

At this time Homay was still alive, so she and I took the guitar and climbed the hill to Me-do-me-pa's house to sing to him daily, and try to be a comfort. He loved it and would ask for his favourite hymns. *The Great Physician* he wanted at first then nearer the end it was *My hope is built on nothing less than Jesu's blood and righteousness, When I survey the wondrous Cross* and *Jesus keep me near the Cross.* I felt myself near the borderland of Heaven those days. Once he asked for "that hymn which says, 'this is the victory that overcomes.'" After we sang it, I read to him the fifth chapter of I John, then said to him, "Isn't it good that it says the victory is our *faith*, not our power to endure?" How his face lit up with joy at that thought, for his sufferings were beyond human endurance. "Ma-Ma," he answered, "I believe now what I always have, that Christ died for my sins and rose again, and I know He is going to reward me."

June is the rainiest time of the whole year at Oak Flat. It is the beginning of the Rainy Season and often for several weeks we did not see the sun—just rain, day and night. That year it was especially bad. On June 8, about one o'clock in the morning I was awakened by a knock at the door. I instinctively knew what it would be. "Yes, Ma-Ma," was the answer to my inquiry, "Me-do-me-pa is going and he has sent Job to ask if you will come to him." Hastily I threw on a heavy coat over my pyjamas, got into rubber galoshes and started out into the night. Me-do-me-pa's shanty is only about a hundred yards above ours, but the ground was so soft with the long wetting that my feet sank into it at each step and I had to have two Lisu, one on each side, pull me up the incline, for we had to climb through the mire of a cornfield. Meanwhile, the rain was drizzling gently down on our heads.

I had brought with me some medicine to be given when his pains were most severe. On arrival we found the shanty filled with people, some sleeping on the floor, some standing, some sitting. Almost to the end, people had persisted in taking their problems to him. In vain he pleaded to be freed from their worries. He even appealed to me, "Ma-Ma, can't you ask the church to free me from these matters? I'd love to help the folk still, but I am so weak, and when they come with their long stories it wearies me so, can't you help me?"

I could have wept. He was so emaciated that his big bones stuck through the dry skin—just a living skeleton, and yet the people still sought his advice. He had been a rock in a weary land so long to them that it seemed as if they could not let him go—they were afraid he would die before they got the benefit of his counsel. I issued stern orders, and I think from then on he was freed. But they still surrounded him. The crowd that night were, at last, not thinking of themselves, and a reverent awe was in the atmosphere as I picked my way through and over them, to the little inner room where the dying man lay.

The death rattle was in his throat; he could not speak, but he knew I had come. I took his so-thin hand in mine, and it returned my pressure lovingly. So I knew he was conscious and I asked Job to read John xiv. 1-6. I felt the Lisu voice might be understood better than mine. After Job finished, Me-do-me-pa gathered himself together for a final testimony. I saw he was trying, so I administered the medicine I had brought, with an eye-dropper (he was too far gone to drink). Then suddenly he began to talk. His speech was so thick that I lost the first part of it, but it went on like this, "I believe what Pastor Job read just now and by His Cross I . . . Ma-Ma, pray for me, that God's will, whatever it be, may be accomplished." That last was remarkably clear. And so I prayed, committing him unto the One who had died to redeem him. As I finished he said in his old natural voice, "Thank you," turned his head and seemed to have fallen into a light slumber. I knew the opiate might do that, and not sure when he would arouse, I left some of the medicine for him and went back home and to bed.

R.S.B.S. was in full swing, those days; there were just two of us to teach, and already I had a very bad cold. With so much depending on me I felt I must not go out into the wet without necessity, and I had left word that they should call me if he roused. It was eight the next morning when we heard a soft sound of weeping, up the hill. Before I could get galoshes on to go, the voices of Job, Luke and others started to sing the Lisu funeral hymn, *Sleep On, Beloved*, and I knew the dear suffering one was with his Lord.

They said the end came too quickly to call me. He slept on until about eight, when he awoke and asked the women to leave the room, "Now your uncle is going to leave you," he said to the men, "Don't make a wailing, but look for me" . . . and while he was speaking he was lifted over the ford.

> Deep is the stream and the night is late,
> And grief blinds my soul that I cannot see.
> Speak to me out of the silence, Lord,
> That my spirit may know
> As I forward go
> That Thy pierced hands are lifting me over the ford.

The funeral was hastened on. All guests who choose to come before the burial must be feasted, and he was so widely known that they feared too great expense for the widow, so he was laid in the grave that very afternoon. His married daughter, Me-do-me, was then nineteen years of age. Thaddeus was ten, and little Philip five.

The Rainy Season Bible School students dug his grave. They wrapped the body in native sheets, tied it to carrying poles, then friends carried it to the graveside, where the heavy coffin was waiting. He was enclosed and lowered, the grave being dug as I had never seen a grave dug before. Above the cell for the coffin which was twice its height, ledges on each side were dug; after the coffin was lowered, the space above was kept empty, but huge slabs of rock, heavier than two men could carry, were placed on these ledges, thus covering completely the coffin cell. Above the rock slabs earth was heaped, and rocks on top of that. Later I planted flowers. On an upright slab of smooth stone is carved a cross and "Me-do-me-pa, Forty-one years, Oak Flat Village, Deacon of the Church." Then on the horizontal part of the cross it reads, "He being dead yet speaketh." The site is in the curve where Sunset Ridge joins Oak Flat Mountain, and is right beside the path out to the main road, over which we all pass so often, so that his memory will yet be testifying to his fellow villagers.

Altogether Me-do-me-pa had been a Christian only about nine years. As a heathen he was little known beyond the precincts of his own village. But after yielding to Christ, he became loved and revered and a power for God, for many days' journey up and down the canyon. How account for that, except for the declaration of scripture, "He that wrought effectually in Peter . . . the same was mighty in me." "But the manifestation of the Spirit is given to every man to profit withal. For to one is given by the Spirit the word of wisdom."

Friend, if God could do so much for an earth person, in nine years' time, what might He not do with you—if you yielded yourself fully to His power?

6

The Prey of the Terrible

THE scene changes. No longer the deep canyon of the
Salween river, but the mountain land of Upper Burma,
about seven days' journey straight west from Me-do-me-pa's
home. We have been thinking so much of the Nests that found
refuge in the Rock, that I wonder if we have forgotten the
Abyss? This chapter is to remind us of the evil power which has
always claimed the Munition of Rocks as his own. And he
still does.

A small village on a hill, under a big tree. Before we get close,
the loud clatter of loose floor boards and rough foot-tapping
ring out far down the trail. A spirit séance is going on! Two
women and a man are calling down the evil spirits. Beating a
copper gong the while, they begin a backward and forward foot
dance, much like our Sailor's Hornpipe, and all the time they
are calling out, "Come down! Come down! Come down!"
Suddenly the clattering stops, the dancers are "possessed," their
eyes become glazed as they go unconscious,[1] and a voice absolutely different from their own comes through their lips. This
day the message is extraordinary.

"Worship God," they shriek, "He has a Son named Jesus
and two daughters. They live in the stratosphere above the
clouds. Cast out your demon altars. God will give you eternal
life. He will raise the dead and the old shall be made young!"
No such message had ever been heard before in those parts.
The onlookers drop their jaws in open-mouthed amazement.

Then the man's demon turns on the two women and scolds
them for not completely healing the sick one, in whose cause
this séance is being held. Whereupon the two women, still

[1] Just one in the village retained consciousness while possessed.

possessed, turn upon the man, and scold his devil, using this new name, *Jesus*. (This was in 1923; fifteen years later I personally visited these people and investigated this story. I thought that perhaps they might have heard that Name in a market and their subconscious mind retained it, but all declared emphatically that it was not so. Never had they heard that Name until the demon séance related above.)

After haggling back and forth, the onlookers beat the gong. The demon-possessed ones stagger, come to, and the séance is over. An animal is then slain and offered to the demons.

The demon-possessed ones did not know what had been spoken through them, so when they asked the onlookers, there was a great babble of talk as to what this strange message could mean. One thing had stood out in everyone's mind; all three demons had said from now on they were not to worship ordinary demons but to worship one, Jesus. Knowing nothing more, they thought that Jesus must be a demon who wished to be their special protector. Very much interested, they decided to hold another séance the very next day, and this time definitely and exclusively invite Jesus to come down.

So the two women and the one man again went through the séance just like the day before, except that it was Jesus whom they invited. And the same thing happened. Again the strange voice proclaimed, "Worship God and Jesus. The old will become young and the dead will become alive." Then there followed new instructions, "When you pray to Jesus, take off your turban, close your eyes and bow your head."

The man's devil again said, "Don't worship demons. Repent of your sins!" Whereupon the two women's devils cursed him and for three years he could not get possessed—his familiar spirit seemed to have left him. But others in the village tried, and got possessed. They could tell it was the Jesus-demon by his catch word, "Worship Jesus and the old will become young. . . ." And new revelations flowed in.

"One day in seven you must rest—don't work your farms."

"Don't drink wine, smoke opium or commit adultery. Be good people."

"Don't thieve."

"Don't give false witness."

"Honour your parents" (a thought utterly strange to all Lisu; Christians of our parts have to be taught this from the Scripture).

As far as I could find out, all the Ten Commandments and some of the old Levitical law was given them, from time to time, by demons. The proof that it could not have come from any subconscious mind is that, although Christianity reached Upper Burma, the natives were evidently taught Christian separation from the world, and to this day the tribal Christians in surrounding parts drink, smoke, and do not observe the Lord's Day. This village of the demon revelations was named Goo-moo, and they were the only Christians who tried to live a separated life, as a church. So the thought of such separation from old pastimes was absolutely, utterly, "out of the blue" to them.

Now, I have deliberately picked out, from all the revelations given, those which affect our thinking; but these were not the only revelations. Oh, no. Satan uses the Word of God, but never without mixing some folly and falseness up with it. So there was talk of one, "God's daughter," very vague it was; but most interesting to Goo-moo were the gifts of this demon. He would say, "Go to such and such a place in the mountains, and you will find a bear." They'd go, and lo! a bear was there and the village had meat to eat. In this way they were enticed into bondage to the demon. All his promises did not come true. For instance, he said, "Build cow-sheds and pig-pens and God will give you cows and pigs." (Lisu usually keep their animals underneath their houses, among the stilts on which the house rests.) But of course it took years to find out that there was no increase in cattle when the demon's order had been obeyed. So it came about that the whole village threw out their demon altars, rested one day in seven, and started to worship Jesus.

Two or three months later, a visiting official of the government noticed that they no longer had demon altars in their homes and asked the reason. On hearing their story he reported it to his superior with the result that Goo-moo villagers received an order to report to the government official at Tow-gow, two days' journey away. There they were told that there was a school-teacher at Fort Pien-Ma, who had books about this Jesus, and

that on December 25, a grest festival was held at Fort Pien-Ma
in honour of Jesus. To that festival they went and made themselves known, I suppose, because later on (which year I do not
know) the school-teacher visited them and the third day of his
stay the Jesus-demon came upon the two women, mentioned
above, and through them said, "Don't study his books. They are
dog books, monkey books." So no one was interested in the
catechisms he had brought along. However, one thing impressed
them—he had taken the gong out of the hand of one of the
possessed women and said, "You must not do this!" whereupon
she came out of her spell—the demon left her. The villagers were
too intrigued with this new way of living, however, for it was in
the early days of their bondage, when to be promised meat by
revelation was thrilling to them; so the Christian school-teacher
left them, baffled.

I have been asked why did Satan introduce the name of Jesus
to these people? I feel it was because he saw that the gospel was
inevitably going to reach them, and so he tried to make the
name of Jesus and the outward forms of Christianity (the Ten
Commandments, etc.) familiar to them under a system which
was really worship of himself. We see that he had succeeded in
his subtlety up to this point in the story.

But it did not continue so happily. Once thoroughly ensnared,
the inevitable trickery began. One day the two women's devils
gave forth a message. "The earth is going to be burned!" they
said. "Jesus is coming to earth! And all unbelievers will be
burned. You, believers, go to a certain place in the mountains
and wait for Him! When He comes He will give you animals
and money."

The whole village packed up. Left their farm work unattended,
and retired to the directed place in the mountains, where they
fasted, eating only once a day, and waited a week without
anything happening, of course. Fooled, chagrined, and anxious
now for the unwatched crops left behind, they returned to their
homes. This happened four times in nine years and once the
whole village almost starved because of it. The prey of the
terrible. Some began to wish to get free from this demon.

One day a Karin teacher came for a night or so. As he left

the next morning, a demon came upon one of the villagers and said, "He won't reach his home—he is going to get sick!" And that night the teacher truly, nearly died—a strange fever seemed to be burning him up. "The demons were very intelligent and knowing," the Goo-moo folk told us, and so obedience gradually became that of fear and terror. Then when the fourth revelation of Jesus' coming was given, it was accompanied by the order, "Don't plant your fields this year." Should they obey? Dared they not obey? There was one young boy in the village who had never become possessed—he had tried, but the demons would not come upon him, the only one in the whole place on whom they would not come—and it was through him, in the end, that deliverance came.

"Dad," said this boy, as the family conference whether to plant or not to plant was waging, "I don't believe that Jesus is coming. Has he not told us that three times already and each time fooled us? We will starve if we do not plant our fields. What I'm thinking is—I'd like to find out the truth about this Jesus. That Karin teacher worshipped Jesus, but he did not go through séances like we do. And he does not get fooled either. And years ago that Pien-Ma school-teacher had books about Jesus, don't you remember? I'd like to take a trip out to where that Karin teacher lives and ask him to come back and teach us!"

"I think so too," said his father. "Take a friend and the two of you go." So the two boys set out. But at the sight of them the Karin teacher became terrified. "Go to your village? Never!" he cried. "Your village is full of demons. I would not dare go to the other side of Schoolhouse Mountain!"

"We were wrong," pleaded the boys, "when you came that time. We did not listen then, but now we are tired of these demons and want to learn the truth. Please come!"

But the Karin teacher would not hear of it, so the two laddies had to return home, sad and troubled. No one to deliver them! However, Mark's father (later the boy was named Mark) had decided. He was going to have food, demon's wrath or not; he was going to plant! A few other families in the village followed them; the rest left their fields unplanted, constantly expecting that Jesus was coming and would miraculously feed them, as the demons did so often in directing them as to where to find game in the mountains. But as time went on—when planting was too late—and the Jesus-demon had not come, wan and thin faces besieged Mark's door, pleading for food. But there was not enough to share with so many. Mark's face grew more grim each day. To be enslaved to such a deceitful, malicious master was intolerable.

Then, one day, into his house walked two fellow villagers who had gone to the Salween canyon to trade.

"Books!" they cried out, waving two Lisu catechisms under Mark's nose. "Lisu books about Jesus! You know we went away over to the market at Sandalwood Flat Village, and while trading our things we saw a Lisu selling these catechisms. They are Lisu books—he could read them so as to make them speak our language, and he was preaching about God and Jesus!"

Great was the excitement in the village. As news spread, more and more people gathered around the two young traders, and many times they had to repeat their story. They had met Andrew, one of the lads that had followed La-ma-wu with the gospel evangelization, in the canyon.

Mark was fingering the books with a tremendous thrill in his heart. "Can you read them?" he asked eagerly.

"Oh no. We did not have time to stay long enough to learn. But other Lisu were learning to read them; Teacher Andrew was teaching them how. Bright fellows learn in two weeks, they say."

"Well, why didn't you bring teacher Andrew back with you?" cried out Mark, exasperated at so wonderful a chance thus slipping away.

"Oh, he couldn't come," they answered. "He could not cope with all the invitations he was getting from people who live nearby. And to our place is a journey of five days—seven days soon, for snow will be closing the pass, and he would have to go around Fort Pien-Ma."

"Well, I'm going," cried out the boy. "If I can't get teachers, I'll stay until I can read the books for myself. Dad, may I?" The decision was made, but there was still the Master of the Abyss to deal with. Not lightly would he lose such slaves to his every whim. Twice Mark started out with a comrade and was beaten back. The first time malaria nearly killed him. How the evil one must have laughed as the wan, pale boy staggered into his father's home—defeated, and nearly dead. That was May, 1933. In October he essayed to go again. A different route he and his companions took, but before they got over the high pass (Mountain of Suffering, the Lisu had named it) his comrades became terrified and again he had to return home, still without knowledge of the way of escape from their terrible master.

But by March, 1934, Mark could stand their cheated, terrified bondage no longer. On consulting with his father, they decided, "The devils have led us astray. If there are people who know the truth and can teach us, we must reach them; better to die trying, than to go on as we are." Mark persuaded his brother-in-law and a neighbour to accompany him, and the little band of three started out for the unknown canyon, over a partially unknown road, and one which involved crossing the great Pien-Ma Pass (11,000 feet high) at a time when there was snow on the ground and new snow was likely to come down and obliterate the trail. A Chinese traveller whom they met told them they could get from Pien-Ma Fort to the Salween canyon in one day, so they got up before dawn the next day, and started. Up, up, the air getting freezingly cold. Snow everywhere on the ground; so deep was the snow that they noticed the tops of trees sticking through the crust they were treading underfoot. Snow, tree-high! Up, up to the lonely pass where no human habitation ever is. Snow blew in their faces. They could not breathe for the wind and the biting cold, so they buried their faces in their turbans and sleeves and tried to get their breath that way. Single file they walked and in utter silence, but praying to the *unknown* Jesus (the *good* Jesus whom the demon had tried to counterfeit) to bring them through to where they could find the truth about Him. As they felt their blood chilling, they bit with their teeth into the flesh of their own arms to increase circulation. Sometimes they would fall through the snow crust and get separated—they could not see their fellow in front of them plainly because of the blowing snow. And then—over the pass—and the descent on the China side. Oh, praise to the unknown Jesus—no snow on the China side!

Hope renewed, how fast the young feet now sped over that rocky descent, through those miles and miles of uninhabited, wild-grass mountainside; then at dusk—a village! Coming in the door of a house, the man there looked up at them and asked, "Where did you come from?" When they answered, "Over the Pien-Ma Pass!" the whole house of people exclaimed, "Oh, don't lie! You could not get over the mountain in this snow!" But they had. Wonderful joy of accomplishment.

But where were the Jesus-teachers?

"Oh, there are white people in the canyon, teaching now," was the unexpected answer. "Their name is Cooke, and they are living across the river at Pine Mountain Village. You will have to go up to Place-of-Action Ferry to get across."

All the next day they travelled beside the roaring Salween, and at night slept in rice-fields by its bank. Early morning of the third day saw them at the crossing edge waiting for the first ferry boat. A young Lisu with a book-bag slung over his shoulder got out of the ferry as it drew up and hooked on to the rocks of the bank. "Who are you?" he asked, eyeing their different costume, for the Burmese Lisu are Flowery Lisu.

"We have come from Burma to get a teacher of the gospel," they replied.

"Oh," he said with interest. "I am the missionary's servant. I am on my way to collect their mail. Mr. Cooke isn't home just now, but Mrs. Cooke is there, and the night before last Mr. and Mrs. Kuhn arrived. Go on up. The road is easy to find. See you to-morrow!" and he sped on and left them.

And now I want you to change your point of view, and see things as we saw them, knowing nothing of all that I have been relating to you. My husband and I were on a trial trip into the canyon. Mr. Fraser always feared that my health could not stand the rigorous life of the canyon, but when we heard that two districts had turned Christian, and that to care for each, Mr. and Mrs. Cooke were having to separate and live six days' journey apart, then we volunteered to move in and take over one district. So Mr. Fraser proposed this trial trip, to see if I could stand it.

There being no mail service quick enough, we could not

announce our arrival, so we walked in on Leila Cooke unawares. It had been about a year since she had seen another white woman, so how warm a welcome we received! And from now on I will quote from the letter written right at that time.

The second morning after we arrived as we were sitting in conversation together in through the open doorway walked three strangely clad but handsome Lisu.

Mrs. Cooke urged them to take chairs, but they stared as if they had never seen such things before in their lives, and indicated that they much preferred the safety of the shanty floor where they squatted down in front of us, a picturesque group with their white clothing and red turbans. As Mrs. Cooke questioned them politely and listened to their rather lengthy answers she became visibly thrilled and began to drop to us short translations of the story told above. "They have come seven days' journey over those mountains yonder," pointing to the craggy peaks with sparkling crests of snow which loomed up across the canyon through the open doorway. "Said they had to bite their way through the snow of the pass. . . . Say they've come back until they can take teachers with them, no matter how long they have to wait. . . . They've brought their own food to keep them. . . . They have worshipped God and Jesus for eleven years without knowing anything more about it. . . This is their third attempt to get teachers."

When the conversation came to an end, the three Goo-moo boys were introduced to Pastor Moses, who led them off to his own house. Mrs. Cooke turned to us and said, "And just think, we have no teacher to send with them!" How sad our hearts felt; nay, even rebellious. I knew a town in America with only four thousand population, yet it had nine churches. And here these brave laddies had walked seven days' journey to learn the Way of Life and there was no teacher to send back with them. Every Lisu teacher in the immediate area had his hands too full already. Word had just come from Mr. Cooke that now, if the Kuhns had arrived, would Mrs. Cooke please come up and visit him for a while! And we could not talk Lisu, just Chinese, which the Burma men could not understand; so we were out of the question, anyway, though my husband burned to go.

"Well," said Mark, "we have brought food and money. We will just stay until there is someone, and in the meantime Pastor

Moses can teach us." So day by day they pored over their books, waited and prayed for a teacher.

A month passed. Teacher Simeon arrived on the way home to Stockade Hill. He had fulfilled his promise of one or two years of evangelization and now wanted to get back and be married. Mrs. Cooke had laid the call before him. It was a hard struggle, for he was already homesick. "But I can't go alone very well," he said. Lisu evangelists usually go out two by two, in case of sickness or other sudden need. The young lad who had gone for the mail stood by listening to this point, but surprised us all by crying out:

"I'll go with him! I'll go! Oh Ma-Pa let me go. I don't know much to be sure, but I *can* teach them to read and pray and sing a few hymns. Oh, do let me go!" And so it was arranged. In Lisuland we almost take it for granted that if a boy proves to be a good servant, we will soon lose him from the kitchen into the ministry. It has happened so often, and of course there is no question of whether we can spare him—the Lord's call comes first. It had happened again. Teacher Simeon postponed his longed-for trip home for a full six months, so when the three inquirers returned to Goo-moo something over a month after they had left, it was to show their fellows two Lisu teachers. With great joy, the whole village started in to learn of Him who was manifested that He might destroy the works of the devil, and deliver them who through fear of him had been in bondage.

During those happy six months, and the year that followed, the Kuhn family moved into Lisuland, and by September, 1935, John was free to follow his never-forgotten longing to visit Goo-moo.

John had the most wonderful time at Goo-moo. His party arrived on a Saturday after dark, and the villagers were all at chapel. Of course the visit was unannounced and unexpected, but as the weary band climbed the mountainside (at the end of seven days' travelling) grateful that the long, hard trek was nearly over, through the dark there came a sound of singing, and as they listened, they heard these words floating down the trail to greet them, like a heavenly welcome:

Have you been to Jesus for the cleansing power?
Are you washed in the Blood of the Lamb?
Are you fully trusting in His grace each hour?
Are you washed in the Blood of the Lamb?

"Before we saw their faces, we heard their testimony!" said John, touched to the heart. Then came the delight of surprising them by walking in the door. How they shouted his name, laughed and wept with joy—the first white missionary the village had ever seen. The man who had been possessed by demons could not resist kissing John—took his face reverently in his hands, and kissed him—much to my husband's discomposure! "There won't be any sleep for us this night, to think that Ma-Pa is here!" cried one. And so on. It was a happy time. Twelve were baptized, this making a total of twenty-five baptized believers and more catechists; for other villages were hearing the Good News and wanting to be taught. At length when the time came to part, there was true weeping and grief. In loving gratitude they insisted on acting as John's carriers, free of charge, on the return trip, and even provided chickens for his meals, though very poor themselves in this world's riches.

Three or four of them made the long journey to the Munition of Rocks at Christmas, for they had heard we were going home on furlough. When that happy festival was over, and it came time to say goodbye, knowing it would be years before they saw us again, both men and women broke down and cried. I was deeply stirred to hear Mark's, "Oh, Ma-Pa!" as he broke from John's embrace and turned to the trail, sobbing.

So when furlough was ended and we were once more back in the beloved canyon, we made plans to go and visit that far away little village in Burma, and see how they had been faring. Lisu teachers had continued to go from our district to teach them, so they had been growing, but I myself had never been there and wished to investigate their story. The account of our trip was written in the November, 1938, circular—the year that Homay and Thomas were married.

LOSS AND A DREAM COME TRUE

"My heart is on it," said Homay to me with happy eyes. "That is what we Lisu say when we can hardly wait for something. I can hardly wait to start for Goo-moo!" That is how we all felt as we waited for the return of the mule, Jessie, and those who had escorted Mr. Peterson and Mr. Christianson to Paoshan. They arrived a day earlier than we expected for their hearts too were "on it," but they brought with them news that simply levelled us to the earth. Charlie Peterson, who in 1937 had buried his beloved comrade, Earl Carlson, arrived in Paoshan just in time to bury our beloved and indispensable superintendent, Mr. J. O Fraser.

I say "indispensable" for we still feel that way. After the first shock of the news there was a forlorn feeling, that, speaking of *human* fellowship, "there is no one now to work for." *How Mr. Fraser will enjoy hearing about this*, was always a first reaction to any joy or blessing, and we still have found ourselves thinking that very thought, only to come to ourselves with the desolate realization that he is no longer here. There was no one else on earth who had such a complete knowledge of the details of our problems and so no one who could share so perfectly in our joys and sorrows. And he never disappointed us in that sharing. He was more than superintendent to us: he was our missionary ideal; a continual rebuke, challenge, and stimulus to maintain at any cost the apostolic methods of missionary work. His brilliant gifts, united to unfailing humility and a sympathy motherlike in its tenderness and thoughtfulness made him our refuge at all times of perplexity and need. To win a smile of approval from him was worth any extra effort. It is one thing to be praised by a person who has no experience of your work; it is quite different to win a "well done" from one who himself is a master in that very line. We have lost a great stimulus as well as an indispensable counsellor.

The Lisu of Oak Flat district asked for the privilege of paying the twenty dollars which the digging of his grave cost.

With the passing of our beloved superintendent, John and I have, perforce, to enter an entirely new epoch of our lives, for life can never again be quite the same without him. But life does not stop for heartache, so on the morning of October 2, a beautifully clear morning after days of rain, we started out to follow the road which had been covered four years ago by that historic journey of Mark and his two friends—a story we told again and again while on furlough. Our party consisted of Ah-be-pa, Luke, Thomas, Homay, Simon, Lucius, A-che (the Cookes' cook who is now cooking for us), Abel as mule boy, three carriers, and then just almost at the last moment the Lord set a seal on our going, by bringing us haphazard into contact with two of the Goo-moo church Christians who had come into the canyon on private business. They were needed as guides and interpreters as we came to Kachin country and needed to buy food, etc.

At the end of a good long travel, the first evening out still found us in sight of our house. We slept at Luchang, from which, across the canyon, we can just barely make out the roof of "The House of Grace," our shanty.

The second day we had to go over the great pass, some 11,000 feet high. Up, up through valley-sides, ravine-sides we climbed. Before noon we had left the edge of habitation and for a long time travelled through forest, dark overhanging, shut-you-in forest, not a human soul or house in sight. Mid-afternoon brought us out to bare rocks smitten with a wind that made you shiver although snow time had not yet come, and about four o'clock we came to the narrow slit between peaks and shouted with joy. At our back the great canyon of the Salween and beyond it China's sea of mountain peaks; before our eyes Burma and another monster net of mountain-tops. We had still quite a little walk over the high cold trail, before the earth fell away from us and we beheld a panorama of unrivalled beauty—the valleys of the Upper Irrawaddy, the sun setting behind the peaks that guard those valleys, peaks that seemed in the sunset to tower higher than those we had left behind and made even the Lisu gasp with surprise; then, as our eyes fell from the glory of crimson sky and jagged silhouette, far beneath us on a little knoll stood the British border fort of Pien-Ma with its neat array of sepoy barracks—like a silent handshake from civilization. It was dusk before we reached them, only to find them deserted—fighting between the tribes people and the Buddhists of Burma had caused the fort to be dismantled for lack of soldiers. We slept that night in the middle of the road, having travelled from daybreak until eight in the evening.

Early on the third day we ran into a teacher of the American Baptist Mission, which has work in Upper Burma, and we travelled with him until dusk. He brought us to a village of the A-Chia tribe where we slept, but first held a service, John speaking by interpretation. This day began our travelling through a canyon of gorgeous beauty, scenic falls every little while, a river of surging foam banked by precipitous rocks with trees which were full of orchids.

The fourth day everyone was so tired that we decided to sleep at Tawgaw although it was only two in the afternoon when we reached there. This is the post office town (mail once a week), a beautiful little place with red-roofed bungalows built foreign style; here there is a district superintendent, a garrison of twenty-six sepoys, a Government doctor, a Kachin school with three teachers (all of these officials, of course, were natives) and a few stores where we were able to buy canned milk and coffee! It used to be quite a town, but a severe earthquake has lessened its population to several hundred.

The schoolmaster made us welcome in his own house, and in the evening we were visited by three superintendents, one of whom had an excellent knowledge of English. They urged us to stay over a day so they could give us a dinner party, but our answer you will readily guess. They spied my guitar and asked for some music, so we had the Lisu sing for them, and they were delighted, calling for piece after piece. The Lisu tribe is despised in these parts, the Kachin being considered *the* tribe, so we were ever so pleased to show off our dear group.

The fifth day is made memorable by monkeys above and leeches beneath. Wooded cliffs towered above us and from these the monkeys kept up a sort of heavenly chorus—I presume warning each other of our approach. High above our heads in the tops of the huge trees which lined our mountain path we heard their "*Oo-a-la! Oo-a-la!*" like an antiphonal choir, but not a one did we see. Not so the leeches; underfoot, the little black wrigglers were legion. They stood on the dead leaves of the path, standing upright on their tails and waving back and forth in the air, for a foot to attack, hang on to, and suck. The mules' legs were blood-streaked that day and our dear barefoot band suffered equally. The vegetation too was distinctly different. I saw tree ferns for the first time—long, straight, unbranched trunks, unfolding at the top into beautifully graceful arms of fern each about ten feet in length. Other trees were tremendous, over a hundred feet high, and trunks big enough to contain an auto. That night we slept out in a ridge near a Kachin village with the canyon to our right, over whose jagged walls of rock the moon peered and then sailed majestically on high. We thought we would again have a good night, but we were to make the acquaintance of a minute fly which stings like a mosquito; a net is but a tracery of open doors for it. Goo-moo abounds with these tiny pests, much to Homay's misery, for her plump, bare ankles made good eating!

The last day was the hardest of all—my, what a day! We started on the road at seven in the morning, stopped for lunch at noon by a sheet of waterfall, the water running gently over a bare face of rock some fifty feet in height, then we pressed on through hot sun and black leeches to the river brink which we reached in the late afternoon. Early we had sighted the big tree by the Goo-moo chapel, high on the mountain of the opposite bank, but it was a different matter to get there. Here man battles Nature with only the most primitive of weapons. There was no bridge across the river and only a raft made of bamboo poles tied together with bark. It was so flimsy it could only take two passengers at a time and even then sank into the water; and there are two currents in the river to cross. When we arrived, the raft was on the other side of the river. Some Kachin rowed over with it, but they had come for a pal and refused to take even one of us, so we had to sit there and just look at the raft. We were four hours in getting across a stretch of water only about two hundred feet in breadth. Word had been called across to send a message to Goo-moo for raft-rowers and at length three men arrived and began the trips. What delayed us so long was getting Jessie and Jasper across, and a horse and a colt that belonged to our interpreter. We tried making them swim, but when they struck the first current they turned back. By that time half of us were on one bank and half on the other, dark had fallen and the rocks in the river bed made it too dangerous, so we had to wait for the moon to rise. Finally, by dim moonlight the animals arrived: tied to the raft by tail and one man holding their head, they had been made to swim for it.

We had no food with us and had eaten nothing since lunch. Goo-moo was still two thousand feet above our heads and that climb before us which is too steep to ride and where the traveller must go up holding on to the mule's tail. A drink of coffee all around and then we began. The trail was through dense vegetation twice our height—I could see nothing beneath my waist; my hands holding on to Jasper's tail were all that was within vision, except for a silver-laced gleam overhead where the moon was trying to penetrate the tropical canopy over us. I could not see where my feet were treading—we had seen big snakes that day and I thought of the leeches, but I was reminded that Christians walk *by faith*, and, throwing my cares on Him in all that stiff climb, I stepped on nothing to alarm me. The heat was oppressive, perspiration simply streamed off me and we thought how merciful that it was only moonshine, not sunshine, overhead!

We came out to a Kachin village (toward the end of the climb we were able to ride a bit), where a black-clad figure sprang out of the shadow and in an ecstasy of delight ran to John, then to me, greeting us. We peered through the dark at him, that attractive smile and those beautiful teeth were familiar—Mark! Our precious Mark; he had not heard of our arrival in time to come to the river side and others of the Christians were lining the roads above our heads. It was a wonderful welcome and two tired but thoroughly happy missionaries that midnight lay down in the little whitewashed chapel with prayers of thanksgiving that another dream had come true and we were actually in Goo-moo!

Come tell Me all that ye have said and done,
Your victories and failures, hopes and fears.

I know how hardly souls are wooed and won;
My choicest wreaths are always wet with tears.

WATERING HIS GARDEN AT GOO-MOO!

We arrived on Saturday night, and Monday morning our boys scattered over the hills to surrounding villages, to announce our arrival and that we would hold a short-term Bible school beginning the next Sunday. Goo-moo villagers came night and morning to us for teaching and also set about building us a sleeping house and a cooking house. It is interesting to watch a Lisu shanty go up: not a nail was in the building of our curly-headed house—I call it that because of the roof! I have slept under slate, tin, tiles, shingles, thatch, and canvas, but this was my first experience under a roof of leaves. They thatched it entirely with the long silver green leaf of the banana tree the ends of which tore and curled back, giving it the tousled appearance of a curly-head just out of bed and not yet reached by mamma's careful comb. Tousled heads are in the majority in Lisuland, so the house quite fits the country.

Then began the Bible school, and I stop to wonder how to tell you about it. God gave us Isa. lviii. 11 as our verse for that session and then wonderfully fulfilled it: "The Lord shall guide thee continually." There were weeds in His Goo-moo garden: strife, self-love, uncleanness, and day by day up to and including the very last day, sins were confessed and matters put right. Husbands and wives were reconciled. Our own dear Mark was greatly blessed. In fact, he said to us that our coming this time had been salvation to the little church here.

The last evening we had testimonies and Mark surprised us by staging a little play of his own inventing. He came on the platform and said, "I am an unbeliever and I have two friends whom I love very much. Come my friend," and beckoned to Sa-mu-ye-pa. On Sa-mu-ye-pa's chest was a placard: UNCLEANNESS.

"Do people listen to their beloved chums?" asked Mark.

"Some," replied his audience.

"Well, what do you say to me, my friend?" Mark asked, turning to Sa-mu-ye-pa.

"I say, 'Do unclean things; think unclean things!' "

Mark: "And I have to listen to my friend. But I have a second friend—come!" And A-che slipped on to the platform with a placard: HATRED.

Mark: "And what do you tell me to do, my dear friend?"

A-che: "Love yourself—don't pay any thought to your neighbour. This is hating him." Then Thomas comes quietly up with a chest placard: JESUS.

Mark: "And who are you? What do you offer me?"

Thomas: "I offer you eternal life and a heavenly inheritance, but to receive these you must break with your two former beloved companions."

Mark: "Teacher Kuhn, what shall I do? I've lived all my life with these two friends."

John (from the audience): "Take the advice of Him who offers you eternal life."

Mark: "All right—off with you!" (and Sa-mu-ye-pa with A-che slink from the platform). "But, Jesus, what will I do for a friend now? Must I live all alone?" (Simon comes on to the platform with a placard: THE HOLY SPIRIT.)

Thomas: "No, dear friend; here is a companion who will never leave you, but will abide with you alway and be your counsellor."

Mark (throwing his arms around Simon): "Thank you, Jesus, I accept Him—now, friends, this is my testimony and I want to ask you this question. Who are *your* friends? And what is your choice?"

The effect of this strange testimony was solemnizing. We got a new impression of our dear, precious Mark this time; the gentleness of his sweet smile is misleading. He is a very strong and forceful character. Just twenty-six years old, this leads him into difficulties with the church as he is apt to be a bit tyrannical and self-righteous in his governing of them. He is upright himself and he expects others to be just as consecrated and does not realize that babes in Christ require more patient handling. His self-righteousness he confessed before them all that week; his "strong hand" I do not think he realizes yet. He needs the epistolatory teaching and is going to make every effort to get to the Rainy Season Bible School.

Luke's and Thomas's messages were wonderful. We see more and more that the R.S.B.S. is already producing wonderful fruit. Goo-moo was soaked this time with the teaching on the second birth and we hear from all over the field of our boy students (the Ma-pa-ra) of last summer preaching this foundational truth.

After the school at Goo-moo we went to Sa-mu-ye-pa's village for the harvest festival. We got a wonderful reception—an aisle of flowers as well as an arch had been made for us. And a little house prepared as our dwelling was so filled with mountain blooms that their fragrance attracted the animals at night who tried to get in to eat them, and caused John some practice boot-throwing, for the door was far from stable.

Parting was, as usual, mournful. The Goo-moo Christians wept so that as we dropped down the mountainside from them, it sounded like the wailing for the dead, and I was relieved when they finally changed it to calling to us like monkeys, after we were too far beneath them to communicate otherwise.

Mark came to R.S.B.S. twice, in different years, but each time could not stand the discipline of it. Strange as it seems, he was much slower to grasp doctrines than his fellows, which hurt his pride, for he was by now accustomed to leadership. He was ashamed when he did not make excellent grades, and got so homesick that each time he stayed only a month or so, and then went home, taking his fellow Goo-moo students with him. The result is that none of the Goo-moo students were well-grounded in the truths of the New Testament.

During the war, the Japanese occupied Upper Burma. Goo-moo again appealed to us for teachers—with the Japanese at Tawgaw and spies everywhere, a little band of them worked their way through to us, and pleaded for Lisu evangelists! One of our young student teachers responded, and at the peril of his life went back with them. We just received one letter from him, in which he said that they were reaching out after another tribe which lives in their neighbourhood, and Mark was learning that tribal language in order to lead them to Christ! But he also told how Mark and Sammy-pa were quarrelling, and the church inclined to split over them. Had Satan been gaining an advantage? The Master of the Abyss will never forgive the fact that they were delivered from his clutches, and he has more than one way of enslaving men. Pride of heart is a Wind from the Snow Height which ignorant Christians may not recognize as heading them toward the Abyss; Satan has used that Wind to render useless more than one promising young disciple. The Sharp Wind from the Bitter Height is still blowing.

K

7

The Soul-seedling Patch

NOW, in thought, we must go back to the canyon of the Upper Salween, to the station of Oak Flat. So much has been said of the Rainy Season Bible School, that it might be well to tell of those sessions now.

Brother Two's criticism that the Lisu church was becoming legalistic, was not without foundation. But side by side with that fact one should put this—that the church did not then have the New Testament, and its teachings on law and grace were not understood. John felt deeply that the time had come to do something definite about this general ignorance, and so the vision of our furlough had been a regular, prolonged season of Bible teaching, with the New Testament in manuscript before the students, if necessary. The Books of Galatians and First Corinthians and some others had been completed by that time. We were able to bring back with us a Lisu typewriter (a portable arranged to type Lisu script), so our very first summer in Lisuland, we began. Mr. Fraser wrote us that he was delighted; he felt that nothing was so needed as a prolonged, continued time of Bible study.

And now I think that quotations from the circulars will be more vivid, for they tell of events just as they happened.

THE SEEDLING PATCH

Picture a great rocky mountain on a lone range. Up through its wild grass and pine-tree studded sides threads a yellow-brown trail. Three-quarters of the way up to its crest the trail slims on to a small brow where some tiny huts are planted, with a long weather-beaten thatched bamboo shanty at one corner perched above a deep drop. Around the great wrinkles of the mountain, about three miles up the ravine's abyssal sides is another collection of huts. Of what importance to the world could such far-away isolated poverty be? Why talk about it! Write every month about it? The world may not care—and indeed it does not. However, Heaven is watching that wild mountain brow with joy and brooding love, and it is Heaven's interest that makes us talk of this place to you. Those little shanties are Oak Flat Village, of course, and Heaven is interested because there is a Soul-seedling Patch here—the Rainy Season Bible School.

I told you before how at the end of May each year, the Soul-seedlings gathered from all parts of the canyon. Such insignificant, barefoot, coarse-clad laddies, climbing these steep wrinkles on Mother Nature's brow, perspiring yet laughing, tired yet hopeful, crawling in here from north, south, east and west like so many minute flies! A passer-by would never dream that there had been a stiff fight in the heavenlies, before some of those little "flies" were set free to come. Yet it was so. Prayer was the only thing that opened some of their barred pathways. And as they came trudging over the muddy trails, their bantering talk lets loose, perhaps, the flash of an angry eye here, or a carnal word drops there, or the lagging steps of that one betrays a tendency to laziness, and we realize each one of them is a son of Adam the First. Did that discourage the angels, I wonder? No, I think the angels are more patient than we. I think the angels were looking with eyes of gentle happiness at the book-bag slung over every shoulder. Inside that little cloth bag was a Book which has turned the world upside down—a Book which tells of a last Adam, who has redeemed all that the first Adam wrecked, and whose we may become by a New Birth. They are not on the Seedling Patch long before they are questioned whether they have experienced that New Birth; because there is no hope of growth where there is no life. But they all have, they say—only they do not know how to appropriate or use that inheritance, so here they are.

Before that first three-months' R.S.B.S. we held a week's Bible study as a sort of "try-out." Those eleven who attended did not all turn out successfully, but they are very typical of the ordinary R.S.B.S. student body. Friends enjoyed that early circular about them, so we reprint it here.

OUR VERY FIRST SEEDLINGS
"Belle, what are you grinning at, there in the corner with your paper and pencil?" asked John, looking up from a moment's lull in his dictation class.

"I'm jotting down some impressions of your pupils, for our prayer partners," was the explanation.

Eleven black heads were studiously bent over books around the long stretch of table at the head of which sat John. The table was composed of one round one, plus one square one, plus two square cupboards all placed end to end, and the students were the Ma-pa-ra (which being interpreted means the Small Teachers, or, as we have called them, the evangelists). Our idea has been to call them all in once every seven weeks for Bible study, so that they have one week of study followed by six weeks of preaching in the villages—putting into practice, we hope, what they learned during study week. Some of the eleven were Ma-pa-ra for whose board the church pays; others were laymen who pay their own expenses. As this little band will be the core of our Rainy Season Bible Classes, I thought you might like to meet them individually. The "grin" was at various boyish characteristics, which I fear I cannot convey to paper.

JUNIA

A stripling, looks seventeen but is really twenty. Lives at Spirea Flat and has been a believer for eight years. Slight, eager, intense, he is the one who started out after the February Bible school "to do God's work," taking nothing, not even a hat. He got bad headaches from the sun, and returned with another Lisu's old cast-off hat, a wreck of felt which was too large and sank down over his eyebrows, giving him an eclipsed appearance. Dear Junia—went off radiant and excited and returned under an eclipse, but only as to his head—his heart was still happy. This is very typical of him. When we were leaving for furlough Junia had an attack of measles, but refused to let that keep him from our farewell service. Hot with fever and speckled like a leopard he walked the five miles to and five miles from Oak Flat; I got quite a shock when I saw that measly face, rapt with attention, in the middle of our audience!

SILAS

Twenty-three years old, from near Horse Grass Level. Had believed for three years. At first we thought he was stupid. The dictation lesson finds Silas laboriously working his pencil. He writes a few words then sits back scratching his head to look at them as if he wondered how he did it; bends to the task once more, carves out two more scraggly words and again stops, tugging at his collar to loosen its grip. Writes two more and then stands up and looks around to see how the others are conquering. When he happens to answer a question correctly he is the most astonished member in the class, which is saying something. But we later discovered that he can surprise everyone by remembering

accurately sóme minor point that nobody else got; alas, that is character-
istic. He has a talent for doing the wrong thing. What he should remember, he doesn't; but the complicated point that we expect will make no
permanent impression on any one is faithfully registered on Silas. In
other words, it is not that he can't study, but because he is incurably
lackadaisical.

For practice preaching the class was told to prepare a message on the
resurrection as Easter was approaching. All did so but Silas, who when
his turn came gave a thoughtful résumé on the death of Christ. John
expostulated, "But when I asked you to preach on the resurrection, why
didn't you, Silas?"

Silas did not know why he hadn't—and neither did anyone else.

In another dictation class John said, "Where have you got to, Silas?"
(They were copying Philippians, which John taught that week.)

Without looking up from his book the lad replied, "The tenth
chapter." There was a roar of laughter.

"But Philippians only has four chapters!" suggests someone. Oh, well!
maybe it was the tenth verse Silas was copying; anyway, he was copying
something. Dear boy, it is a shame to laugh at him. He has a sweet disposition, never gets angry and takes all the embarrassment with a smile.

Lucius

Twenty years old, comes from Village-of-the-Olives, the only child
of Christian parents and supported by them in these study groups—
not a Ma-pa-ra yet. He is quick as a flash, sits next to the bottom of the
class, but leads it. John says, "He stretches his long neck around the
corner of the table—and misses nothing." Quick of mind, his thoughts
outrace his tongue so that his words often come forth on the stampede.
Has the shyness and high-strung mettle of a thoroughbred colt.

Luda-Peter

Twenty-five years old, lives at Luda, has believed for nine years.
Some would say he is the handsome one of the group, has suave manners
with a graceful poise. A good speaker and an excellent song leader; has
a splendid knowledge of the portions of the Bible already translated.
Is a pleasure to teach, he is so bright, but one has indefinable feeling that
these points are but an attractive shell and that the centre is hollow.
This lad needs prayer or something. He has not been dismissed from the
ministry because he gave a testimony of blessing after the February
Bible School, after which he was sent to the backslidden village of
Water Buffalo Mountain and won three families back to the Lord. It
may be there is a spiritual revival in store for him.

NATHANAEL

Twenty-two years old and a Christian for two and a half years only. Lives at Horse Grass Level. Is stocky, pleasant-looking, with a broad forehead and an open countenance that begets trust. Study does not come easily to him; he ranks next to Silas, whose right to the bottom of the class, however, is beyond dispute! Nat has good solid qualities and surprised us by his sermon which was thoughtful and well delivered.

JOB

Thirty-two years old, comes from Stockade Hill district, has believed for eighteen years; is the man who first brought the gospel to these parts. Small, slight, pockmarked, undignified; with his hat often stuck on a side corner of his head looks more like a horse jockey than an evangelist. Perhaps the most insignificant-looking member of the class, but as far as we know, the greatest soul-winner Lisuland has yet produced. Job has so few natural gifts, and yet has been so used of God, that he is a monument of what God can do with any man who brings Him nothing much more than a heart of purposeful devotion. Now I am going to tell you something . . . just lest you think that we are all saints here and sit with halos around our heads! Job is not a "glowing" listener. Nay, he is the very opposite; I do not suppose there is one in the group who nettles his teachers (we all testify to this) with inattention as Job does. He is not really inattentive, as you will learn to your surprise some day when you hear him giving that message of yours to which you thought he had not listened! But he is just incurably restless. You spread your very best prepared eloquence before him and—he picks his teeth, or fiddles with his ear; he squirms and wriggles and finally turns around and stares at each of his neighbours. If perchance your subject should really require his thought, then he is less inspiring than ever; back goes his head, his jaw drops wide open, his eyes roll up to the ceiling—the most vacant of faces, you would never guess that this is Job thinking hard. But it is. You have to know Job. When you know him you love him—and love makes allowances.

CHO-A-TSEH

Twenty-two years old, from Goo-moo in Burma; acted as Job's escort home, but we pressed him to stay for this week of Bible study. He has a very affectionate, almost girlish manner. Simply adored John, laughed hilariously at all his jokes, and was never happier than when holding his hand and exclaiming, "Oh, Ma-Pa!" The week's study made a bigger change in him than in anyone; all of a sudden the "gush" seemed to leave, and he became thoughtful and quiet—gave the most satisfactory testimony (to my thinking) of any, in the last night's testimony meeting.

ARISTARCHUS

Twenty-two years old (cousin to Gaius) from Sandalwood Flat. Has believed for five years. Has a very shy, super-sensitive nature; lips that twitch and work like a rabbit's. Goes around with an awkward and self-conscious manner, even sometimes has a hang-dog look and a furtive glance as if always expecting life to hit him a blow. But when he stands up to preach, all that falls from him like a cloak; he speaks fearlessly, directly and with a quiet insistence that his audience understand his point. Has probably the deepest prayer-life of any in the group, but is so unobtrusive and quiet with it that few know. This boy left a position where he got his food and sixty dollars a year for the ministry where he gets his food and sixteen dollars a year! This is the wage for the Ma-pa-ra; Job, Luke and Andrew get more for they are "teachers," i.e. "Ma-Pa." The white missionary is Ma-pa-da-ma or Big Teacher, but to his face usually called merely Ma-Pa.

RUFUS

Tall, thin, pockmarked. Twenty-three years old and a believer for four years. Reminds me of a cowboy. No shyness about him; willing to try anything once, and frequently quite pleased with his "try." Alert in mind but not much sign yet of a spiritual mind. Capable, willing— "One thing thou lackest."

JONAH (Sah-gwey-chee)

Twenty-two years old, from Village of the Olives; a believer for six years. In temperament he is the Simon Peter of the class. Warm-hearted and impetuous, he is the most appreciative and responsive, as far as words go, of any in the group. Resourceful and energetic, he is a natural leader, but has the Peter-weakness of acting first and thinking afterwards! Deep-voiced, a rapid speaker with a bright mind. Jonah (and Titus) keep Lucius on the *qui vive* for first place.

TITUS

Twenty-two years old, younger brother of Andrew, comes from Stockade Hill, is a layman supporting himself. Has believed for sixteen years, but declares he was only "born again" this spring of 1938. He is a marked contrast to Jonah; as coldly calculating as the other is affectionate and impulsive. Titus is usually alone, Jonah is often found hugging a pal. Jonah receives the doctrine with bursts of appreciation; Titus says little, but a gleam in his eyes and a certain quick intaking of breath reveal his interest. They sit together, not because they are attracted to each other, but because they want to get as close to the teacher as they can. Titus has a shrewd, sharp business sense and—dimples. He knows "where he is at" (which is not true of Jonah) and his artistic impulse covers all his books with drawings. He has another gift—the loveliest tenor voice I have heard in Lisuland. John said, "When Titus sings it touches the heart, somehow brings the tears, doesn't it?"

Now I have told you about our boys, and I wonder if you have been able to see them—really. I wonder how much you have noticed. That they are all very different, yes? That they are very young? But then youth has enthusiasm and heroic loyalty to offer to its King, very often; Robert M. McCheyne did most of his work before he was thirty, did he not?

These extracts from circulars throughout the years are not given in chronological order, but we have been consistent in always giving the same name to each character. When we got more than one "John," for instance, we numbered them; we actually had First John, Second John and Third John at one school! Just plain John, of course, is my husband!

And now for our first R.S.B.S. when Homay and Me-do-me-pa were still with us, and the church just recovering from the bewilderment of Brother Two's days. Those days had done some good—the church's self-complacency was shaken, and they were willing to listen to the answer to the question, "What is wrong with us?"

May 28, 1938, was a great day. On that day the students for the Rainy Season Bible Classes arrived in groups at intervals all day long. Those from the south came first, among them was Aristarchus returning from a trip in Horse Grass Level district where he reported thirty converts from heathenism. The party from Luda district arrived next; among them was a new believer —so new that he did not even know how to read, but had carried his own food supply for the three months' study and came prepared to learn. He bought books immediately on arrival, and the next day I found him drifting about our house, his books hugged to his bosom, his mouth wide open, and his eyes the same, as he investigated how these white people live. We nicknamed him "Brand-New."

"Ye must be Born Again"

This has been our central theme. Opening day was given to prayer and fasting, with some good results. Mrs. Yang made a confession with tears, and the consecration service at night saw some young lives given over to their Master's use.

But before and after this, Charles Peterson and John spent time in interviewing privately practically every student with definite questions on their own regeneration. With the exception of Brand-New, there was not one who did not give a satisfactory answer, and it was surprising to me to see how many of them date their "New Birth" to our April study week when Job gave a message on John iii that stirred everyone. We decided the Lisu church leaders (for, as you remember, this is mainly an evangelists' Bible school) need to be saturated with this foundational doctrine, so every day in practice preaching class each student, as his turn came, had to give a message on the New Birth. I wish you could have heard Job, Luke, Aristarchus and Nathanael.

As if this were not enough, Mr. Peterson gave a message on the same subject every night for a week, so it has been quite uppermost in Lisu minds. Each week-end the student body scatters (girls included), going into the villages on this side of the river. Some of our boys must walk over twenty-five English miles, take three services, walk back the same distance, and do it all between Saturday morning and Monday morning when classes start. Not one of them has failed us so far. Our hearts have been touched by their weary but happy faces as they run in to shake hands early Monday morning, having just completed such a journey. Every week but one they have had to do it in the rain, and Lisu don't usually have raincoats or umbrellas. No wonder the missionary learns to love his Lisu until he can say with Paul, "It is life to me now, if you stand firm in the Lord." The first week-end our students reached about five hundred Lisu; the next over seven hundred; and this last week-end a still greater number. Between the early classes on Monday we have Report Hour when each gets up and tells his experiences. Don't you wish you could listen in?

But to go back to our first week: June 1-4 were days of heart preparation messages. Then on Saturday Andrew walked in. It was a crowning joy and there is evidence that prayers for him had not been in vain. He arrived a sick boy, with a heavy cold which developed a strange puffy rash all over his body, but he said quietly, "I have never been sick since I've been up there, and now when I come to study God's Word I get ill! I believe it is an attack of the devil," and he steadfastly refused to be downed by it; he not only continued to come to classes

but at the end of the week he led everybody in the examination on
1 Corinthians.

LISTENING IN

How we have wished we could share with you some of the glimpses
into these Lisu hearts. The only way I could think of was to jot down
a few sentences from their prayers, now and again as I heard them.

"Lord, I'm not worthy to be Thy slave and Thou hast made me Thy
friend. I am worthy of death, and Thou hast given me eternal life."

"Thy name is written on my heart and my name is written on Thy
hands, so we cannot be separated."

"Lord, Thou art my refuge; if I had not Thee I would have no hiding
place."

"I used to pray to Thee, Lord, just for what I wanted; I never thought
or cared if Thou didst want anything. But oh, that was wrong, please
forgive me. Now I desire what Thou dost want."

"Lord, give strength to our teachers; help them so that when they
teach, we may see the face of Jesus."

"Let Thy name be always in our hearts. Let it be as a perfume there."

> For mankind all, Thy love is shown,
> Yet seems't to be for me alone;
> I claim Thee for my very own,
> My Jesus.

Doesn't this verse—spoken probably by a white voice—find its echo
in these Lisu heart cries?

We have some little notes slipped to us now and again. Here is an
extract from a boy who had just had a talking to, on putting the will of
God before his own will; "If ever you have any exhortation for me,
please give it quickly. I won't be offended. If there were nothing in me
to correct, I would not be in here."

This from one who regularly failed in every examination, but who
showed by his preaching that he was assimilating the new truth: "I would
like to say a few words to you by the Blood of the Lord Jesus and in
His Name. I have no ability to study the doctrines of God and the Lord
Jesus. Although I study in the school, I cannot think up the answers,
Big Brother Kuhn. But although I can't memorize I have received the
truth that Jesus Christ died for me on the Cross. Now all that I have, my
spirit and body, are His, I have given up all to Him. I can never forget
His Cross. You have taught me much, Big Brother, and it has brought
joy in Christ. Thank you so much. Although I cannot memorize His

doctrines, because His Blood was poured out to purchase me, I must always be happy.

In the days of 1938, Homay was still with us, of course, so her name appears in the circulars.

BEHIND THE SCENES

If you were able to pass through the House of Grace between hours, you would behold in the large living-dining room, in one corner near the window, a little Lisu lady bending her turbaned head with an anxious expression over a large book of loose manuscript leaves and with pretty plump little olive hands, typing away earnestly at a typewriter which was bought in Lancaster, Pa.! This is Homay, and without her and her typewriter this Bible school could not possibly have been held. She types out twelve copies of each Book we teach, so that as we teach these new and strange Epistles the students are able to read with us—if they could not do that, they would never understand, for the Pauline letters contain many expressions which the Lisu language does not possess and which have to be coined and carefully taught. Lately I have had to teach "fellowship" and "example." When we first said "ja-la-ko" no one (but Homay, Luke and Job who had previously learned it) knew what we were saying; we had to explain not only that ia-la-ko meant fellowship, but what "fellowship" really is.

This reminds me of Trench's book, *The Study of Words*. He calls attention to the fact that no people can have a word before they have the experience which the word illuminates or describes. He says, "There is no such witness to the degradation of the savage as the brutal poverty of his language—rich in words which proclaim their shame, poor in these which attest the workings of any nobler life among them." He had doubtless never heard of the Lisu, yet this is true of our natives too. Words to express sin in various forms are plentiful—they tell you with gusto how to skin a human being alive, but if you asked them what holiness was, they would not know, they had no word for it. Their language had no word of course for *redemption*, or *justification*, or *grace*, but it also had no word for *religion*, nor for *exaltation*, nor for *conscience* nor many other things. Just yesterday I had the word for *humility* on the board and Lucius asked what it meant. He said he had never heard of it before. And when we gave a message on conscience even Homay came to us and said she had not understood what that word meant in the scriptures, and did not know that she herself possessed a conscience. Yet the Lisu language had a word for God, i.e. *Wu-sa*. They knew *Wu-sa* but they do not worship Him, and there seems to me to be evidence that the Lisu race once had a higher knowledge of life.

I want to slip in another picture from the week-end evangelism as it is so typical of many things Lisu.

"The Father is always Watching"

It was communion week-end, and A-che and Lucius were commissioned to take that service at Squirrel's Grave Village. As the Salween is now, of course, swollen, they had to cross by rope bridge. There was quite a party to cross, for other Ma-pa-ra were going to take services elsewhere on the west bank, and also Juliet with two girl friends from Runaway Horse Ascent had to be helped over too. Those three girls studied with us the whole month of July, paying their own way. Altogether there was such delay at the rope bridge that the two boys around which this tale hangs, could not make their destination that day, but decided to sleep at a Chinese hamlet where there is a Christian Lisu family. But by the time they arrived there, dark had fallen and as robbers have abounded this year, the Lisu family had closed and barred their door and were all inside. Approaching the house they were stopped by a clear call, "Stand or we shoot!" As the Lisu poisoned arrow has to prick the skin in any point to bring death they "stood" very quickly and obediently.

"Don't be afraid of us!" they called back. "We are only two Ma-pa-ra on our way to Squirrel's Grave Village to take the communion service. We want to sleep with you to-night."

"Humph!" comes the retort from mine host. "Ma-pa-ra eh? Maybe you are and maybe you aren't. How do I know?"

"Well," calls out Lucius, who knew them personally, "Pu-ra-pa, you ought to know me. I am Born-on-the-Road from Village-of-the-Olives." (Some of you thought I made up Lucius' heathen name myself; I did not. His uncle named him that in fun over the event, and the name stuck. More people know him by that name than any other.)

"Oh; yeah?" came a sarcastic drawl, this time from the roof of Pu-ra-pa's house, where mine host had climbed up better to protect his family. He was armed with a huge bow and poisoned arrows, a big knife and a long spear. "It is very likely that young Born-on-the-Road is in this place at this time of night. Quite handy to borrow a good fellow's name, it is." (Lucius had not visited this family for years.)

"Let's run for it," whispered A-che, "and sleep in the bush to-night."

"No," answered Lucius. "If we run he will think for sure we are robbers and shoot, and just one prick . . . you know!" Then patiently our laddie tried again.

"I *am* Born-on-the-Road all the same, and my pal is A-che from Luda and we are on our way to preach."

"Hm. If you are Ma-pa-ra then you can sing. Tune up a hymn and perhaps we will believe you." So out in the dark, hungry and weary, our two laddies sang *The Holy Spirit is with me*. But from inside the house comes a girl's voice. "Dad, there are a lot of backsliders nowadays that can sing hymns too; you had better be careful."

But just then the mother of the house had an inspiration. There was a peek-hole near their door, so she stuck a pine torch through it, causing the light to fall on the two boys' faces. "I know Born-on-the-Road," she began, then changed quickly: "Why it is he, sure enough! Come down, Dad. It's all right! My, my, my——" and then the doors were thrown open and welcome and cordiality flooded the tired pair. What laughs they had telling us of it! But more than one Lisu thief has died this summer from the poisoned arrow of a stout hearted crop-defender. That in none of the week-end preaching excursions was any student harmed is a matter of thanksgiving to God.

I hope you have not forgotten that this is still a story of little Nests above a dark abyss, but with a Rock-shelter who "follows" them.

ODDS AND ENDS

Our youngest student was informed just the evening before, that through the unexpected sickness of the one previously scheduled to go, he alone would have to be responsible for the week-end services of Knoll Village. He had never had such a responsibility to shoulder by himself before, and the next morning before breakfast he dashed into the bedroom of our bachelor missionary (blessed haven to the anxious student heart) and planted before that astonished gentleman his Lisu Gospel, a paper and pencil. "Write me a sermon outline on 'Seek ye first the kingdom of God'!" was his graphic order, whereupon he disappeared to go eat his breakfast, happily confident of the results, just like any American boy who slips a nickel across the drugstore counter and orders a cone to be ready in five minutes—and neither was our Lisu laddie disappointed. When he dashed in to get it and go, there was an outline ready for him!

From another circular:

Our "Baby" sits next. Lucius is taller than I am, and a splendid athlete, but in years he is our baby. He is responsible for the ringing of the gongs, and we persuaded him at night to take charge of John's gold watch. He was very reluctant to put his strong, inexperienced fingers on that delicate, ticking gold disk. Then sure enough—the worst happened. We heard his shuffling step in the next room one morning when I was combing my hair and a concerned young voice came through the bamboo mat wall—"Ma-ma, the watch *has died*! It doesn't go now."

Quickly remembering that we had neglected to wind it the night before, I told him not to worry, but to put it on the desk. Later a few twists and the familiar *tick-tick* came back. I immediately sought out our worried Baby. "Lucius, the watch has come back to life!!" My, what a smile. If only that watch will continue to live, Lucius' burdens will be light.

Our strongest (one who has carried my two-hundred-pound husband on his back through the rain down a slippery mountainside) stood baffled before the problem of how to remove a paper-clip. He had been asked to help me to rearrange some exhibition writing samples which were clipped to a string, and I was quite unconscious that paper-clips were a new thing in this young life. I turned to find him earnestly doing his very hefty best to unwind the wire spirals, which was the only way he could see to get rid of the thing. He had it well on the way to wreckage before I saw him and cried out, "Oh, that isn't the way! See!" and in a second I had whipped off the neighbouring clip before his astounded gaze. "*A-geh!*" he exclaimed in disgust at the ease with which things can be done if only you know how!

Our cleverest (as far as examinations are concerned) had desired to find him a private nook where he could practise the conducting of our newest musical attempt, which you shall hear about in a moment. He chose the corner between his cabin and the pig-sty, quite unconscious that he was in view from Ma-Ma's window. I happened to look out and there, singing and waving his hand, he stood, leading the pigs with unction and fervour in Handel's *Hallelujah Chorus*!

This sounds impossible (perhaps the pigs still think it is), but Mr. and Mrs. Cooke while at Bana translated this wonderful piece of inspiration into Lisu, taught it to Luke, Homay and A-che, and sent it back with them. Luke is now teaching it to us of the Bible school and though I have heard it more than once in America, it has never so thrilled me as when our Lisu sing it. They *love* it and sing it with all the passion of their hearts. "The kingdoms of this world are become the kingdoms of our Lord and of his Christ"—oh, how that rolls out! how the soprano sinks, then lifts! how the bass climbs up to meet it and the tenor like a bird swoops under and then soars over. It is inexpressibly grand—praise God.

Jonah[1] had been teaching in Goo-moo, Burma, earlier in the year, and came home all enthused with the reverence and order of the service of Mark's leadership. Lucius has just been elected Village Service Leader; the two boys are second cousins, so Jonah was not long in inspiring the other to join him in an effort to maintain the same order in the chapel at Village of the Olives. John spoke at the big noon service, and shortly after he began I noticed Jonah slip to the back of the chapel and take his stand near the door with a long stick in his hand. When any youngster in the audience began to get audibly restless he received a stern poke in the middle of the back by the aforementioned rod. It was a silent but vigorous reminder that if he did not listen he might later have to deal with the broad-chested young man at the other end of the stick. And he listened.

Up at the front Lucius was seated. A husky young farmer near him grew tired at the unusual inactivity of listening and decided to sprawl his limbs over the empty bench in front of him. As the first brown leg was casually journeying through the air, it received a sharp tap from Lucius and quickly withdrew like a frightened snail into its proper place and was not seen to wander again. What we had always considered impossible—order in a Lisu service—had been accomplished by these two determined youngsters.

Memories of August seem to be marked by sunset scenes; the first is trivial but illuminating.

The village of Oak Flat was not directly on the banks of the Salween River, but rather perched on the mountain wall of a tributary which runs into the Salween. To reach the real bank of the Salween, however, was but the matter of five minutes' walk to the west over a path which curves, zigzags and then drops down to a slender wooded ridge which we long ago named Sunset, for there we would go at the cool of the day to keep tryst.

One evening in early August we went down to Sunset Ridge for a school-family picnic supper. We white folk took rugs and cushions to sit on, but these children of the hills did not seem to notice their lack of such possessions for they merrily and

[1] Christian names are given to converts by anyone who is asked for them. In this case it was Job who gave Jonah his name.

quickly pulled each a heap of soft leaves from nearby bushes and sat themselves down on the top of their thrones. In the centre were black sooty iron pots containing boiled corn and chunks of boiled pork, and the extras—the dainties and decorations—for our feast were well supplied in the sweets of loving smiles and cheery banter, and by the matchless panorama of the sun as he entered the mountains of the western bank, spreading out his canopies of gold, then pink and finally twilight silver. As the latter fell softly around us, Titus and some pals, the first to finish eating, gathered at our right and sang to us, *Hallelujah, what a Saviour! Hallelujah, what a Friend!* One by one the others joined in and the falling dusk was filled with the melodies of our favourite hymns, for at the end of each they turned to us to make the next choice.

The next memory is quite different. It was the evening of August 18. I had been feeling slightly discouraged, wondering if we teachers were not too ordinary in our own spiritual lives, wondering if the boys' hearts were being penetrated with the Word the way we wanted them to be, and so on. At sunset time I slipped out for the usual tryst, but this time decided to go up the mountain instead of descending to Sunset Ridge. The evening wind was blowing cool and sweetly in my face and I turned to the upward path which cuts across a ploughed field first, and suddenly turning a corner I came upon Junia and Lucius who were descending, apparently from the same errand on which I was bound. They passed me in smiling but self-conscious silence, and I was reminded that those two were scheduled to take between them the week-end services at Village-of-Knoll the coming Saturday. We had continually urged our boys to "keep tryst" and to pray about such things, but who did, and where they did, I had no notion. These two, being such young-sters, had evidently felt their weakness and I had stumbled upon their little effort to fortify themselves.

Pleased and gratified, I continued to climb, when I heard a voice on the trail above; wishing for solitude I decided to avoid him so turned and broke through the wild bush to a place higher up. The mountains were a darkening grey flecked with white clouds, the passion of sunset colour had long passed and the cold, steady beauty of night seemed to steel one's heart to fresh strength. The One I had come to meet was not absent, but I might not tarry, so after a while I arose and returned to the trail; I feared the bush at that hour, and perhaps the student had left. But no, before I came in sight I could hear his voice clear and strong, "O Father God, help me to learn this Book——" and then I knew he was praying. I tried not to listen and glided more swiftly and carefully onward, but a curve of the path and I saw him, kneeling before the open scriptures, his face right down on the grass even with his knees and his voice cutting the still air with all the freedom of one who believes himself to be entirely alone in the woods. He did not see me at all, so occupied was he, but my first glance drew a second, for I could hardly believe my eyes were telling the truth, and as I stopped to look I heard him say distinctly, "O Father God, I hand over my whole body, soul, and spirit to Thee—do with me as Thou willest," then with thrilled heart I turned and fled down the path out of sight and sound. What I could hardly believe was this, that praying lad was not our Aristarchus, nor any of the spiritual leaders of the student body, but that boy alone on the mountain consecrating himself to his Maker, was our dear little *Brand-New*.

The third scene is that of our consecration service at Sunset Ridge the evening of August 26. Our last week we were to have guests, as you shall hear, so the preceding week we viewed as the last we would spend together as a "family," and the last night of that week we betook ourselves to the open for a bonfire service.

Though that was in the rainy season, never had there been a kindlier one; especially was August wonderful—heavy rain at night and in the early morning, but clear and sunny hours through the day. We had prayed beforehand and asked our dear Giver of all good gifts if He would not add a starlit night on August 26 to His list of generosities, and He was pleased to do just that! As we set out for the spot at sunset, I thought I had never seen the heavens above so beautiful. The mountains were a jagged line of dark blue and scattered over the pale upper hemisphere were clouds which had caught and held the last fire of the now invisible sun. Our world was a dusky mass of jade topped with pearl and rose, which shifted and paled as if it were breathing and then all quietly melted away to give place to a slight moon and faraway stars. Night comes swiftly in those parts.

Soon a different scene held our eyes, a tent-shaped tower of flaming boughs which cast light and shadow on a wide circle of dear faces, all tender with the thought that this was our last family night together, and all grave with expectancy as my husband John arose and came forward to give his message on "Sacrifice." At its close he called for all those who wished to consecrate their lives completely to God from henceforth to come forward and kneel with him, and one by one they came. As far as we could see—for some were in the shadow and one might not pry on such an occasion—every one of our beloved students sooner or later joined the inner circle. Hearts were then poured out to God in prayer, and afterward on happy risen feet they gave glad testimony. From a letter written at that time:

And now the evening is far spent—my watch has stopped but the pale moon has journeyed far across the sky. The word comes to stand and form a friendship circle; fresh boughs are heaped on the low fire and the flame soars and sings with joy as it reaches upward, casting its golden light on a great circle of fifty faces, glad smiling faces, while our Youngest tosses his head with rapture and calls out "*Ka-chi:* (Joy!)" at the beauty of the scene. A hymn or two, the benediction, and we break up, but memory has still a last gift for us. Pine torches are lit to find us our path back to Oak Flat, for the moon is a mere curved wisp in the sky; as we climb the trail and reach its highest level we stand a moment, turn and look back and there behind us, flickering through the pine boughs like living golden jewels is the string of pine torches flaring out bravely into the dark and suddenly lighting up beloved faces which lift themselves laughingly toward us, and then as we turn once more to the path the music of dear voices pursues us lovingly through the night to our very door.

At the end of each Rainy Season Bible School, we held closing day exercises. The students elected their own chairman, song-leader, and valedictory speakers. They marched in to music, and at the close of the service, each received a certificate with his rank on it (honours or just pass, etc.). Here is an account of Closing Day, 1939—that summer the Tabernacle had been taught.

One Closing Day

"Homay-y-y! Oh . . . are those flowers for your own room? Say, don't forget to pick some for the boys, will you?" The broad little figure laughed up at me.

"Just like last year, Ma-Ma?"

"Yes—everybody must wear a flower." Then, as I passed Brand-New on my way to the chapel—"Don't forget to go to the House-of-Grace and get a posy for your buttonhole!" brought a smile to his well-scrubbed countenance. Brand-New was looking quite civilized now.

The chapel floor was strewn with fresh pine needles—a fragrant joy which elicited an exclamation from one young Lisu girl, "Isn't it nice to have a celebration!" Up at the front was a temporary platform for the student body, at one side the portable organ, and opposite at the other side a table with a small model of the Tabernacle on it, which Job was putting in position preparatory to explaining it briefly. Caleb and Simon were flitting excitedly around, recalling memories of last year when they were both in the *Hallelujah Chorus*. Sickness kept both of them from attending more than one week this season, much to their sorrow.

"Caleb, give me the signal when they get close so I can start the march," I requested, and met with a quick, smiling assent, followed later by a briskly waved hand, and then the twenty-three young people, single file, with measured step came slowly up the aisle. Thomas, handsomely attired, after having passed Homay's careful scrutiny, led the procession; each was well groomed with a bright zinnia tucked in somewhere and there was an impressive and pleased silence as Chairman Christianson motioned them to sit down.

But alas! dignified occasions have been hitherto unknown in this land of the mannerless. I was just enjoying the solemnity of it all, when Luke, who was song-leader for the day, started out of his seat in consternation, "Where's my song book?" Then turning, he shouted at some invisible person in the audience, "*Did you bring it?*"

"Of course I did," came a female answer from the middle of the women's side. "Here it is," in tones of wifely indignation that he should doubt her faithfulness in public. It was handed up the aisle, and our dear song-leader, unconscious that he had ruined the dignity of the occasion, sat back in his seat with a sigh of satisfaction that now he was equipped for what lay ahead.

Titus was the first valedictory speaker. He was resplendent in black sateen with white anklets climaxed with pink shoes. The young monkey had coloured some white tennis shoes with beet juice (he is on good terms with our cook!) and appeared before us red-footed if not red-handed. He spoke on "The Dragon"—tracing Satanic appearances through the scriptures, but especially in the book of Revelation. He was good.

Job came next with the model of the Tabernacle. He got along well until he came to the coverings which he had been warned before-hand not to attempt to expound. But, seeing so much interest in his audience, he felt buoyed up and (like some of the rest of us) plunged in, with the expected result. "And this," says he, holding up the white curtain with easy assurance, "was made of goat's hair." But goats are not white in Lisuland. A sudden fear smote him. In horror, he turned and called over his shoulder in a stage whisper to Ma-Ma, "*Was it?*" Whereupon his congregation grinned.

Andrew was the other valedictory speaker, and with his usual quiet composure spoke on the "Lamb of God," tracing that doctrine from Genesis to Revelation. Cath Christianson thought he was the best of the day.

A recess for lunch was followed by the afternoon meeting when the rest of the student body were to give five-minute testimonies as to the different books studied this summer—John being chairman. Apart from Lucius, who was confined to bed with a sore foot, each one spoke a few words. Nosu-Mary and one or two others were quite perspiry, but got through safely. Junia's was short and simple; he could not afford to perspire, he had too many clothes on. He evidently had decided to put on all the respectable garments he possessed, so as to be sure he had selected the right one.

Luda-Peter, who, unknown to himself (for we publish only general results), led the whole school with a percentage of $97\frac{3}{8}$, got so nervous he began to pull the bark off the low beam over his head and wandered considerably from what he had promised Ma-Ma he would keep to, with the consequence that he mixed up shittim wood and almond wood, but otherwise made no heresy.

The Rainy Season Bible School for boys asked for the *Hallelujah Chorus* again this year, so they are practising it these evenings. Much of the success of this noble oratorio depends on alert and instant obedi-ence to the leader. If that is missing you will find yourself singing, "Ha——" with lusty enthusiasm all alone while your neighbours bury their noses in their sleeves and snicker; and you have a miserable feeling that public prominence is not what you covet after all. For who could sing the *Hallelujah Chorus* without enthusiasm? "*The kingdoms of this world are become the kingdoms of our Lord and of his Christ. . . . King of kings and Lord of lords—Hallelujah!*" Why, to know that we are actually going to see that accomplished some day it sends the blood fairly racing through one's veins, with the joy of it. Ah, but if you "Ha" at the wrong moment—like Rhoda did last year on closing day, just because she was in the front row and too self-conscious to lift her head and watch the leader—it rather takes the glory out of it. Alert, instant obedience, that is what makes team work such a thrill. May none of us have to hang our head on *That Day* because we were not ready to obey!

Chapter Six gave a glimpse of the Abyss and its Master. This chapter has shown the Nestling and how it cuddles down into Shelter of the Cleft of the Rock, when that Shelter is pointed out to its bewildered ignorance. The dangers of legalism are best combated by teaching "the word of his grace, which is able to build you up, and to give you an inheritance among all them which are sanctified" (Acts xx. 32).

The stiff Wind of Legalism—it blows in the West too. Christians sink so easily into thinking that to follow Christ is just a set of *do's and don'ts.* Our R.S.B.S. students carried the message of grace everywhere over the mountains. John could only be physically in one village at a time, but through the R.S.B.S. students, the message was preached in ten or twenty different villages on the same Sunday. And throughout the whole year, all over the field, the students continued to preach grace and tried to point out legalism. Quietly, sweetly, the transformation came about. Not that the church was now perfect—far from it; for that Wind also seems to blow where and when it listeth—but the trained evangelists and the whole deacon body changed in their attitude, from set laws for set offences, to consideration of each case on its separate deserts. And throughout, *striving to get the mind of Christ on each matter.*

As you paged through the story of the Seedling Patch, have you sensed what a privilege it was, to be a participant in God's work there? And as you continue to read, and see how far-reaching the lives of some of those humble, barefoot laddies became, do you not think that to lay before them God's full plan of salvation is a great joy, a worthwhile use of one's life? One furlough I met a lady who said to me, "I have no interest in anything but my house and my garden. My house and my garden are my life." I thought how pitifully poor she had confessed herself to be; even though hers was a large expensive home and mine a mere shanty on the wild mountainside. For in imagination, I saw the uplifted faces of our Hephzibah classroom; thought quickly through the years of study and companionship with them; saw the dull empty look of ignorance change into that of shining radiant possession. And my heart cried out, *What a waste! for her to spend that human life and sympathies on a wooden house and a dirt garden, when God's spiritual house is calling out for living stones and His garden has Seedlings of Eternal Destiny that need to be trained!* But the West is full of human beings (church-goers, many of them) who live just for *things*. When that lady dies, she must leave behind her house and her garden—everything that spells life to her by her own confession. When I die, I know I shall see again my "living stones"; and I shall comrade with my precious Seedlings throughout eternity.

> The angels from their home on high
> Look down on us with pitying eye,
> That where we are but passing guests,
> We build such strong and solid nests;
> While where we hope to dwell for aye,
> We scarce take heed one stone to lay.
> *Unknown.*

8

A Thief Who Laboured to Give to Others

"*Let him . . . steal no more*"
EPH. IV. 28

Youth, O Youth, can I reach you,
  Can I speak and make you hear,
Can I open your eyes to see Me,
  Can My presence draw you near?

Is there a prophet among you,
  One with a heart to know?
I will flash My secrets on him,
  He shall watch My glory grow.

For I, the God, the Father,
  The Quest, the final Goal,
Still search for a prophet among you
  To speak My word in his soul.

*And He does reach them; conquer them; captivates them until they
yield to Him that valiant and glorious self-abandonment which
belongs so markedly to youth.*

SUNDAY. The big noon service had finished and I hastened
down to House of Grace to get behind the dispensary table.
The Lisu come to the Sunday noon service from many miles
around, and so it is an opportunity to get medicine for their
sick ones. As I measured out ointment and pills I was conscious
that Luke and another were hanging around in the background
of the crowd. At length, the last medicine-seeker satisfied, I
turned to see what was wanted.

"Ma-Pa and Ma-Ma," said Luke briskly. "This fellow wants
to confess his sins!" Then, turning to the young man, he added,
"Now go ahead."

The repentant sinner was not an attractive Lisu. He had stubby hair and a hang-dog, on-the-defensive manner. This was all the more emphasized at the present moment by the embarrassment of his situation. But, pulling himself together, in a low guttural voice, he began.

"Ma-Pa, Ma-Ma, I have sinned against you. The second Christmas you were here, I came to the festival to see what it was like. But I wasn't born again then, and . . ." Here it was hard going, but he straightened up and went on doggedly: "I saw a pretty bag hanging on your wall and I stole it. I want to be a Christian now, a born-again one, and I wronged you in something else too. I got some medicine from you once, and instead of returning the bottle to you, I sold it, and kept the money. Here is the price of it and I will pay you for the bag when I can get the money, later on." And he put a half-dollar in my hand, his feet shuffling nervously and his face sad and ashamed.

"Well, friend," we replied, "we are glad to see that the Holy Spirit has been working in your heart. When you start in to follow the Lord Jesus, it is good to clean up your past as much as you are able. So we shall accept this money. But this is what is called 'conscience money' and we do not keep such ourselves. We do not exhort you to repentance in order to get things back from you." So, putting the money in Luke's hand, "We shall give this to the Lisu church. And we hope you will study God's Word so that you may grow spiritually. Where do you live?"

"At Squirrel's Grave Village," Luke replied for him. "Across the river there!" and he pointed west through our open doorway.

"Well, you talk with him, Luke," we suggested, for Sundays always saw many Lisu wishing to consult with us on different problems, and we could not spare much time to any one person. Later this boy was named Gad, so we shall just call him that from now on.

A few weeks later I was pleased and surprised to hear that Gad had gone off on a preaching trip with Jonah! The latter needed a companion, and the self-confessing thief offered to accompany him (and incidentally get lessons in reading and writing), and so it was arranged. Gad carried Jonah's load and helped in small ways, and in his spare time pored over his scripture portions.

Each April, before R.S.B.S. began, we called in the evangelists for a week's Bible study, and to hear reports of their work. When Jonah arrived, lo and behold Gad was with him, and in his customary shamefaced manner asked to be allowed to study too. He appeared very dense in class, and I would have regarded him as hopeless if it had not been for his industry. Being new he was very slow at writing and copying the Bible notes we gave, but after classes, when the other students rushed off to the athletic field, day after day, Gad was to be found sitting before the blackboard laboriously copying all the notes he could find. Once I reprimanded him, "Gad, it is recreation time now. You ought to be down on the playground with the other students. You'll get too tired writing for such long hours at a time."

He looked up at me. "Ma-Ma, please let me finish. I'm slow because I'm new, you know." I had not the heart to discipline him for it. The willingness to labour hard in learning the Word of God is not very common. I dared not quench it. So I left him to copy, and copy, and copy until long after dusk had fallen.

In all Bible schools, even shorter ones, we endeavour to have one class a day in practice preaching (Homiletics being too high a name for the results!) and my husband and I have never forgotten Gad's first attempt at a sermon. He was such a babe in things spiritual that he really had nothing much to say, and embarrassment drove out any idea that he might otherwise have had. But we must all begin some time, so we would not excuse him, though he begged we would.

"All of us here know that you are a new believer and have not had time to learn much, but get up and try, anyway."

So, with his hang-dog look and deep guttural voice, Gad rose to his feet and tried. A most painfully boring succession of platitudes followed. He was, like other beginners, trying to remember what his Lisu teacher had last preached, and reproduce it. The result was incoherent and unconnected, but every now and then his fact lit up and looking at us earnestly he would say, "And we must not sin! We just mustn't sin." That far his face was filled with inspiration, but at the next step, panicky at his empty thoughts, he would make a desperate grab after memory and scramble on with more muttered platitudes, only to bring up again the one fact that he was sure of. "We must not sin! We must not sin," he would say again with that earnestness in his face. As a sermon it was ridiculous; but at least the one thought that was his own, he had driven home.

"Well," was our judgment upon it, "Gad has evidently learned one important thing, and that is, that *sin* comes between man and God. And that if man wants fellowship with the Father, he must first deal with the sin question. He was not able to put it so clearly, but he left that feeling with each of us, did he not? So, as a first attempt, his sermon is not a total failure! Now learn one thing from this. *The part of God's message which will be most potent from your lips is that which comes from your own personal experience of it.* Gad has learned what sin can do, and his earnestness on that point was a blessing. It is always so. What has blessed our own hearts is sure to have a message for others."

> For he that serves his Lord, must holy be,
> And he that labours must be free from guile,
> And he that sows be filled with purity;
> And he that speaks the message of the Word
> Must first receive the fulness of the Lord.
> *M. B. Whiting.*

Gad flushed with pleasure, for he had expected the worst, in criticism, and nothing but the worst. And I think everyone else had too, so it was a good thing for all.

At the end of that week, when we were discussing where each evangelist should go until R.S.B.S. brought them back to us again, Junia spoke up, "Ma-Pa, may Gad go with me? He says he'd like to!" I turned then and really looked at Gad. Could it be possible that one so shortly out of sin had a secret hope to become a preacher of the gospel? Though he would not dare voice it, so early, that hope evidently was already in his heart, and at the close of the week he and Junia trotted off happily together.

June, 1939, circular tells this part of the story:

Earlier in the afternoon Junia and Gad had arrived—the latter with the mumps! They were merely on their way to teach the new inquirers at Squirrel's Grave. Gad looked so funny with his great swollen jowls, but he never thought of stopping work as long as he could speak (for, of course, he had no knowledge of infection until we told him). Squirrel's Grave was his home, but he meant to testify there; he could read and write now and thus teach others. And this was typical of Gad.

> In His Name who, meek and lowly,
> Died to make poor sinners holy,
> Stumbling oft and creeping slowly,
> Great Lord
> Guide me by Thy truth, O Lord.

A few weeks later:

Titus, Jonah, Gad and Junia arrived last Saturday night and all are busy to-day getting a schoolroom built—last year we met in a part of the church but it was most inconvenient, so this year a school house, or rather bamboo Bible school is going up—the first Bible school building the Lisu have ever built, at least in these parts.

Later: We have a brand new building this year, with seating accommodation for thirty and it has been filled so far. It is nice to have room enough to go around and inspect their work. This was not possible last year. Our Bible school building is named "Hephzibah" and I suppose it is the poorest little Hephzibah in the world—just bamboo mats for walls, bamboo mats for roof, and earth for floor. It has no need of windows, for mats do not reach to the roof, and it possesses no door—everything is nice and airy. The "desks" are crude slabs of rough wood held up by tree boughs driven into the earth, so they don't wobble! I love it. Its poverty does not worry me in the least—in fact I have been thanking God these last few months for the privilege of being asked to minister among the poor. If their lives were not so drab and ugly, so toilworn and uninteresting, Jesus and His messengers might not mean so much to them.

And now we must leave Gad starting in with his real book work, to trace a development which was later to affect Gad himself.

We must go back to the end of our first Rainy Season Bible School, and let us watch how God began, almost immediately, to use this study of His Word not only to tell the Lisu tribe, but also to reach out toward other parts of the country where His Name was not yet known.

Two weeks' journey to the east of us (over the high Mekong mountain range, and a sea of other mountains to the far-away, famous gorge of the Yangtse River) lay a great unopened tribal territory which we called Yongpeh. At the close of our first R.S.B.S. in 1938, a letter from Mr. Andrews, a missionary labouring near Yongpeh, reached us. The circular of January, 1939, tells of it.

Some time ago we received a request from a missionary north of Tali, asking for evangelists to be sent to him, as he felt there were Lisu in his neighbourhood who would respond if appealed to in their own language, and he wished to start a Lisu work there. Our beloved superintendent wrote us, in almost his last letter, saying he hoped the church would give heed to this request from another mission, and so we laid it before them as a solemn trust from the one who has gone to heaven. They replied by sending Aristarchus and one other younger Christian named Secundus. We have requested that they be sent back to us by June, so as to continue their studies in the Rainy Season Bible School.

The next month's letter contains a report from the two young evangelists themselves.

They spent twelve days in arduous overland mountain travel in order to reach their base of operations. Part of Aristarchus' first letter here reads something as follows:

Sometimes we walked up into the night, and other times we were on the road at the cock's crow. We were tired and cold and my partner almost cried. And just now they are pressing men into the army. For this cause, while we were on the march an army officer told us to become soldiers. But we answered them that we did not care to be soldiers. We were bound for the country of Lichiang, where the Pastor lives. However, the officers nearly forced us into the Army. On the other hand, God did not allow them to touch us, neither were the two of us given into their hands. Exceeding and unending thanks to God! This little experience, however, is not worth mentioning as suffering.

The writer is a Christian,

ARISTARCHUS.

April, 1939, brought us the following report from the two.

Yongpeh City.

To the Christians in the church of Oak Flat:

To the church at Oak Flat which we love and wish mutually to behold, Aristarchus and Secundus in the name of the triune Father, Son, and Holy Spirit greet all you Christians with a letter. Are you Christians of the church at Oak Flat all safe and strong, dwelling peacefully in the Lord Jesus? We would like very much to know and we thank all the brethren for praying for us.

As Secundus and I came from Oak Flat country to Ya-pi market we saw some Lisu homes and people. But leaving Ya-pi on our journey to Lichiang we crossed much country where we saw no Lisu homes or folk. Eight days after arriving in Lichiang we went with the missionary and two evangelists from the Lichiang church into the country round about to teach. Leaving Lichiang without accident and travelling peacefully in the Lord we reached Yongpeh country, thank God. It is three days from Lichiang to Yongpeh and we had to cross a mountain range. From our Oak Flat to this place is some little distance! Yongpeh is a city like Paoshan, with a big market and the people around are all Chinese. There are lepers also in the city.

There was no preaching of the gospel there, so we pity them. Therefore the Lichiang missionary borrowed a house and now they have services. On the evening of January 30, the gospel began to be preached in this church. Please pray for the Chinese of this place.

Also on Chinese market day countless Lisu come. A half-day's journey from the Chinese city brings you to the Lisu villages and there are so many Lisu you cannot describe them! Moreover, the men and women resemble the Lisu of the Luda district. Many of them have a knowledge of Chinese. Please, brethren of the Oak Flat church, village by village all of you, pray more and more for these Lisu of Yongpeh.

My companion Secundus and I on February 2 went to the villages where the Lisu live. We went to village by village and preached the gospel. When we taught them they said, "We have never heard this story before nor seen any kind of Lisu book. Please pray for us!" Their words and our Lisu words are about one-third different. Kindly pray for us while we are in this country that we may walk in the Spirit and sow the seed of God's doctrine. Now there is another thing; in this country the money we formerly used we never see here. There may not be any traffic in opium. People have been killed for planting it. Over a thousand soldiers have gone from this place but none has ever returned home. How is our Oak Flat country now?

Now there is one more thing with which I would like to acquaint you brother Christians. In the middle of this Yongpeh district there is a people called the Lolo, over one hundred thousand of them. They are like wild people and steal and rob all the time. More than this, when they seize Lisu and Chinese, man or woman, along the road, they lead them away and make them slaves in their own country. None of the Chinese officials dare discipline these people. Pray that these folks may cease to be robbers and their hearts become tender—and constantly pray for us two, please. Now that is what we have to say. We are well and strong in the Lord. Many thanks to God.

The one who walks and writes to you is the Christian,

ARISTARCHUS.

I was perfectly thrilled over that last paragraph, for he had undoubtedly come upon the *forbidden territory*—that tribe of Lolo which the Chinese have never been able to conquer and for which prayer has gone up in our Mission since before I came to China, at least.

R.S.B.S., 1939 (when Gad first came), did not bring the two boys back to us as we had asked. Mr. Andrews wrote us the reason.

Requests for a teacher had come pouring in on Aristarchus and Secundus. To cope with the spread of the work, they had separated, but still there were calls they could not answer. To leave at such a time with no one to replace them seemed disastrous. As it was, all they could do was to make clear the way of salvation, teach a simple prayer and perhaps a hymn, then pass on to others. How they longed really to establish the church in the truth. When their backs had to be turned on the new believer, Satan would send out his sharp Winds from the Bitter Height, and if they had not been taught how to shelter in their Rock, how would they ever stand? So of course we wrote our consent that they wait at Yongpeh until reinforcements could be sent to relieve them.

Mr. Andrews paid the little infant church a visit and wrote to us of the happy time he spent there. "How they hunted the mountains for idols!" he said. "Some thirty-five families have cast out their demon altars . . . this means that about two hundred have confessed Christ as Saviour. It was a blessing to see how they came to the meetings and to hear their singing. Seeing a Lisu with his Catechism, I asked him to read it to me, which he did with such liberty and joy that the tears came to my eyes as I sat and listened. Wonderful indeed. 'As soon as they hear of me they shall come; and thy people shall be willing in the day of thy power.' The Lolo also have asked the evangelists to come to their villages and teach them."

In this way began something which we hoped would grow—the Lisu tribe reaching out to evangelize other tribes. The white man cannot hope always to be in China; the native church should be trained to care for and evangelize its own countrymen.

Now to go back to Yongpeh. The very first of these thirty-five families to turn Christian was a local official, Chiu Teh-tsi by name. His is a wonderful and rare story of a heart prepared. If I remember rightly, the two evangelists were having rather a lonely and defeated time of it, when they "happened" upon this man, who, immediately he heard the gospel, was thrilled with it. He invited them into his own home and questioned them eagerly, and with great intelligence; then made his decision telling Aristarchus that he had long been seeking after *the truth*. Upon casting out his idols and ancestral worship, this dear man wrote us his testimony in Chinese, but alas, that letter is lost. Another from his pen will appear later. A quotation from a circular will introduce it:

"AN HANDFUL OF CORN . . . UPON THE TOP OF THE MOUNTAINS"

Twilight—the day's responsibilities over—I turned once again to the orange-brown path which slips in and out among green foliage until it falls away into Sunset Ridge on the banks of the Salween. There, at the end of the day, I like to keep tryst. The ridge is growing old . . . just as I am. Its rounded youthful form has been stripped of so many trees and bushes that it is thin and spare now, but it is still a quiet spot and it possesses a *forward look* which is incomparable in grandeur and never fails to silence the soul into worship. As I sit on my favourite grey stone, the opposite bank of the river towers up before me into jagged peaks, navy blue in the falling dusk, but with soft wreaths of pure white cloud wistfully clinging to their great shoulders. Peak behind peak—they trail away into the steel-grey skies with an enticing lure—*Come, find me! Come, find me!* and you feel quite sure that heaven and the Prince of Glory and all the host of loved ones gone on ahead are just over the border, and so in the quiet of the evening you feel *close*. That is the time and place to lay all the day's ruffles cut before Him and ask His dear hand to smooth them out. And when the inner peace is matched to the outward, I sometimes ask Him for a word, and often, so often—with unfailing kindness He has given it. He knows just what word will mean most, and that evening He opened the Book for me and pointed to Ps. lxxii. 16—"an handful of corn . . . upon the top of the mountains . . . the fruit thereof shall shake like Lebanon."

"An handful of corn"—it just described them. Our little handful of corn-kernel students who we hope will fall into the ground and die to self and bring forth a harvest of other kernels for Him. But the handful of corn was getting slimmer every day—how could one believe that its fruit would increase until it was like the great trees of Lebanon?

Do you remember we told you of an official in the Yongpeh district who had turned Christian under Aristarchus' exhortations? Well, the very next letter from there told that this dear "first-fruits" had passed the border country, and now is with the Lord. As I sit and look at that sky trail, and in the evening dusk feel "close" to those on the other side, I remember that Mr. Fraser's last request to us before he went Home, was that we would try to send a messenger of Christ to Yongpeh district. And now he and that new convert have shaken hands—isn't it wonderful? We aren't so very far separated, are we? We never know when it will be our turn to slip heavenward. A letter from that new convert is a voice, now, from beyond the sky trail.

To the Oak Flat Church: May 20, 1939.

The two teachers you sent to Yongpeh, namely Aristarchus and Secundus, are now in the Sha-pa village teaching *God's clear road*. We are very fond of one another. In the Lord Jesus we have peace.

These two are working very hard for God, changing our superstitions and lifting us up to walk the *great clear road*. Up to now there are over forty families trusting Jesus and of men and women over two hundred are studying the books. But then there are still a *few thousand* who do not believe in Jesus. These unbelievers are all in the hands of the devil; please pray to God for them.

That everything is in God's hands is our great joy. (They say he died with his testimony still on his lips.) Thank God and thank you.

I would like you to announce to the church that the most important thing in this note is that Aristarchus and Secundus are going home in a short time. We have only escaped from the devil's hands a few months; and we of Yongpeh do not know anybody who can read Lisu characters and we cannot do without them. We thank you because you have been expending your hearts in order to bring us into the faith.

CHIU TEH-TSI.

The following is an extract from Aristarchus' letter announcing Mr. Chiu's decease:

... Now among the brethren who have believed there are some Lisu but most are Lolo ... of individuals about two hundred and fifty. They are now at this time working on building a chapel. They have already finished two chapels of about thirty feet in length. Thank God.

Moreover, after they had believed, the Lisu official (the one whose letter is above) and another Christian went home to God. But the believers were not saddened. In fact, it was the duty of Secundus and me to comfort their hearts from the scripture, but some of them comforted us saying, "Don't feel badly." This is a sign to us that we have cause to thank God.

Another thing, the believers here are meeting with trial and seduction from some people Satan is using. This country where Secundus and I are, is close to that governed by Szechwan. And in that place, here and there robber bands are continually stealing people. Seven years ago about seven hundred of them (Wild Lolo of the Forbidden Territory!) came to this village where we are now, and burned their homes. They drove before them their cattle and many of their young men and women.

Needless to say, we did not request that Aristarchus and Secundus come home immediately; still it was not wise to let them continue on without Bible study under a competent teacher, so all during 1939 R.S.B.S. we were hunting in our hearts for the two students whom we should ask to go and relieve Aristarchus and Secundus to come back to us.

Again the 1939 circular gives a description of each member of the student body, but as repetition becomes wearisome we will quote only what relates to our story.

... And next to him sits a young fellow, face lowered, looking up at you with such a black scowl you would think he was planning your murder. Oh, no, dear friend, this is just poor Gad *trying to concentrate.* He reminds us of Aristarchus—such an unattractive surface, a slow working mind behind it, but, we trust, a sincere desire to do what is expected of him. I hope some of you take a liking to Gad—a prayer liking.

The women's bench is over at the back next the door—right next to Gad. Gad is not the type to distract a girl's thoughts. (Is that naughty? I'm sorry. I really like Gad, even if the girls don't.) Homay, Dorcas, Rhoda, Elizabeth, come as they can, and women visitors also but the only enrolled females are Mrs. Yang and Nosu-Mary.

R.S.B.S., 1939, was a happy school. I quote from the circular which reviewed it at the close.

Quite without our intending it, last year's R.S.B.S. held the key-note "regeneration," and quite without our planning it this year's one had a keynote also—it was "identification," our union with Christ in His death and resurrection. Many were the testimonies of what a blessing this study had been to our dear laddies. I listened to them with gratitude but with no excitement, for I know full well that to learn it in the classroom and to experience it alone on the field are often far apart. They do not need to be, but they often are. After a class on Rom. viii, Andrew said to me, "Ma-Ma, are there Christians nowadays who remain carnal *all their lives*?" Blessed innocence; may it always be that to learn a truth is to practise it, in their lives. But to put identification into practice necessitates suffering—there is no easy path to dying to self and living to God. My prayer for them is—may they recognize the opportunity to die, when it comes. I was myself blessed by these few sentences in a letter from our revered Miss Frances Brook: "Brokenness is the place of blessing. Broken personalities letting the fragrance of Christ out; broken purposes meaning power; broken plans meaning life; broken periods meaning glory. The corn of wheat breaks when it has let itself go to the ground and the embryo is free."

As I sat listening to the closing exercises I thought how much we had for which to thank the Lord. No student failed. Brand-New, Levi and Mrs. Yang did not write examinations and so were not "graduated," but of the other twenty, ten got over ninety-four per cent. There were no spectacular ones, this year, but several little incidents made us feel there was real progress. For instance, there was not one dissension between the students, large enough to come to our ears; last year there were three. We had no worries about misbehaviour; there was only one exhibition of temper on the playing field, Rufus the culprit. And with many there was a gradual growth which has been a quiet joy to us. I would like to mention Gad, Ephraim, Pade-John, Daniel and A-che as gladdening our hearts, these in addition, of course, to those who have been an undiminished joy all along. This summer A-che won a woman to the Lord in Water-Buffalo-Mountain Village and telling us of it later she said, "Now that's a fellow who loves folk." Little things like that show us the study of His Word is not in vain. Also we would like to praise the Lord for the safe journeyings made every week-end through stormy and dangerous weather, yet not a student was hurt by falling rocks, of which there were more than usual. Can you not see how God has been answering your prayers for us? And not least was the way the food supply kept up. In fact, I fear the "shepherds" were better fed than the flock, this summer.

Heading the list of unexpected joys was Gad! And now the designation of evangelists, their work and field for the coming year, was before us. Who were to be the exchange teachers with Aristarchus and Secundus?

Tall, good-looking, clever Luda-Peter had led the school that summer in marks, and my husband suggested him for Yongpeh.

"He is expecting to be married this winter. I do not believe he would like to be sent so far away," I demurred.

"Oh, that is an American thought, not a Lisu one," answered my husband impatiently. "I don't think he'd mind in the least. Any of our boys would be thrilled to go. Whom did you think to ask?"

"I thought of Daniel and Gad," I replied quietly.

"Gad! Why he's only a beginner! What on earth! Why, I want to send our very *best* to that great field! You know it was just about Mr. Fraser's last request before he died, that we should respond to that call for help. Gad! Humph." And in some disgust John turned away.

But I had been noticing the once-upon-a-time thief—noticed how hard he worked, how blamelessly he tried to live. Life is a powerful testimony, more powerful than clever words. Gad's daily life impressed me more than Peter's.

The next day my husband approached me with a rather sheepish grin. "Guess you win, Belle! I suggested Yongpeh to Peter yesterday. His face fell and he answered slowly, 'If it is God's will, I'll go, of course——' but his face told enough for me. Daniel, on the other hand, is glad to go. So I think I'll send for Gad and sound him out."

Gad limped in, and stood looking with a hang-dog expression from one to the other.

"Don't be afraid, Gad," cheerfully assured the missionary. "Nothing wrong. We've just called you in to ask if you would like to go with Daniel to Yongpeh for this next year?"

It was like pressing an electric button. His form straightened and his face flooded with light. "Oh, I'd like to *so much*!" he cried. But I had noticed his limp as he came in, and on inspection saw that one leg was just a row of ulcers from knee to ankle.

"How can you go, Gad, with a leg like that! There are twelve days of hard mountain walking before you get to Yongpeh, you know!"

"Oh," says Gad, looking down at his leg, "it will soon heal up. We don't have to go immediately, do we?" and he turned from kill-joy Ma-Ma to scan anxiously Ma-Pa's face.

"Oh, no," was the answer. "Job has to escort you and he is not going for a month or so yet."

"Well, I will be all healed by then," he replied with great relief. "Thanks ever so much!" And he limped off joyfully to communicate his good fortune to the others. The circular merely records:

> To exchange with Aristarchus at Yongpeh: Daniel and Gad. Job will escort them over there, as they must pass through Chinese territory and neither speaks much Chinese; then Job will remain to give the new believers a month of study before returning to his post at Ludá.

One fine autumn day, the little band of three set out on the long trek to a pioneer field, where many of the people were of a different tribe. "Go ye forth," He said.

I do not possess copies of any of the correspondence that ensued during that year of hard, faithful labour. Up and down the mountains the two plodded, teaching little groups of inquirers here and there, or entering heathen villages to proclaim their wonderful Word of Life. There was no hand-clapping or praise of men to urge them on, or comfort when the way was hard and lonely. They must adjust themselves to a different dialect, different food, and different customs, and all without any human help, except what they could give one another. And the field was so large that more often than not they had to separate in order to meet the calls for service. We, on the other hand, were so busy with a very full programme that we did not write to them as frequently as we would have liked to, and as they deserved.

Now back to the circulars. May, 1940, says:

> The safe return of Gad and Daniel from Yongpeh brought the news of over a hundred more souls won to Christ there, and one of them was coming along for teaching—Yongpeh James. There are now some six hundred Lisu in the Yongpeh area who have turned to Christ. Isn't that wonderful? In your joy do not forget that this is a mass movement.

... God will start His winnow going some day, but let's not be afraid of that—even in a mass movement *all* is not chaff.

That summer of 1940 we had four different tribes represented in our R.S.B.S.: Chinese, Lisu, Nosu, and two Lolo, one of whom Gad brought back with him, and all had to study the scriptures through the Lisu language![1]

There were three from Yongpeh: John and Peter have already been mentioned, so there is only James to describe. He was one of the newest converts—out of heathenism only about nine months. He could read but had not yet learned to write very well. He was only a laddie of twenty years, with a rosebud mouth and, the first few weeks a very worried brow. To ask him a question, even the simplest, was to petrify him. Poor laddie! He was a picture of Atlas—in Lisuland—with all the world on his shoulders. It was a joy to see the care smoothing out and smiles beginning to come. He sat next to Luke, whose duty it was to mother him!

Gad was with us all that summer, and it was easy to see that the year's preaching and testing, so far from home, had done him good. His hang-dog look had largely disappeared, and when it came to his turn in practice preaching, although he never was an outstanding speaker, he had something to say.

The end of R.S.B.S. came, and again the evangelists were allocated for the year. To Gad fell the honour of a field to himself. Previously he had always been just a cadet-evangelist; now he himself was to be in charge. He was sent to Hollow Tree district, about four days' journey to the south, a large area containing Shan and Lolo, as well as Lisu. We like to send the evangelists two by two, but this time there were not enough to go round. As always, Gad was quite happy to be given the difficult place.

"Don't worry," he said, smiling. "I don't mind. I'll be all right." Knowing how plucky he had always been, we let him go.

> Yet not in solitude if Christ anear me
> Waketh Him workers for the great employ!

---

[1] All had previously learned it, of course; many of the tribes are bi-lingual.

Oh, not in solitude—if souls that hear me
Catch from my joyaunce the surprise of joy.

Gad was hoping for this kind of companionship, and we felt
if once he got there, God would surely give it to him. Nevertheless, he was going far from home, so our "alone-boy" was much
on our hearts.

That winter, we ourselves hoped to visit Little Daughter in
Chefoo. As we must pass near Stockade Hill, we had decided to
stop off there and give a short time of Bible teaching. That district had been given no teaching help since the New Testaments
arrived, except the school at Longchiu conducted by Mr.
Peterson and Mr. and Mrs. Crane. It had been a good school
and appetites were whetted for more study. We could give them
only three days, but about one hundred gathered from all over
the district. One result was that Claude, a Lisu who had received
a good Chinese elementary education, offered to go into the
Lord's vineyard. We immediately told him of Gad's need of a
companion, and off he went to Hollow Tree. Little did we dream
how much Gad would need Claude, as soon as he arrived.

"God's Country" for Christmas

It was a crisp, fresh December morning when very early we started
out from the dark little Lolo hut where the past night had been spent.
It was cold, riding muleback on that high mountain-top before the sun
was up, but there was the hope of reaching home that day, and when the
pale yellow beams glinted on the great quiet peaks across the canyon
from us, warming the grey rocks and tinting the tree-studded sides into
genial colour, we thrilled and were glad to be alive. Our path took us
over a great cap of mountain whose fawn grass velvet sides dropped
down from beside our feet some two thousand feet to the green, winding
Salween River below. Everywhere the beauty of God's country, its
meditative quiet, its kindly hospitality, its open-trailed freedom was
spread around. I took a deep breath of the untainted air and said to
myself, *Back in Lisuland! I feel as if I could write a circular again!* For I
had a slightly guilty conscience—I had not written from Chinaland that
last month. Somehow the noisy rush of city life, with its conferences and
truck-travelling in between, had left my pen dry. There had been
blessing, but somehow no leisure to think out its record. But during that
early morning ride I knew what that exiled Israelite of long ago meant
when he cried, "How shall we sing the Lord's song in a strange land?"

Back in God's country the desire to chat with prayer helpers about Him and His work once more flooded my heart.

But why Christmas in Lisuland when we had planned to spend it with Little Daughter at the coast? War conditions, including the bombing of a bridge on our route out, seemed to close the door. Though heart-strings tugged for little girlie, trusting the wisdom of His faithful love who has never failed us in the past, we came back to spend the day with our Lisu children, and their love and welcome certainly comforted us. God is always so good to us—Charlie Peterson had reached home just a day and two nights before we arrived, but he had cleaned house, unpiled stored-up furniture and boxes, spread his own lovely new bedspread and other fresh-from-furlough possessions all throughout our rooms—well, the only rooms that had not been dressed up to welcome us nor fixed in any way were Charlie's own! Then we had brought a grand present for everybody in the person of Orville Carlson!

"The Least of Those You Love"

"All our joy is touched with pain," someone has said. Christmas Eve, as the line-up from the south—Horse-Grass-Level Village and Hollow Tree district—waited to come under the arch, I eagerly looked for Gad. Claude, I saw, and so thought for sure Gad would be there too, but I could not see him. So when all the greetings were over, I asked where Gad was. A quiet fell over them, then they answered, "Gad has gone home to God. He died around the first of December." (Probably, as I learned after, from relapsing fever.) The news was an awful shock, and could not be forgotten. As he was the first of our Rainy Season Bible School students to fall asleep we held a memorial service for him on the morning after Christmas. Orville Carlson had been appointed to speak by interpretation at that meeting and it was peculiarly fitting, for two of Gad's brothers were present. One, at least, had come purposely to meet Gad, not having seen him for over a year, and the news made him very bitter against the Lord at first.

Orville had been through the same thing. His first arrival in Yunnan had been filled with the joy of an unexpected meeting with his loved brother Earl, only to be met with the news of Earl's Home-going at Luda. As Orville movingly recalled his own grief, questionings, and how the Lord tenderly met them, there were many wet eyes in the audience and I am sure Gad's brothers got an answer to their *why?*

After Orville Carlson, Gad's fellow students and workers one by one gave short testimonies of different things in his life that had blessed them. Some of them have already been recorded in this chapter—his confession of stealing a book-bag from us and the restoration of the money, which began a new life for him. His fearless and faithful work at Yongpeh were mentioned. Rather an austere, very exact and unemotional character though he was, his faithfulness to his appointed task was almost everyone's testimony.

Claude had been with him at his death. He said, "Gad knew he was going. Many of his people came crowding in to see him and he spoke to them, gave instructions as to the disposal of his things and then said, 'I know for a certainty that I am going Home to God. All of you behave as you should,' and with that he fell unconscious, and passed away." Wasn't it lovely that he died exhorting men and women to walk in the light of Calvary's sacrifice? It was typical of him that he could not put it beautifully. He was not a gifted teacher, but one of the testimonies concerning him was that his fellows grew to know that he never was flippant—he always meant what he said, and he said it.

The last letter we ever had from Gad, not thinking it would be his last, we did not keep, but it ended on a note that none of his letters had ever had before. He never exhibited affection, yet this letter had a love-longing phrase at the end, a non-translatable Lisu love-sigh which means, "Oh, you dear ones." Then after it he wrote, "The writer is the least of those you love—Gad." One of the reasons the news of his departure brought tears was that I never had showed him how much his faithfulness and willingness for hardship were prized. But there is One with him now, who will see to his reward. In thinking of Gad I am reminded of a verse my grandmother loved and wrote in my autograph album:

> A noble life is not a blaze
> Of sudden glory won.
> But just an adding up of days
> In which good work is done.

What is love to Christ? F. B. Meyer says, "You would like to love with a strong, undying flame—but perhaps you fail to distinguish between love and the emotion of love. They are not the same. We may love without being directly conscious of love. . . . *They love who obey.*"

Gad never could gush. Even if he felt "a strong, undying flame," he would not have known how to put it into words, or even into manner, *but he did know how to obey.*

Gad died, trying to "give to him that needeth." The great Abyss of Sin had once made him shudder, and the tender shelter of the Cleft Rock (the forgiving grace of the Lord Jesus) never ceased to comfort his soul. But comfort was not all he desired. He was ashamed of that past; he wanted to express gratitude. With that thought in his heart, Gad set his face towards service. The raw Wind of Sickness whipped against him but did not stop him. The moaning Wind of Loneliness made him shiver but it also taught him to snuggle into the Shelter of his Rock. Thus when unexpectedly (he was still in his twenties) that bleak Wind of Death came whistling over the Abyss, he was so disciplined to self-forgetfulness that it failed to produce any terror, just concern lest the younger nestlings around him, who had had less opportunity to study their Rock, might be needlessly overwhelmed.

9

The Unseen Missionaries

"BELLE!" My husband looked up from a letter he was reading. "We shall have to go to Luda after this R.S.B.S. is over. Here is another letter from Mr. and Mrs. Cooke" (they were on furlough then—it was 1939) "asking us again to give their Lisu a little oversight. I'm just ashamed we have not gone yet. And it is such a *wonderful* field. I've always wanted you to see Luda; you know that."

"Well, my dear"—I sighed a little—"you know we tried to go last year, but the rains drove us back. I'll go now if you want me to, but you know what Mr. Fraser said once, that that trail up the canyon is the hardest travelling in all China. I could never walk it. "

"You don't *have* to walk it—we have Jessie and Jasper!"

"But the Cookes say you can't use a mule on those mountains!"

"That is because they are both such splendid walkers. I don't believe they have ever tried to use an animal much. Probably felt safer on their own feet. But I've been up there too, and I believe our Jessie and Jasper can do it!"

"All right, I'll go then," I agreed.

"Three cheers!" exclaimed Friend Husband, jumping up enthusiastically. "Then I'll go over and talk with Luke, and we shall arrange a grand party of deacons and Christians to go with us. The last letter from Job said that Village-of-the-Three-Clans is split with quarrelling, and it is having a bad effect on the community. Cath and Vic Christianson are here now, and they can look after Oak Flat. Do you agree?"

"All right," was the answer given more cheerfully. And now I'll let the circulars of those days tell most of it.

December 12, 1939.

Let Him lead thee blindfold onwards,
  Love needs not to know;
Children whom the Father leadeth
  Ask not where they go.

Tersteegen.

"BLINDFOLD ONWARDS"

We thought we were going to Luda for just three weeks. It happened that five of our Ma-Pas had to go back to their home in the Stockade Hill District for one reason or another: Luke to take his little daughter to school there; Job to be present while his dead father's estate was divided; Andrew, Titus, and James for other reasons. It seemed just the time for us all to unite in giving the Luda district a bit of help—a shower of love and grace—before going our separate ways for the winter.

One bright November morning we started out with the best evangelistic party we could assemble—Luke and Lucius, and two of our best deacons. Job also was to meet us at Luda. So, full of hope that God was going to give us revival blessing, we began the trip.

For six days we travelled, with adventures every day, but I will quote mainly those parts of the narrative that touch the problem at Three Clans.

THE RECEPTION

The last morning a happy, long, serpentine tail of us wagged along the river road. Rock formation was entrancing. At one point was a huge wall as smooth as if the missing part had been sliced off with a cake knife—a cake hundreds of feet high. At its feet approaching us was a little band with a gaily bedecked horse. "What is this—a wedding party?" I asked Peter.

He smiled knowingly and said, "No; not a wedding party." Then the supposed party began to shout and wave to us, and here if it was not a reception committee from Three Clans Village! Their service-leader A-ge-tsi and many others—and the red-trimmed horse was for us to ride, if you please!

But this was not all. Farther along we met someone else, who handed John a written invitation for the evening meal! Still farther on was a shout and along came the famous A-deng, who had paid forty cows to redeem his wife so he could marry her. With a bamboo tube in one hand, a tea kettle in the other and a grand smile on his face, he invited us to drink out of the kettle's spout—honey-water, but cold.

"Oh, take a good drink, Ma-Pa," he said. "I've plenty more here!" patting his long bamboo tube. Still farther on were some more Three Clans folk with *hot* honey-water—much more palatable, for the Lisu do not strain off the wax, and cold wax bits were sticking in my mouth. At the riverside, before the ascent to Three Clans Village, they had made a second raft (for at that time of the year we did not need to go over by rope bridge) to get us·all across more quickly, and on the hither bank were still more folk waiting to greet us with hot tea! At the top of the hill was an arch of wild orchids and a long line (Lucius counted over a hundred and then lost tally) for Three Clans is a big village, "the New York of Lisuland," says John.

We never had been given such a reception before, but our elation was short-lived. Alas! it was not all affection (though some undoubtedly was), for Three Clans had an axe to grind. The three main clans in this village were at loggerheads over some mountain plots left them by their ancestors, on which valuable wormwood had been discovered, and they all were in hopes that John would settle the dispute. Each relay of the reception, then, was not the lovely thought we had imagined, but a different clan trying to gain our favour. One side would not come to meet us with the other side, and each was afraid the other side's attentions would outdo theirs! Alas and alack for the missionary who takes things at surface value!

We had not brought Luke and party just for pleasure. They scattered over the hills to give a loving ministry, but before doing so they assisted John in the long and tiresome discussion meetings over this wormwood. More or less all day and late into the night our party pleaded with those dear folk to be forgiving and generous toward one another, and to accept the church's decision rather than take the disagreement to the heathen official for settlement. Though respectful and loving (I want to say that for them), they simply would not listen. John refused to make a decision—in fact, Ah-be-pa and all said that it was impossible—so they "went to Egypt" for aid, with the result we had expected.

The Chinese official came to inspect the disputed fields. They had to carry him on their shoulders free of charge, kill a pig and feed him royally, and then he went back home and sent them this word: "First tax—for weariness of feet"—the trouble of inspection, but the title amuses me, for his precious feet never touched the ground, so to speak—"$220.00; after this is paid me I will give judgment," which means the tax for that, and the tax for writing out the document, and other incidental charges will be made later after he received the Weariness-of-

Feet Tax! Result—the quarrellers are sitting around holding their headaches and groaning. Now my husband will say that is an exaggeration, but it just describes the woeful countenances I have looked upon. The devil surely is a hard master, but men won't believe it until they feel his blows.

Three Clans was only one out of many villages in that great Lisu district, so John decided that we had better change our plans and stay three months, instead of three weeks, and tour the whole district. In the meantime, word of the seemingly hopeless condition of Three Clans could be sent home, and the Lisu prayer partners could get under its burden.

With that decision made, we entered into the Christmas festivities.

December, 1939.

God's Christmas Gift

We had not expected any gifts this year. Notice from the Chinese post office said that after last July all parcels from abroad containing— (then followed pages of forbidden imports which seemed to include everything that a missionary uses)—would not be allowed to cross the Chinese border, so we concluded all gifts for us would accordingly be confiscated. Nobody knew we were to be in far off Luda for Christmas anyway, so the possibility of a private celebration never entered our mind. We set our hearts to forget what Christmas used to be like and to make it a happy day for the Lisu. But His Name is *Wonderful* and part of the wonder of Him is revealed (to those with eyes to see) in the way He thinks and takes care of even very little things which add to happiness.

But the first was not a little thing. Some weeks before Christmas we had heard most astounding news—that Mr. Morrison, a missionary of another mission to the north of us, had already received his Lisu New Testament! A little later we received a note from him, asking if we could spare him some of our Lisu hymn-books. Very crafty were we. We immediately sent him a load of them with the request that he lend us some of his New Testaments! He was most kind and gave us all that he had left—not as many as we had hoped but enough for us missionaries to have one each—and we were able to send one to Job and one to Luke. Oh, the joy of owning a copy—it has not left me yet! I felt as I turned its pages that God had given me all the Christmas gift I needed to make me happy, but He had yet more in store. The evening of Christmas Day, carriers from Oak Flat unexpectedly walked in with mail, and in their bag was our girlie's Christmas gift to us—a new photograph of herself; and also two small packages from America (containing things forbidden to cross the border! Was the postal examiner asleep that day?) In one of them was some candy, so we had a white man's Christmas after all. In those days of China's turbulence, no one but God could have timed mail to arrive like that!

Job, very busy as all Ma-Pas are during the festivity, wrote us later: "I got the New Testament you forwarded, Big Brother; thank you. I was very pleased to get it. That evening the festival was on, so I was too busy to do more than glance at it. All night I was so happy I could not sleep, so at midnight I got up and studied it. I am ever so delighted. Thank God."

The time had come for Luke and Job and the others to bid goodbye to us and start on their long trek to their homes in the south. As our little band of dear comrades dropped out of sight down the steep mountainside, and we turned back to the mission-ary shanty, it seemed cold and desolate. I noticed a watery look in my husband's eyes, and I could hardly keep the tears of loneliness out of my own. Leila Cooke had once written from that very same house, "I feel as if I've jumped off the edge of the world," and now I knew what she had meant.

We felt sorry too, that the evangelistic party which had come to Three Clans with us with high hope that God would use us, had to return with the knowledge that all our labours, exhorta-tions, and teaching had seemingly been in vain. But there remained one hope. The returning party carried with them letters to America and England, *to the prayer partners of the Lisu Church* and when those faithful, *unseen missionaries* got to praying, things might happen. We had explained the Three Clans problem and had given details of the need. Keep this in mind as the story unfolds to you just as it unfolded to us. We saw nothing, felt nothing, but turned our attention to the large district, full of villages, around the village of the Three Clans. We left the latter

to the Lord, and to the *unseen missionaries*; for we had done all
we could without them. Now I quote:

The evening of December 30, returning from prayer meeting, we
heard voices in the servants' shanty. Peeking in, who should we see
but Simon, Caleb, and another Plum Tree Flat boy—Joshua. The little
bamboo hut rang with shouts of mutual joy, and the loneliness which
had haunted us since arriving here seemed to melt away before the
warmth of their comradeship. They had come, not for themselves, but
to give several months to the Lord in either forward evangelism or
teaching. Everyone is food-conscious these days, and most young men
are making strenuous efforts these winter months to make money by
trade or other work, with the hungry future in mind. Seth, Simon, and
Caleb are all married men, each with a little one to care for, yet they
are putting His Kingdom first, for they know there is a spiritual dearth
in Lisuland worse than its physical need. Seth we did not see, for he had
been retained in Oak Flat District in the absence of Luke, Thomas,
James and Job. I wish I could pray down some special blessing on those
three and their brave wives, but it comforts us to realize that the Lord
is more careful to reward faith than we could ever be.

Sitting around the wood fire, John said to them something like this:
"Well, Mr. Fisher of Lanping" (an independent missionary) "has asked
for teachers to evangelize the Lisu around his district, but our own Luda
field is in such sad need of teachers that I'd like to split you three—find
a partner for Joshua and send them to Lanping, keeping Simon and
Caleb here in this field to go around the villages and teach." Hugging
their knees, the boys looked up and said, "Anything you decide is all
right with us. We want the Lord's will, that is all." A young Luda
Christian was present, and the next day John asked him if he would be
Joshua's partner—he knew the road across the mountains and could act
as guide and helper in general.

"I have to be back to plough in March, but I will be glad to go until
then," he answered. So we named him Thaddeus, and he and Joshua
left early on New Year's morning to mine for Christ in the mountains
around Lanping, a Chinese city some five days' journey east of here.

New Things with the New Year at Luda

To reach the missionary's home at Luda you must first prepare for a
terrible climb, perhaps two thousand feet up from the banks of the
Salween. Luda Mountain is gracefully knobby, and the village itself is
spread over these tiers of knolls. It is a village of over four hundred souls
and, as you climb, to right and left and in front of you are these rounded

swells of the mountain with Lisu homes perched on their flat tops. Daniel's family live toward the bottom, so you may perhaps first meet his pretty little sister shyly waiting at the roadside to shake hands, as we did.

After this breath-taking ascent you follow a bamboo-trough water-course around the side of the knoll on which the chapel is built, and above you on the next mountain knob are two native bamboo shanties at right angles to one another. The one facing you is marked on the door "Mr. Cooke" and the right-angle one is marked similarly "Charlie," only, of course, in Lisu. As you pant up through the hillside garden to Cookes' front door, you notice a big tree down to your right and beneath it a roughly fenced enclosure. That is God's garden, where two precious grains of wheat have fallen into the ground to bring forth fruit more abundantly. Weather-worn wooden crosses are roughly carved "Sylvia Ward" and "Earl Carlson," with texts which I do not remember. Significantly, opposite the large tree which shades their sleep is a huge old stump.

"That was a devil-tree in the old days," said John to me. "The people used to worship it, and when they turned Christian they were still afraid of it, so Job said, 'I'm not afraid of it! Bring me an axe and I'll cut it down!'—and that is how it fell."

Up behind the simple shanties winds a road to further mountain tiers, where Peter and Dan live, and crowning all is a precipitous mountain peak out like a gingerbread loaf. I looked everywhere, on arrival, and inquired for Leila Cooke's waterfall which she had so enticingly described in her circulars, but saw none, and no one seemed to know of it. Then one day it was revealed, and this is how it happened: it snowed. Lucius was hoping it would, for in all his twenty-one years he had never seen it snow. From the low-lying Village-of-the-Olives, when the clouds cleared after a rainstorm, he had seen that the opposite peaks were white, and once only someone had shown him a wee bit of the white stuff brought down from the heights but that was all he knew of snow. One morning early, toward the end of the Bible school, I heard Lucius go out the kitchen door; then came a great yell, "Ma-Ma! It's *snowing*! *A-bo! A-bo!* (Oh my!) It comes down just like the rain does! *A-bo! A-bo!*" An hour later an excited laddie was showing us a snowball. "Is this what you used to throw at one another when you were a little girl in America, Ma-Ma?"

"Yes, Lucius; only do not pack them too tight or they will hurt."

"I'm going to put mine on the stove and see what will happen," and away he trotted, while John and I exchanged grins, but allowed him to make his own experiment. Soon he reported. "Yes, it turned into water.

They had told me you could cook with snow, but I did not believe them." Well, he himself had to cook with melted snow for some days after, for it continued to storm and the water ceased flowing. Gradually the snow turned to rain, and it was then, in the quiet night that we heard a steady, thunderous sound. *It was the waterfall!* Dry weather had turned it into a mere dripping, but the storm had brought it back to life. It falls in tiers down the ravine which faces Cookes' house and can be heard but not seen from there.

In January, 1940, we toured the district of Luda, and in the course of events came to the village where Mary of the Nosu tribe lived: we called her Nosu-Mary.

In the Home of Nosu-Mary

These are Yunnan's golden winter days—a chill nip in the air, but until February, clear skies and little fear of rain or snow. This is the time to travel, so on the second of January we set out to visit the southern part of this field, with Nosu-Mary's home particularly in mind. We visited eight villages, holding service and sleeping in six of them, and also held a baptismal service in one of the cold mountain streams. It was an exciting journey for we rode Jasper and Jessmine, though many folk said animals could not possibly go over those trails. Undoubtedly little horses would have been of small use and how grateful we constantly were to friends at home for their gift of our big mules. In several places, we had to say to those begging for a visit, "Fix the road for our mules to pass and we will come." One place was a rock ascent where we could not even "ride by tail," for the mules had to spring up it at a run. Another place was a face of rock about thirty feet high broken three times by earth ledges some ten feet apart. Against the rock leaned the now familiar knotched-sapling ladders. Truly no animal could climb them, but they found a detour through dense growth which "Jas" and "Jes" could traverse after having all harness removed.

What a difference a frame makes to a picture! Mary against the frame of her dainty cousin last summer had seemed so loud and unattractive. But up here among her own wild mountains, and especially against the frame of her own mother, Mary shows up quite golden. I think, of all the women I have met who have loud, piercing voices, Mary's mother ranks among the three most outstanding. (One was an elevator girl in Canada, one is a Chinese woman in a poor, mountain-top village, and the third is this little old Nosu lady!) I heard her about fifty yards away before ever we met. "*Eh-eh*, now isn't this just *awful*? They told us you weren't coming till Saturday, so we have no flower arch made to welcome you. It's perfectly *dreadful*, but there was nobody home to make it, and we can't help it; you will have to forgive us," and so on, was shouted in a continuous stream as we appeared around the curve of the road and came toward her. But oh, what a kind heart—she had prepared a nice room in their long bamboo shanty, killed a pig for us, and evidently searched the mountainside for food, for nowhere were we given such a variety of vegetables as in that generous house. Tall, jagged, most quaintly picturesque peaks encircle the little dell where Mary lives; and a full, happy, gurgling stream at the bottom, night and day seems to testify that a person *has* to talk loudly if she is to be heard above its chatter.

Like most husbands of talkative females, Mary's father is a silent partner, but he listened to our messages with such a glowing countenance, and at parting put a leg of pork into my hand, a practical token that he was one with the rest of them in good deeds. Mary is the oldest child; she is followed by two brothers and a sister. One of the boys was very ill some years ago and all expected him to die. Later Job heard of him. "Why, is that fellow still living?" he exclaimed. "He ought to be called Lazarus!" And the name stuck. So Mary and Lazarus live together in the house by the rushing stream. Lazarus now is twenty-one, plump, healthy, and a very keen student.

The village is a small one and the chapel one of the tiniest we have been in, but those who worshipped there were among the best taught and the most interested we have met in this district. Isn't that a good testimony for Nosu-Mary?

A gladness greeted us shortly after our return to Luda Village. Aristarchus, Secundus, and a new convert named Yongpeh-Peter arrived from Yongpeh! Tired, thin and worn, our dear Aristarchus is just the same as ever. When John asked him to give a word about the work at Yongpeh at the Saturday Prayer Meeting, he got up in the old awkward way, with the same old awkward "*Ahem . . . Ahem*," and then sailed into his testimony. "Now this is *not* the work of Aristarchus, nor is it the work of Secundus. This is the work of *God*." After plainly emphasizing that, he went on to tell of four hundred and thirty-five adults and children in Yongpeh who now own the name of Christ.

Another great joy on our return to the Cookes' shanty was the arrival of the Lisu New Testaments, packages and packages of them—enough for everybody!

"Now we really must have a February Bible School!" cried John, and at the following chapel service in Three Clans Village, he stood up and said something like this: "Now that the New

Testaments are here, and the missionaries are here temporarily, we really must have some teaching on the Word of God. I am going to send word out all over this district and invite *anyone who wants to come*, to join us in study for the month of February. We go back in March. Now you folk at Three Clans were a heavy disappointment to me in the Big Matter, when I asked you *for Jesus' sake* to rather suffer yourselves to be defrauded than to dishonour Him by quarrelling in front of a heathen judge. You did not do it, and my heart is sore." Here there were many nods and tears in a few eyes, in the audience. The Three Clans believers were not individually hard-hearted; it was just that they were in bondage to the law of the clan and did not know how to get free. "Now I am going to ask one other thing of you. Don't say *no* to me. I am going to ask *you* to entertain the students of the February Bible School—one family to feed one student, or even two students, for one month. Now that is not a lot. Hands up, those of you who will promise hospitality to one student for the month of February!" And hands went up all over the chapel. Dear souls, they wanted to do right. They were just enslaved to wrong and had not the courage to break away. So the Bible School was held. I quote from the circular:

The February Bible School was just ending. It almost failed once. It is hard for people who have lived an active outdoor life and never been to school all their days to keep their noses in books for a month on end. By the middle of the month numbers had dwindled somewhat. A delegation of Nosu interviewed John on that rainy, cold, miserable day. "We must go home. Dan's sister-in-law died of typhus last night and we daren't stay," they announced. It was true that the typhus epidemic then raging in other parts of the canyon had reached Three Clans Village, but only in Dan's home, which is the very highest in the village and so easily segregated, and it proved later that his sister-in-law had not died. John pleaded with them to trust the Lord and not go, but they shifted uneasily, and it was plain they meant to leave. There was only one thing left to do. John and I went into our bedroom, shut the door, and asked the Lord of Calvary once more to vindicate His victory there, over Satan and all his powers. We said no more to the students, but not one of them left, and the school finished the month triumphantly. Oh, how well we know that it is not *we* who do the work; feeble little us-lings whose best arguments were but as empty air to those restless, frightened students. And in the blessings poured out finally, we had to stand and just look on and marvel; like Jannes and Jambres of old we must admit, "This is the finger of God."

Bible school teaching days are very difficult ones in which to write circular letters. Although thrilling to the teacher, they make poor "copy" for the writer. Every day is just the same in events, and it is impossible to appraise the work justly. Often the student who gives the most brilliant testimony of blessing received, does not turn out afterward so satisfactorily as the lame-tongued one who could not put anything into words—so that the writer does not know what to record. Many of the students of that February Bible School could not even read properly, and to judge from appearances some learned practically nothing all month. Yet experience has taught me in Bible teaching not to walk *by sight*: His is the Word of *Life* and somehow it does bring life, though it may fail to do so in certain individuals. After the school had closed there seemed to be an epidemic of quarrels and fleshly outbreakings that *seemed* to betoken that the study had produced no results. But the last two days, March 11 and 12, without any explanation that we could discover a sudden and astounding change took place.

Before we tell of that astounding change, I must announce that the February School ended with wedding bells! A double wedding took place, A-che to A-nyi-ma, and Aristarchus to— whom do you think?—to Nosu-Mary! Feeling he needed a wife, and hearing that one girl had come all the way from Luda to Oak Flat to enter the R.S.B.S., he concluded, without knowing more of her, that she must be the right material for a preacher's wife, and he proposed on the strength of that! We do not recommend to all and sundry this way of getting a wife! but merely record it.

Great were the preparations. The mud chapel was decorated with pine needles and wild rhododendrons, and to endeavour to instil decency and order into the service, Caleb and Lucius were posted at the doors to refuse entrance to anybody after the ceremony had begun. A bench was placed in front of the officiating minister, and on it the two wedding couples with their attendants were to sit.

All went beautifully, in tribal eyes. The brides, according to Luda custom, entered the chapel with an old skirt or blanket over their heads, so that they could hardly be seen at all, and stood thus beside the bridegroom until asked to be seated by the minister. At this crucial and breathless moment the calamity happened. Caleb and Lucius, anxious not to miss the ceremony (the bride is frequently too nervous to answer properly and it is often fun), forgot the doors; and a young fellow, knowing he must be late, but eager to see the evangelists' wedding, broke through. Before anyone could stop him or even realize his entrance, he had dashed up the aisle searching for an empty seat, thought he saw one in front, and planted himself hopefully on a corner of the *bridegroom's bench*! With one simultaneous cry of wrath and horror, the bridegroom's bench arose, two stalwart and indignant doorkeepers dashed down to the front, and before the luckless guest knew what he had done, five pairs of hands fell upon him, and he was evacuated bodily to a place of less honour.

Decorum having thus been restored, the ceremony proceeded. A-nyi-ma shook so much that I went close to her in case she collapsed utterly, while Mary refused to answer anything at all—she just tittered. But then, if the brides did not do anything unusual Lisu weddings would not be any fun. To the Lisu the *pork feast* afterward was the most important, anyway. And so they were married.

Now we were coming to the last days of our stay at Three Clans and the most significant part of this story remains to be told. In fact, I would not have told any of it, if it had not been for this last part. *For the whole material of this book is dependent on the truth I want now to emphasize.* That truth is this—the slaves of the Munitions of Rock could never be freed by so feeble a thing as missionary witness and effort. They are held under a Tyranny of Darkness so strong, that only God is stronger! Only tremendous spiritual forces, working on the ground of the Atonement of Calvary, can bring Light to those sightless eyes. That spiritual force is *the prayer of many*. The prayer of one or two missionaries or converts *is not enough* to break such bonds.

We had reasoned, we had opened up the Word of God to the

Three Clans, until their souls shivered with conviction, *but they still could not see the way out,* still they could not muster up the courage to break the custom of years. But by March the friends at home had received our appeal for prayer, and had gone to their knees in intercession. Then, and then only, this little corner of Satan's kingdom began to shake. We felt it. Notice again how that last circular read. "The last two days . . . *without any explanation that we could discover* a sudden and astounding change took place." When I wrote that in April, 1940, a letter with the explanation was already written and on its way, *but had not reached us yet.* And the letter was written in human ignorance of how the victory had come.

Those last two days we sensed that the atmosphere of the village was softening, was changing, and the night before we left to return home, my husband got an inspiration. I will let the circular now tell the rest:

The last night before we left to return to Oak Flat we held a service in the chapel. John had decided to make a plea for the abolishing of the "law of the clan." That law was, that if any member of the clan gets into trouble *whether he is guilty or not,* all the rest of his clan must back him up financially or otherwise. So if one man decided to steal a plot of farm land, his whole clan would have to help him steal it. If any man fail in this loyalty, when his time of legitimate trouble comes, he must face it alone—the clan will not help him.

John had prepared a set of paper arrows. On one set was written, "I have no desire to practise the law of the clan"; on the other set was written, "I desire to practise the law of love." That last service together John very simply drew their attention to how Satan was binding them to sin by the law of the clan, and though it would be costly to break away from it, followers of Christ are bound to the law of Christ which is love—love toward *all* men, not just your own clan.

"Now I am going to ask all who henceforth will break free from the law of the clan and follow only the law of Christ to come forward, take the clan arrow, and burn it in the fire here. If you do this, I will give you a love arrow to keep always." Then he waited. There was no excitement, no play on emotion, but deliberately and slowly, one after another leaders of the various clans came forward, took a clan arrow and burned it, giving at the time a short testimony, received a love arrow and returned to his seat. Some twenty did so—all the important leading fighters *but one man.* (I always myself remember his name was "Lamb" because the word, with the exception of tones, is the same as the Lisu name for Lamb. The change in tone gives it another meaning of which I am ignorant, so I will just call him the Luda-Lamb for our convenience although never was there a worse misnomer.)

Lamb sat silent, head down, looking up at John through shaggy eyebrows. My husband ignored him for the moment and turned to some famous old quarrellers. He publicly named the disputants and asked them to stand, seek each other's forgiveness and shake hands before us all. They did so. I myself have never been present at such a scene as God gave us to see that night. Two brothers who had not spoken civilly to one another for twenty-six years were among those reconciled. Then John quietly sprang a surprise. "Now, a certain man present has held a quarrel with the Oldest Brother" (of the two just mentioned) "and I noticed that he did not burn a clan arrow. Luda-Lamb! Are you going to be the only one in the village to refuse the law of love?" The old woman sitting next to me sat up and whispered excitedly, "Oh, yes, yes—*those two*!" But the Lamb sat silent and obstinate. He is one of the most powerful personalities in the community and was at the bottom of all the wormwood fighting. I whispered to the woman, "Pray for him! Pray for him!" and while we did so John said sadly, "Well, I am afraid we must say of Lamb like that one of old, 'he went out from us because he was not of us.'" Then, just as John was about to close the meeting, suddenly Lamb stood up and clearly and definitely made a public apology to his long-hated enemy, who likewise apologised, and they two shook hands.

Luda-Lamb then came forward, plucked a clan arrow and burned it in the fire and took away an arrow of love. It was wonderful. Only God could have done it, and only God can maintain it, but He has decreed that you and I must help Him by putting our spirit with the Holy Spirit in "groanings that cannot be uttered," which is the travail of intercession.

That night, after we had returned to our shanty, I said to my husband, "John, that was more than your own inspiration. I'm going to note this date down and see—I'm sure someone in the homelands has been very specially praying for us." And the date went down in my diary.

We returned to Oak Flat. Some two months passed. Then one day when the mail had come, I called out to my husband, "John, read this, while I go and get my diary!"

It was a letter from a dear prayer-warrior, in a small town

in North America, a Mrs. K——. It read something like this:

BELOVED CHILDREN:

I must write and tell you what happened to-day. All morning I could not do my housework, because of the burden on me concerning the Three Clan Village, so finally I went to the telephone and called Mrs. W——. She said that she had been feeling the very same way and suggested that we phone Mrs. J—— and all go to prayer. We did so, each in her own kitchen, this morning we spent in intercession for those quarrelling clans. We feel God has answered. You will know.

I consulted my diary. Night with us is morning with them. It was the very time that we felt the "astounding change" of which I had written in the circular. It was the same twenty-four hours that the clan arrows were burned!

Now these prayer-warriors were not seemingly of the earth's mighty ones. Mrs. K—— was delicate, had a heart condition. Mrs. W—— was expecting a serious operation, and Mrs. J—— was going blind. All three were elderly women, too frail physically to cross the small town and gather in one place, but each in her own kitchen was joined to the others in spirit, and the strength of that extra intercession, in addition to what all the prayer-helpers were sending forth, pushed the battle over the wall.

Our Lord differentiated between the strength of demons. (Matt. xvii. 21.) Some strongholds of Satan require more spiritual force to overthrow than others. And it is not surprising if numbers count in such battles.

I have been helped in this matter by an analogy from mental telepathy. But I do not want to be misunderstood; prayer is *not* mental telepathy. Science can never explain prayer, though it does profess to explain mental telepathy, and tells us that there are such things as wave-thoughts, which exercise influence upon the one to whom they are directed. Just supposing that to be true, how easy it is to see the power of missionary intercession. For wave-thoughts would emanate only from the soul and so are limited. Prayer, on the other hand, emanates from the spirit, the only part of man that can reach out and touch God as well as man. How simple, then, the power of the prayer closet: many spirits working together with God the Holy Spirit for the liberating of a human soul, or a village of souls. Thus, as man has been able to advance in his research of mental telepathy, it is not surprising that those who "by reason of use of their senses exercised to discern" can tell when they have prayed through to victory. The unseen missionary, the prayer-helper, has here an effectual weapon against the Sharp Winds from a Bitter Height, which is the last word in spiritual warfare. Remember the parabolic picture of this in Exod. xvii. 11-14. Joshua on the battlefield won only as Moses on the mount kept his hands of intercession lifted high. Even in that work (some think Moses a type of Christ as our Intercessor) Moses *had to have human help.* The missionary on the foreign field must likewise have other spirits to aid him with the battle in the heavenlies. Explain it as you wish, it is a fact, *and it works.*

The Lisu work has had wonderful prayer-warriors in the past; but many of them have been translated into His Presence. We are needing prayer-warrior reinforcements. And China, all China, needs them too.

> If radio's slim fingers can pluck a melody
> From night—and toss it over a continent or sea;
> If the petalled white notes of a violin
> Are blown across the mountains or the city din,
> If songs, like crimsoned roses, are culled from thin blue air—
> Why should mortals wonder if God answers prayer?
> *Ethel Romig Fuller.*

10

"Jes' Pebbles"

De sunflower ain't de daisy, and de melon ain't de rose,
Why is dey all so crazy to be sumfin' also dat grows?
Jes' stick to de place you're planted, and do de best you knows,
Be de sunflower or de daisy, de melon, or de rose,
Don't be what you ain't, jes' you be what yo is.

.   .   .   .

Pass de plate if you can't exhaust and preach.
If you're jes' a little pebble, don't try to be de beach.

UP to now, this book has been mainly about outstanding Lisu Christians, those who could "exhaust and preach." The biographies also have been of those who have completed their course. It is not safe to write of those who are still in the running—if one had written of David, for instance, before the Bathsheba incident, he would have been accused of "misrepresenting." All of us are possible Davids. But I would like to say that the *power* which wrought in the lives of Me-do-me-pa and Homay, is *still working* in other lives just as attractive. That power is still as potent, and you may correctly pray for the Homays and Me-do-me-pas still being stormed upon by the blasts of Sharp Winds from the Bitter Height—for there are many of them. You may pray also for those *who would be* Homays and Me-do-me-pas if they had their opportunity to hear the gospel—there must be many of them, too.

There are also some who are "jes' pebbles"; and a real picture of the Lisu church is incomplete without its "pebbles."

OLD BIG

Old Big, a rough country farmer, accepted the Lord the first

time he heard of Him, when La-ma-wu and his party first took
the gospel to Pine Mountain Village. His hut was on the lowest
level of the village, but his mansion in glory. Until he died, I
never heard of his dishonouring the Lord in any way. On
Sundays he used to sit up near the front, and the light on his face
was never dim.

Sometimes in an audience a speaker will notice one face
particularly because of its shining sympathy—always such a face
is of untold help to the preacher. Old Big was like that—a tall,
lean old man with a countenance of kindly wrinkles. He was
delighted with the music and kept pressing forward until he
was next to the organ and finally sat down on the same box
as a prodigal boy. A favourite hymn was chosen and Old Big
knew every word by heart. How his face glowed as he sang—

> I shall know Him, I shall know Him,
> When redeemed by His side I shall stand;
> I shall know Him, I shall know Him
> By the print of the nails in His hand.

There he sat with such a light on his face, seemingly unconscious that beside him was Prodigal, the boy who had been at fault
with his daughter. When the beautiful song was ended and the
voices had dropped into silence, I could not resist leaning across
the organ and pointing a finger right at Prodigal. "When *we*
see the Lord, we shall be ever so pleased, but when *you* see Him
you are going to be terribly afraid!" I said. And while his startled
eyes held mine I reminded him of the sin which stood between
him and God—and his head hung down like a shot.

There is a word of St. Augustine's which I like; to me it is
the only answer to Peter's, "*To whom, Lord, shall we go?*" He says,
"And he who loveth Thee . . . goeth . . . but from Thee well-
pleased to Thee displeased."

Old Big was facing his Lord well-pleased, and his wrinkled
countenance was one glow of beatific joy; but Prodigal was
facing the same Lord displeased, and his head hung so low you
could not see his face.

Sunday in Lisuland was a different day from all the rest of the
week. First of all there was a before-breakfast service for just our

own village, when from up above us and down below us our neighbours gathered together at the Lord's feet for an hour or so. Then followed breakfast and after a while folks from the other villages began to gather. To right and left thin brown trails crawled up the mountain's giant sides, and gradually over them came, trickling single file, village after village of worshippers who approached like tiny armies of coloured ants. Immediately on arrival most of them ran into House of Grace to shake hands with Ma-Pa and Ma-Ma—and it used to be to hear the victrola, but it was broken later. Almost always one of the first of these eager greetings was from dear Old Big, whose village is near, just down by the Salween bank. I always looked forward to his beaming smile and loving handshake. About sixty-five years old, his kindly face was a token of "the adding up of days in which good work is done." Some others of the Lisu saints may have given us heartache or worry from time to time, but never Old Big. Behind him came his sweet, happy-faced wife. Lisu couples if they love each other never show it in public. True, the happy newlyweds sometimes cannot help letting out a beam or two, but it is not considered good form. This old couple were the exception, however, and it was lovely to watch the simple pleasure they took in each other's company. Charles named them Zacharias and Elizabeth in these latter years, for they truly "walked blameless." They were not rich, but so often, in shaking hands, an egg or two or some other like gift, was slipped quietly to their missionaries. The first-ripe corn each year was faithfully brought to us, and if they killed a pig, a bit of the pork would be sent up the hill as a gift to Ma-Pa and Ma-Ma, or to any of our missionary guests.

I still chuckle over the recollection of a visit we had some years ago from the British Consul of those parts. A very tall, dignified gentleman with a monocle, he was. Old Big heard that a white man visitor had come to House of Grace, and supposing, of course, that it must be another new Ma-Pa, and having just killed a pig, he trotted up the hill to present the gift himself. I was not aware of it when he walked in, until I suddenly heard him saying in Lisu—which His Britannic Majesty's Consul did not understand, of course—"Ma-Pa,

we're so glad you've come. I've brought you a bit of pork!"
I turned around to see my elegant guest adjusting his monocle downward toward a strip of greasy pork tied in the middle with a straw for carrying, which was being confidently held out toward him with the left hand while Old Big's right was pushed forward for the expected handshake. I took in the situation in a second, and could have hugged the dear kindly old saint—but I feared the Consul felt otherwise! I quickly explained the situation —in English!—and my guest proved to be a good sport, for he shook hands with Old Big while I rescued the pork and delivered it to the care of his valet!

Because of its connection with Old Big, let me quote here from the circular which told of that Consular visit:

May 27, 1941.

"Oh, Ma-Ma, look at all the pack horses coming up the ridge! *A-bo*, they are still coming; I've never seen such a caravan in these parts. What can they be hunting?" This question took me running to the window, and as I watched and wondered I suddenly remembered a letter received the month before, telling of a proposed journey of the Tengyueh British Consul up the Salween canyon.

"The English Consul!" I exclaimed. "Whatever shall I do? How can we entertain a Consul in this bamboo shanty? Oh, John-n-n!" But the great gentleman was already coming over the trail, and John, having no time to give advice, ran out to receive him.

He proved to be a six-foot, well-built Englishman—a real gentleman. He was not a Christian, but was not a hypocrite either. He made no pretence about his standing, but said that he respected Christianity and, if anything, had a leaning toward Roman Catholicism, "because of its beautiful ritual." He was really very enjoyable and endured us for two nights and a day with all the courtesy and niceness one could wish. After he left he sent us a letter which I copy below. The "Ma" and "Ho" whom he mentions are two Lisu Christians he hired as guides from here on. This is his letter:

H.B.M. Consulate,
Tengyueh, Camp Chihzelo.

DEAR MRS. KUHN:
In choosing paper to use to write and thank you very much for your kindness and hospitality to me at Maliping (Oak Flat), I have been at pains to choose a large sheet which may leave some clean paper for your students.

Officially I am glad to have had the opportunity of meeting you; and privately it was a pleasure. I very much enjoyed my halt at Maliping [*isn't he a good sport?*] and the rest refreshed me much.

Ma-fu-yi and his friend were of the greatest help to me, and the journey, though certainly arduous, was very enjoyable. The mules made it all right, with only two minor accidents, but after the first accident . . . the head muleteer became frightened and hired carriers for most of the loads.

The scenery was certainly impressive; but I was equally impressed with the work that you and your colleagues have done in this part of the world. At one time travel along this route was a matter of some danger; but now wherever I went I was received with friendliness and courtesy. Even though I was obviously no missionary (I use tobacco a lot) people seemed to take great pleasure in shaking me by the hand and wishing me "*hwa-hwa.*" There appeared a very real sense of companionship when Ma and Ho met other Christians and shook them by the hand. At An-a-ma-po [one of the newly turned villages this year] many of the locals produced well-thumbed hymn-books from their bags and started shouting them at me, and at night I went to sleep to the sound of hymn-singing from the local chapel. [But I must be frank and say that the hymn tunes were neither so musical, beautiful or suitable to the mountains as the wilder Lisu songs.] And while halting before starting to climb up to Bya-lo-shih one of the coolies hired by the muleteers produced a *Lisu Hymn-book and Catechism* and a simple Chinese religious work from his pack and passed the time by reading to me. It was certainly most impressive.

Yours most gratefully and sincerely,

M. L. GILLETT

The mention of the large sheet of writing paper is in laughing reference to a remark of mine that we use the blank backs of all letters not private (including his!) for scribbling paper for our R.S.B.S. students who are too poor to afford much writing paper.

The account of the hired Lisu at Bya-lo-shih especially thrilled me as he must have been one of the small group there, which group first found Christ by Luke's testimony that night in the rice-field as we went up to Luda. "Ye know not whether shall prosper, this or that." Only one believed then, but others have since, though teachers seldom get to that part, it is so far away.

Old Big did not escape from the Sharp Wind of the Munition of Rocks. At the very outset of his Christian life he was faced with the problem of the two wives he had taken as a heathen. That is a very worrisome Wind: it blows up heated discussions with relatives-in-law, and Old Big might not resort now to his former solace of an opium pipe or drink of wine, to help endure taunting words. But somehow he was led to a solution, and somehow given strength to endure. The wife that did not love the Lord, was put away, and eventually married someone else. Safely out of that spiritual monsoon it would not be long before others blew up. Sometimes inclement weather would destroy much of their crop, their year's food; once it was a nephew hired to help him, but misbehaving. "If I dismiss him, Ma-Ma, his parents will make it hot for me. But"—and I remember how his face set—"the most important thing is *eternal life.*" He felt that God required him to rule his house after a godly manner and, Wind or no Wind, he did.

In 1943 we told of Old Big's death from a fever:

Yesterday as I took the weeping widow in my arms to comfort her, and tried to tell her how that dear, good, shining face was worshipping in heaven, this his first Sunday there, she whispered to me, "Yes, but Ma-Ma, I won't be able to see his face in chapel." And in my heart I had to add, "And so say we all." Too old to learn to read, he always sat up close to the front and with radiant countenance did his best to memorize hymns, texts and sermon outline, so that I had long regarded him as my special Sunday joy. During the week he held services in his own home for his neighbours and preached and sang from memory.

"Pebbles in a brook polish one another"—thank God for the pebbles of His Lisu church.

The Infant Brigade—and a Goatherd in Particular

"Ma-Ma! The new goatherd has come!"

"Oh, all right, Homay, I'll eat supper with you all, seeing I'm alone to-night. I'll see him then. Show him his room and make him comfortable."

A new servant always meant a girding up of one's loins to attack the disagreeable. Leila Cooke once described breaking in a new cook, in words something like this: "You must teach him not to throw egg-shells behind the stove, that the sweepings of the kitchen floor will be discovered if pushed behind the door, not to throw dirty dishwater on the floor, and if he gets jam on his fingers not wipe it off on the wall." Every word of it is true. People at home have servants, too: the bottle of milk that arrives on your doorstep, pasteurized and ready to drink; the gas which comes when you turn on the jet of your cook-stove; the water in your faucets and the electric light button on your wall. In Lisuland, water has to be carried up several hundred feet of mountain on a human back, usually. Food grains must be pounded out and husked by primitive foot-mills. Salt and sugar arrive in stone-like lumps and must be granulated by hand, and so on. House-helpers are indispensable, but not always agreeable. I have always tried to receive these trials in the form of servants, however, as an answer to the old question, *What is that in thine hand?*—in other words, as human souls to influence for Christ. *I have not always been successful.* Moreover, as pointed out before, when we do meet with success, they get called into the preaching ministry and we may not but relinquish them, and start in with a raw one, probably not nearly so easy to deal with. Goatherds are not a very close contact, however, and at supper-time I was introduced.

I beheld a little fellow (looked like nine years old, but they said he was seventeen!) seated on his haunches, with his head lowered and staring at me with the glare of a little wild animal. I did not feel comfortable.

"All right, I said, as pleasantly as I could, after we had shaken hands, "let's eat. Perhaps the new goatherd will ask the blessing?"

"Nope. Won't. Can't."

I was astounded! What a beginning! There he squatted, still staring at me, this time pugnaciously, a sort of hit-me-and-I'll bite-you look on his face. I turned to Homay. The church found servants for us usually, and only those who were Christians were allowed to enter our employ.

"Isn't he a believer?" I asked.

"Yes, Ma-Ma, though not baptized yet." She was doing her best to be sympathetic, but the corners of her mouth were curling with the desire to laugh. "He can't read or write."

"But *every* Christian knows how to pray!" I continued, dissatisfied. Then, catching the look on her face—she was ever a lover of peace—"All right, I'll pray then," I agreed, and the meal started in silence.

Diminutive in size, but not at all in thoughts of his own importance, Goatherd seemed to think that he must take care that no one took advantage of him. He used to glare at me, and snap back his answers just as viciously as a little chipmunk, so I mentally labelled him that! He did not milk any more faithfully than he pleased, either. One morning we would get a quart of milk, the next perhaps a little over a cupful—but woe betide me if I tried to point out that goats don't go dry that fast! Many times we would have dismissed him for cheekiness if it had not been that he was the only son of a widow. She was blind and needed part of his wages. So we struggled on.

A year later I decided that I would not have an eighteen year-old in my house who could not read! Goatherd *must learn*, so at evening I called him in, told him nicely that it was good to know how to read God's Word for himself and that I meant to teach him. But he made not the least effort to learn. His body was there, for he came each night *if called*, but that was all. An evening is difficult for a missionary to spare, and I seemed to be wasting it all. I was almost in despair. Then the Luda trip, just narrated in Chapter Nine, took us from home for three months and Victor Christianson took over the teaching of Goatherd.

The next March, when we returned to Oak Flat, Mr. Christianson said, "Goatherd can read now, and is learning to sing! I've named him Amos! You'd be surprised what a nice singing voice he has!" This was as good as it was astounding. I wonder if the reason was not much due to the fact that the previous summer, when Goatherd had been very ill with typhus fever, Mr. Christianson had nursed him as kindly and tenderly as if he had been a dear chum, instead of an unsatisfactory servant. Now, if this were an ordinary story, I would tell you that from now on, *Love* did its work and the chipmunk became a sweet saint. But these are not made-up stories. The truth is, that although Amos "allowed" us to educate him, he still often played when he should have worked (one evening he had to report *four* kids eaten by panthers, only the little heads left,

o

while he had been playing) and still was saucy when it pleased him—to me at any rate. Now I will quote from letters of April, 1940.

HEAT MISTS

Heat mists come unannounced, veil all the lovely familiar mountain forms and take the colour out of life, and they are a parable, for there are times in human days when happiness seems to depart and just the drab and commonplace are left. I knew I was in for one such again, as I stood on the upper road and watched the long beloved line wend its way on to Sunset Ridge and drop out of sight over its farther edge: John, Lucius, Cath and Victor Christianson, and a wriggly tail of carriers. Without the loved faces for over six weeks what a desolate stretch lay ahead. John and Lucius were going to Chinaland because John's new appointment as superintendent of the China Inland Mission work in West Yunnan made a hurried survey necessary. Cath Christ-ianson was going out for medical advice and Victor to hold meetings at Hollow Tree District. There was no reason for me to go, and every reason for one of us to remain, so here I was. Duty with the sparkle of companionship is a happy thing, but alone with more or less unfamiliar faces (for Homay and Dorcas had left us and Job and party were not yet back) it looked very drab.

At evening, I thought, there would be inspiration as usual at Sunset Ridge, but for the first time the Ridge failed me, for heat mists had truly and physically come and filled up all the canyons and covered with a grey dull film every outline of beauty which would please one's soul. No, no comfort anywhere *without*, but within? No Heat Mists can blur out Him who is our fountain within, and as perhaps some of you are facing a drab period when all the colour has seemed to depart from life I would tell you how He comforted me, for He has given peace and quiet happiness.

I have been through Heat Mists before, and I know that there are three things I must do. First, remember that this has come only *to pass*. How often have I thanked Dr. Page for that story of his; there will be some of you who have not heard it, so here it is. An idiot boy was seeking for guidance in the old magic way of shutting your eyes, opening the Bible and diving your finger on to a spot at random. He had done it three times in different places and each time the book and finger came to "and it came to pass that . . ." He pondered anxiously, then the light broke. "Why, of course," he said to himself, "this trouble came *to pass* not to stay." So the first thing is to remember that Heat Mist days are not eternal—they have just come to pass, that is all.

Secondly, be sure that they are an opportunity for more abundant fruitfulness. That is always their purpose. It was the ugly confinement of prison which brought Luke's Gospel, Paul's prison Epistles, Bunyan's *Pilgrim's Progress*, and Rutherford's undying letters into being.

Thirdly, tears or no tears, just go on and open your eyes to see God's edelweiss. That is what Miss Carmichael calls the *little* happy things sent to cheer the greyness of the Heat Mist days, as the edelweiss cheers the mountain-climber at a bleak, hard place. "The bright flowers of the edelweiss waiting to be gathered among the rough rocks of difficult circumstances—and they always find, I think, that far more than the toils of the climb, they remember the places where they gathered the edelweiss of God."

On the very first day I found an edelweiss. His name is Joe (I refuse to speak of him as Joseph; he has not attained unto that yet). He is one of the two new servants that replaced Homay and Dorcas, and the breaking-in of Joe into an American cook was one of the Heat Mists which had confronted me. I suppose every missionary woman dreads the hour-by-hour trial of training a new, raw servant.

Joe is a little old man in a nineteen-year-old skin. In other words, dignity, solemn dignity, under a pimply skin, small eyes that never look straight at you—for that would not be proper; bristly hair that by no amount of water and plastering can be made to lie flat, but with an honest heart which makes up for all. Joe *wants* to do well. The new girl doesn't; she merely hopes to hold her job. When Joe breaks a dish he is flabbergasted. When the girl does, she tells you about it with a careless laugh and if you don't show equal lightness she sulks. We prefer them to be flabbergasted.

Well, that first day at noon, when I was trying to drown loneliness by hard work on the Rainy Season Bible School preparations, Joe came solemnly into my room with an air of gravity and mystery which made my heart sink, wondering, *What has happened now?* Coming up close, he cast his eyes to the northeast corner of the ceiling and said in a low tone of confidentiality, "Just set the table for one, eh?" Blessed aspirant to butlership—if I had been a heathen I would have thrown my book at him for reminding me of what I was trying so hard to forget, but being a Christian and his "Ma-Ma" I got rid of him as quickly as possible and then sat back and laughed. Joe expands to his fullest stretch beneath the glory of being the missionary's cook. You should see the swell of his chest as he sets the table in the presence of his admiring fellow villagers, who know nothing of the mysteries of tablecloths and cutlery! Yes, quite unconsciously, Joe helped me over a hard place, and I am grateful for him.

Passionate devotion to the things which are vital delivered Paul from bitterness of soul, from anger and ill will. Disappointments and hardships . . . may be used for the perfecting of character and for the glory of Christ.—C. R. Erdman.

The above thought was a blessing to me; truly turning to things which are vital clears up self-pity and puts the pep back into life. I decided to teach a class in the evenings, calling in the servants as a start. They assembled, and on looking them over I named them the Infant Brigade, for they are all just beginners. They do not look particularly promising. Joe was one of the first to come in. He sucked in his breath noisily and exclaimed with a happy little laugh, "This is unthinkable"— meaning perhaps, that now the dignity of Bible student, as well as of missionary cook, was about to descend upon his already burdened shoulders.

The laundress and house-cleaner is the girl mentioned above. Our beloved Homay found that she could not take care of her baby and look after us too, so she withdrew from our home, but not from our hearts. Gruff-Growl's daughter delightedly promised to take her place, but she has proved to be not strictly honest and unless the Lord changes her heart she will have to be dismissed. She seems to like to join the evening classes, however, and of course is welcome.

Next are Mule-Boy and Amos. (It costs a great deal less to keep goats and a herd than to buy canned milk.) Mule-Boy is Simon's younger brother with the family hot temper, and added to it a graceless tongue which has nearly cost him dismissal more than once. In fact, the reason he still is here is only the compassion of Christ. During our visit to Luda one day I found a Lisu Gospel in a wrong place. Opening it to find the owner I saw written inside in ill-spelled scrawl, "My beloved Testament." Mule-Boy had won it as a prize at the Christmas games, and has taken to Bible study since then. This year he can both read and sing, and even applied for baptism! Not at all graciously, but with obvious interest, Amos is now a member of the Infant Brigade.

My big edelweiss of these weeks has undoubtedly been Yongpeh-Peter. As you know, Yongpeh-Peter and Yongpeh-John, converts of only a year, were sent here to learn the doctrine in hopes that they will return as evangelists to their own people so that the China Inland Mission can gradually withdraw from those parts. But both boys know how to burn charcoal, so in the day time they burn for us (Mule-Boy is kept at home to learn from them, with an eye to the future) and at night I teach them. Peter is big, twenty-five years old, plain-faced and very quiet in voice and manner. He does not impress you at all, until some day you are in a difficulty and a gentle voice beside you says, "I'll attend to that for you, Ma-Ma," and in a twinkling and without fuss or words your problem is shouldered and, in course of time, satisfactorily solved.

Others beside myself are beginning to see this. Joe runs to Peter now, when he finds it hard to decipher his growing cook-book. One morning early, while still at my devotions, I heard the shanty door swing open and two come running breathlessly in. Peter's feet arrived at my bed-room door and Joe's nose was pressed against the bamboo matting wall. A serious problem was shaking the little cook's universe. "Ma-Ma!" came his voice through the matting, "what and where is *maple flavour-ing?*"

"It's in the square bottle."

Simultaneously from the door and wall came a sigh of relief. "Oh, the *square* bottle!" and forthwith they turned and rushed out again. Who got to the square bottle first I do not know, but I'm sure Peter likes to be consulted. He is better with his hands than his brain. When it comes to study, Yongpeh-John is much more showy, but I praise the Lord for Peter. He was once married, but four years ago a band of Wild Lolo carried off his beautiful young wife and she has never been heard of since.

Yongpeh-John, fat, round, and pleasant, is the last member of the Infant Brigade. As he has but lately joined us I do not know him very well. Can you see these six, gathered around our table at evening time, making most awful noises in their effort to learn a new hymn; struggling laboriously with the New Testament letters, and after reading, trying to bend unwieldy minds to the task of getting *thought* out of those symbols as well as words? Baby lessons these, but these are foundation days. This is the kind of work that the Ma-pa-ra must do in the villages as new believers are brought in. Joe—girl—Mule-Boy—Amos—Peter—John—not very wonderful material, but Teacher Job began as Mr. and Mrs. Cooke's goatherd. At any rate, even though they are not lovely, shall we not take the crude new believers of His church into our hearts and prayers also?

Moses' mother made an ark of bulrushes that death might not swallow her child. Who thought that the small babe would one day *shake Egypt?*
—From Bishop Taylor Smith's Bible.

If we but notice God's edelweiss He will send us more. Spoiled children are those who will not allow you to console them. You will remember that all those winter months, our leading Ma-pa-ra had been away down south. The day they were expected back they did not arrive, although we had built a flower arch of welcome for them and put wild rhododendrons in their rooms. The next night it was raining and as the Infant Brigade was in the midst of preliminary acrobatics on the phonetic scale we heard a gunshot. Immediately we were all out of the room and into the dark and rain as if *we* were the bullets. I called out to Joe, "You stay and mind the house" (for a thief had entered a few nights before), which, poor fellow, checked his speed and made him turn back in groaning obedience. Pushing up to the trail I could just discern other villagers emerging from their huts. A white horse was coming with someone leading it—Job! Wasn't it like him to arrive first and all alone. Oh, how good to greet again those you love!

I have told about that arrival in Homay's story. The Infant Brigade could enjoy such evenings. Slipping into the cosy circle around the fire in Luke's hut, or our own servant's shanty, they could listen while these more mature Christians talked. Very often the talk was just good-humoured storytelling of their trips and experiences, with lots of laughter interspersed. Even a small, illiterate "chipmunk" like Amos could not help but be a bit broadened by such contacts.

Amos was not accepted for baptism that year, however, as his work was so unsatisfactory. It was pointed out to him that if he really believed in his heart he was saved *then*, but that *new life* always manifests itself sooner or later, and that for the sake of those watching the church, we felt that we wanted to delay his baptism until his life more nearly matched his profession.

At the end of one month of careless work, after giving the wages to each servant I went to my room, but soon was surprised at the appearance of Amos who, with a crimson face, held out his hand to give me back his money.

"I don't want it, Ma-Ma," he said with much embarrassment. "I don't deserve it." I nearly fell over with the shock. It was the first sign of a conscience he had ever shown. Trying quickly to seize such a grand opportunity, I pressed the wages back on him, and gave him a talk on it being required in stewards that a man be found faithful, and told him that mere money will not repay the cost of faithless service.

Amos was meeker and nicer for quite a few weeks after that but gradually the old spunkiness and carelessness would return. Nevertheless, his books became very precious to the laddie; he began to take them out to the herding with him, and studied constantly. Gradually too, he began to pray in public, and a year or two later, Luke passed him for baptism.

It was in 1942, I think, that Amos decided to leave us. By that time he had saved enough money from his wages to buy a small farm and set up for himself. His blind mother and sister also lived with him and I was glad to see him ambitious to become something. I knew that he would have to work far harder on the farm than he did for us, and probably make less money, but he would be growing into a useful member of the community, so we gave him our blessing, and he left us.

Little goatherd! He had developed one of the truest and sweetest tenor voices in the whole church. May be when I get to heaven I shall see my once vicious little Chipmunk, with transformed, radiant, face, glorifying God among the choristers there.

ROMEO AND JULIET

It was in 1939, while visiting villages on the west bank of the Salween, that we came to one called Runaway Horse Ascent. In the little chapel there we were attracted to a sweet young girl, obviously the most spiritually minded among the women. On inquiry we were told that she was going through a trial. One of the young men had proposed to her and she wished to accept him, but there was an ancient feud between their families, and the parents of each side bitterly refused to let the marriage take place.

"Then we must call them Romeo and Juliet!" I laughingly said, and we henceforth referred to them by those names.

Their love had persisted, and their parents' bitterness had also persisted, but Juliet said she would say *yes* to no one but Romeo. I turned to take a good look at this lad who had won such a loyalty of affection. He was not attractive. True, there was an honesty and earnestness in his eyes and a strength in the ruggedness of his face, but there was also an ugly tubercular gland on his neck.

Our first contact with Romeo left an impression on us that he was but one among many. We saw that he was manly and honest but so were (and are) many of his neighbours. One does not notice a pebble much at first.

A year passed; that winter we had spent at Village of the Three Clans, and on our way back to Oak Flat, an accident occurred which drew Romeo to our attention. Again it involved a horse-riding escapade, but not with trusty old Jasper. In descending the canyon from Three Clans, we had met with a raging stream whose bridge was broken. Jasper and Jessie could not ford such a torrent, nor could they be expected to cross on the one or two wobbling planks which were left, and over which we ourselves had to cross, so from there on we all had to walk. After many miles, at noon the next day, we met Romeo's uncle, who pressed us to stay at his village that night.

"Only if you will get a horse for Ma-Ma to ride up the hill," said our Lisu. "She's tired walking; you should not ask her to climb to your house." Thereupon the old man gave up his animal to me, but it was much smaller than Jasper. Halfway up the slope it suddenly jerked back, missed its footing, and fell over backwards with me still in the saddle. My head just missed striking a sharp rock, but my ankle was badly sprained and I had to be carried into Romeo's little shanty. There I was introduced to his sister, a sweet-faced girl about twenty years old, who was full of sympathy for me. She gave me the best bed they had, and set in to cook something for me to eat. The house was a model of neatness and cleanliness.

"I'm awfully sorry Ma-Ma's foot hurts so," she said as she worked, "but it is all in the Cross, isn't it? There must be suffering if there is to be blessing. And none of ours is to be compared to what our Lord went through for us."

I turned and looked at her. She was talking as naturally as any other Lisu lassie would have about where she found her firewood, but her thoughts were those of a mature Christian! I have never met a Lisu girl of her youth who was so acquainted with the deeper things of God! In silent amazement, for she talked on as she worked, I got my foot into an easier position, then said, "Will you tell me, little girl, how you became a Christian?" Her answer ran like this:

"It was about six years ago when Teacher Andrew was in these parts. Brother [Romeo] and I both decided at the same time to leave devil worship and to trust God. But father bitterly

opposed us; he said he would take away our share of his land
when we refused to worship the demons and went on praying
and studying the Books, so he thrust both Brother and me out
of his house. Mother was dead, but uncle, here, had turned
Christian and he said he would let us live on his land if we
would help him in his farm work until we could clear a farm
for ourselves. We had to work hard"—her hands were calloused
and rough—"but oh, we were free to worship God, and Jesus
has been so precious to us! We've been very happy in this little
house, and when Father married again, we moved over here.
Of course we go over and help him now and again, when his
farm work is heavy, but we come back here to live. We have
peace here." She lifted such a bright, serene face to mine, that
I loved her on the spot. Romeo was away from home. He had
heard of the missionary hospital in Burma where Thomas had
been helped, and where they did not ask for fees from Christian
Lisu, so he had taken all the savings of his and his sister's (gladly
given) to pay his road expenses and had gone off to see if they
could heal his tubercular glands.

The next morning, when it was time to leave, I found that
Romeo's sister was one of our porters. "Oh, it's all right, Ma-
Ma," she said brightly. "I am accustomed to carry heavier loads
than this, and the village men are not free to go to-day."

When we finally parted, I had a picture on my heart of a
clean young soul, determined to follow her Lord wholly no
matter what the suffering. Why had not someone told me there
was such a girl in those parts? Were there many more like her
that I had never heard of? Was her brother, Romeo, as fine as
she? "Yes," said the Lisu; "the two of them are just the same:
They are good and earnest."

The next winter we took our trip to Stockade Hill and the
south. I believe it was on the way down that we met Romeo
on the road, coming home, fully healed. A broad, open-faced
young fellow, we just sensed trustworthiness, and manliness, as
we looked at him.

"No; they did not charge me a cent," he answered. "They even
paid me, because I worked for them carrying water for the hospital.... Yes, thank God, the gland is healed. Go in peace, Ma-Ma!"

We had to part, he going north and we to the south. I thought pleasantly of the joy of the little sister waiting to welcome him back, and of sweet Juliet's shy pleasure that her one-and-only was now free from the disagreeable sore on his neck. They would see one another in chapel, and sometimes on the mountain trails, perhaps. Then our own journey commanded our attention.

Months passed. A year or so passed. We were back at Oak Flat discussing the possibility of a girls' Bible school. "There is one girl I want to have—Romeo's sister," I said to the Lisu teacher conversing with me.

"Oh, Ma-Ma, don't you know?" he said, amazed at my ignorance. "She is dead! When Romeo got home from the hospital she was ill with a fever, and she never recovered."

"Oh," I cried, sitting back, heart-broken, "why didn't someone tell me?"

There was silence. The Lisu were puzzled at my interest. There are hundreds of girls in the Lisu church; some die every year. One cannot report everything. These white people take the strangest fancies! Romeo's sister was a good girl, but not very able at singing or writing—big things in the Lisu man's eyes. Why be so interested in *her?*

But Ma-Ma was obviously interested in that family, so they replied: "Perhaps you don't know, Ma-Ma, that Juliet is dead, too? She died before Romeo's sister did. Lots of people died from that epidemic of typhus."

Oh, poor Romeo! I was speechless. *Lest I should have sorrow upon sorrow*—the words pressed themselves in upon my numbed feelings. By this time my thoughts had stirred the group around me and all were quiet, thinking of the tragic grief of one young life—of the Bitter Wind that had blown upon one small Nest.

"How is Romeo? If I had only known, I think I would have tried to go and see him," I said. He lives across the river and about two days' journey from House of Grace, which is a long way if there is not an important reason for going.

"Oh, he's all right. He's living alone in their little hut. He does not complain, and he goes to church regularly. But his neck has started to suppurate again. It certainly is hard for him." Again a silence. "I think he's going to try to come to R.S.B.S ," said one. From then on, Romeo was definitely on my daily prayer list.

And in April, 1943, he came. His tubercular glands had inflamed, and as that disease is infectious, and the Lisu sense this and fear it, it was arranged that Romeo sleep alone and cook his own food separately. It was a joy to teach him, and his mature, experienced mind simply licked up the truths of the Word. That year we had tried splitting up the R.S.B.S. into three periods of one month each, so in August he promised to return and join us again. After all had dispersed to their homes, at the end of the April study, word gradually filtered through to us that Romeo had begun teaching his fellow villagers every night, and that they had built a little mud chapel.

August saw Romeo gather with us once more for further study, and during those few weeks God gave us a revival such as we had seldom experienced. Our little son, Daniel Kreadman, was born on August 1, so I was not able to teach that session, but the students would often come after classes and talk with me. When they spent one whole night in prayer, I was awake most of the time and with them, of course, in spirit. By the time the school closed I was up and around, and one day I had a talk with Romeo alone.

Of course he had been much on my heart. By that time our own China Inland Mission Hospital at Tali had been opened, so I wrote to them and told them of Romeo, and asked if they would take him in and treat him free of charge, in exchange for simple duties like carrying water. Their affirmative answer had just come, so with much joy I told Romeo of the new opportunity for healing.

"Thank you, Ma-Ma," he said, but without display of any great thrill. He hesitated a moment, then said slowly, "I don't think I will go, thank you."

"But, Romeo, it would mean healing for you!" His noble face was lifted up and had a far-away look in his eyes. Quietly he said, "I do not despise their kindness, nor yours, Ma-Ma. Please thank them for me. But it is this way. I believe this sickness of mine is aggravated by lack of nourishing foods, such as you white people can get. As long as I stayed near a hospital it would be better. I came home to my native diet and the old trouble came back again. So if I want to stay healed, I must stay all my life near a hospital."

Here his eyes came back from the far distance and looked straight at me. "Ma-Ma, it was good for my body, being in the Burma hospital, *but it was not good for my soul!*"

"I know. I know," I said sadly. I had been told that the native nurses there had tempted him constantly.

"And where in Chinaland would I get *food for my soul* like we have been having these past few weeks?"—and his arm pointed out to the little Bible School House up the hill from us. "No, Ma-Ma. Many thanks to them, but I will just stay here—" his eyes flooded with tears, but on his face there was a light I have never forgotten. "Yea, though my life be now at a point to be shed as wine over the burnt sacrifice—still I rejoice" (*Phil. ii. 17; Arthur Way*).

I knew he meant to give what remained of his life to the service of God, and I stood silent, thrilled, yet with tears.

His disease was too dreaded by the Lisu to admit of a travelling ministry among them. He would not have been welcome in many homes, so he specialized on his own village. In the daytime he worked his little farm as he had strength; in the evening he taught all who would come. His village, and more especially the Village-of-Wheat-Level above it, had been notoriously "rotten" (to use the Lisu word). Nazareth never had a more hopeless reputation. "Can any good come out of Wheat Level?" has been the cry, with tears, from its Lisu pastor's heart. But as Romeo taught a wonderful little group began to collect around him. A young girl whom we named Leah-the-second came two years in succession to our Girls' Bible School, and fine young boys came from Romeo's group to our Boys' Bible School.

Now, if I were a fiction-writer I would stop there. I do not fear the truth myself. I know the God behind it. But when God's providences take an unexpected turn, shallow thinkers make shallow and dishonouring remarks. One would expect Romeo's offering to have been "crowned with success." But God does not always deal so with His loved children. In His Word, one of the pictures which has so deeply moved me is that of Paul at the end of his course, aged, alone, in prison, writing his very last letter to far-away Timothy. He, earth's noblest, standing at the judgment seat of earth's vilest (Nero); and not only that inexplicable paradox, but the saint in his old age, after a life simply poured out for Christ, has to write, "This thou knowest, that all they which are in Asia be turned away from me" (2 Tim. i. 15). The work of his lifetime, apparently, lost. And also "at my first answer no man stood with me, but all forsook me." Desertion, seeming failure, and the rattle of Nero's chain on his wrist. That is the way Paul's life ended to the shallow onlooker. Time has proved that what *seemed* like an ill-reward, has really been a wonderful reward. No one doubts now that Paul's reckless giving to his Lord was recompensed, and neither did he doubt, even under those seemingly contradictory circumstances. "Notwithstanding the Lord stood by me," he wrote on. "I have . . . fought a *good* fight . . . henceforth there is laid up for me a crown." God's *near ones* know His faithfulness.

As we were packing up to come home on furlough, a letter arrived from Romeo. It stated tersely that Leah-the-second and A-fuh (one of the boys) had sinned. It was a heartaching disappointment, but my biggest ache was for Romeo himself. He had so hoped to be a fruitful servant to his Lord. I quickly wrote back a little note of comfort. He answered with a word message which thanked us for our love, and said that he was getting weaker physically, but would go on teaching. We left the canyon, and a few months later Romeo's trials were ended for ever.

Wait for the light and it will surely come; for even if our Heavenly Father should, in our last hours, *put us to bed in the dark*, we shall find it morning when we awake.—*Spurgeon.*

Morning. And *Jesus*! . . *Juliet*! . . . Sister! "Jes' a little pebble." . . . Will his Lord say that?

THE MISSING LINK

Two days' journey to the north of Romeo's little home, the mountain ravines become truly abysmal. The Lisu there are unspeakably degraded. The strength of Satan seems unconquerable. That territory we call The Heathen Patch because it is a patch of heathenism between two areas which have largely turned Christian. For many years evangelists and prayer-partners have thrown their labours and prayers against it, only to be seemingly thrown back. Of late years the edges have started to crumble very slightly.

One day in 1943 I was handed a letter from the young evangelist in charge of that district. "Ma-Ma," he wrote, "one of the converts up here is coming to study at the April Bible School session. His name is Chi-lee. Pray for him."

That school was Romeo's first school with us, too. But of all the students expected, I was most interested in seeing our first scholar from The Heathen Patch. On assembling day his teacher proudly brought him up to shake hands. I think I must let the circular of that month describe him.

Then from farther in the deep ravines comes Chi-lee. I wonder what you would think of him? Transplanted just as he is into your parlour, you would doubtless come to the conclusion that the Missing Link had at last been found! A mop of coarse black hair chopped off without regard to order, low brow, small eyes, shapeless wide-spreading nose, protuberant jaw, dirty white garments like potato sacking, and forever scratching himself hither and yon—not fleas this time, but the *itch*.

"Can he read?" I asked his teacher after shaking hands. (Wouldn't it be awful if a *missionary* were the one to find the Missing Link!) "Yes, read and write," answered his sponsor proudly. Well, that was hopeful. Evolution monkeys can't do that.

I was preparing to teach Peter that year, and as we had a staff of only three, we could not grade the school. When I stood up before them, there was Luke's intelligent face, and right beside him the Missing Link, blinking his small eyes at me hopefully. I had a sinking feeling for a moment. Then inwardly I thought, *Well, I cannot hold up the whole class for the sake of one or two. I'll just have to go ahead, and the dear Link will have to lope along after us as best he can.*

Chi-lee listened well, but when it came to examinations he did not get a pass. But what did *that* matter? He was the first student from The Heathen Patch, and after a decent haircut, a lesson in washing his clothes, and sulphur ointment to conquer the Unmentionable, he really looked amazingly different. That was quite satisfactory progress for just one month's study! He himself was full of joy, and testified to blessing, so we parted happily.

"Be sure you come again and study in August, Chi-lee!" we called out.

"I sure will, Ma-Pa, Ma-Ma; pray for me! Stay behind prayerfully!" and he and his party were over the hilltop and out of sight.

There is no mail in the canyon. Letters do not come unless someone is coming on business, and can take them. Two months passed before I got a letter from that district. It was from his Lisu teacher and announced, "Chi-lee has gone back to God," the Lisu expression for *dead*. I could not believe my eyes. Then earnest investigation discovered this.

On return to his home, Chi-lee had gathered together the young people of his village, and started to teach them what he himself had learned. The heathen were furious.

"It isn't enough that you yourself go to the White Man, and learn this doctrine that makes our demons angry at us," they railed, "but you must bring it back, and start teaching it here! Stop, or we'll kill you!"

But Chi-lee went on teaching. Then one day his house was burned to the ground; he lost simply everything. His father, afraid, refused him shelter, so he was driven into the wild jungle to live under a shelter of boughs and branches which he roughly put together. From there he wrote me of his trial, but the letter did not reach me until it was too late. The handwriting was so neat I could hardly believe he had written it himself, but his teacher said he had. The Lisu evangelist was far away at the time. Chi-lee's letter expressed no regret that his witness had cost him so much—he just stated the above facts and asked us to pray for him. But before his plea reached us, he had died from the malignant malarial mosquitoes lurking in the long grasses of the wild mountainside.

Chi-lee was fruit from our Heathen Patch territory. But there are many more great areas, and there are still other whole tribes which have never yet heard of the gospel of the grace of God. I know of one area of the Lisu tribe, about two weeks' journey from our Lisu, where live thousands of people. Some of them heard this wonderful doctrine was being preached out in Chinaland, and a little party made the trip of two or three days' journey to that missionary lady and asked her to come to tell them also. *That was ten years ago.* Ever since then, that lady (now over sixty years of age) has been trying to find someone to go to those Lisu, and up to this date no missionary has ever been resident among them. (Several made trips at various times, and report that the district truly is there and the Lisu number thousands.)

Ten years they have waited. Do you think that when they called for gospel messengers, *God* did not respond? It could not be. He gave His most precious Son that *all* might know and receive eternal life. I think that *man* did not respond. It costs something to leave loved ones and the comforts of civilization. I believe that *each generation* God has "called" enough men and women to evangelize all the yet unreached tribes of the earth. Why do I believe that? Because everywhere I go, I constantly meet with men and women who say to me, "When I was young I wanted to be a missionary, but I got married instead." Or, "My parents dissuaded me," or some such thing. No, it is not God who does not call. It is *man* who will not respond!

Our dear Missing Link is in heaven, and took a little fruit along with him, too. I am sure his one talent received a "Well done!" from his Master. But I am wondering what God is going to say to this *other kind of Missing Link*—the Link missing from His chain of witnesses to the uttermost parts! "My flock became meat to every beast of the field, because there was no shepherd, neither did my shepherds search for my flock, but the *shepherds fed themselves*, and fed not my flock" (Ezek. xxxiv. 8).

Satan's stronghold towers up triumphantly. The awful abyss gapes wide beneath them. The Sharp Winds from the Bitter Height are still blowing. Oh, will *you* not help point out to the terrified little Nestlings, that behind them is the Cleft of the Rock, so close, so sheltering, but so *unseen* unless you and I go to them?